The Rome Escape Line

Sam Derry

The Rome Escape Line

The Rome
Escape Line

The Story of the British Organization
in Rome for assisting Escaped
Prisoners-of-war 1943–44

by

SAM DERRY

W · W · NORTON & COMPANY · INC · New York

Author's Foreword

I wish to acknowledge the great help given to me by Mr Peter Lord in producing this book; for the very many hours he spent wading through documents, checking records, taking down pages and pages of shorthand notes, and his unfailing patience and enthusiasm in typing the script.

This book has been written unbeknown to Monsignor Hugh O'Flaherty, C.B.E.: one of the finest men it has been my privilege ever to meet. Had it not been for this gallant gentleman, there would have been no Rome Escape Organization. I sincerely trust that nothing I have written will cause him any pain or embarrassment.

I should also like to refer to the great debt of gratitude I owe to Lieutenant-Colonel John Furman, M.C. and Lieutenant-Colonel William Simpson, M.C. I fear no words of mine can adequately express my admiration of the wonderful work done by these two courageous officers during those months in enemy-occupied Rome.

S. D.

1960

Contents

Illustrations

between pages 124 and 125

1

Road to Rome

THIS is madness, I thought, as the carriage door whipped open, and I plunged from the speeding prisoner-of-war train out into the Italian morning sunshine. I had jumped on the spur of the moment, and I still wince when recalling how the stony track rushed up to hit and bounce me, and then rose to hit me again, fearsomely close to the deafening roar and clanking of the carriage wheels. The air was blasted from my lungs in a sudden, overwhelming flash of multi-coloured pain.

I first touched the ground in an ungainly crouch, pitched forward, skidded on all fours, and, after an eternity of seconds, scraped to a spread-eagled halt, flat as a deflated inner tube.

I lay waiting to be shot.

Incredibly, inexplicably, the shots never came. Maybe if the German guards fired at all they did so while I was hurtling through the air and bouncing along the ballast. The north-bound train, with its nailed-in cargo of British prisoners-of-war, raced on towards Germany, the terrifying clatter of the iron wheels faded rapidly into a confused rumble, and then to blessed silence. Still only half aware of reality, but satisfied that I remained in one piece, I could scarcely believe my good fortune. I had broken every rule in the escape-book, and should have broken every bone in my body.

Train-jumping was the gateway to freedom for many British prisoners during the Second World War, but it was a hazardous business from which satisfactory results came rarely if the rules were not carefully observed. I was better placed than most to know them, and if I had stopped to think before jumping I should probably not have chosen the moment when the crowded prison-train was blundering through the Appenine foothills at rather more than thirty miles an hour, but would have waited for it to slacken speed on a gradient; nor would I have jumped in the broad daylight of morning, with the friendly cloak of night still far ahead; nor while the train was in a deep cutting, with steep banks on either side, and no possibility of a dash for cover.

Moreover, I was inadequately clad for escape, without food, money, documents, maps, or even any clear idea where I was, and—final folly—I had jumped from the wrong side of the train —that is, the side from which guards, leaning through windows, could the more easily raise their carbines and fire back along the line.

By all the rules, if I avoided breaking my neck, I should have been peppered with bullets, or failing that, the best to expect was that the train would be stopped, and a detachment of unsympathetic guards sent to reclaim me. As it was, I was so grateful for my luck that I could overlook the hammer-blow pains and a violent stabbing sensation in the right leg. For the second time since falling into the German bag in February, the previous year, I was free again. I could hardly refrain from laughing aloud.

After the night in a dim and airless railway compartment, the glare of the summer sun hurt, and I had to screw up my eyes, and shield them with an unsteady hand. I looked back along the track towards Sulmona, northward along the track towards Germany which I had said I would never reach, and along the tops of the embankments. Nowhere was there any sign of life or movement.

Content in spite of the nagging pain in my leg, I dragged myself up the steep bank, and surveyed the Italian landscape, yellow and dusty green under a blue sky. It was farmland, but scrubby, and studded with the stony outcrops of the foothills, and, although I knew little of the Italian rural economy, it was fairly obvious that it would not be densely populated. The combination of few people and a certain amount of cover, in the form of rocks, bushes, and occasional copses, was promising, for while I was grateful to find myself in one piece, I realized that I was in no condition to travel far. With more bruises than I had ever collected on the pre-war rugby field, I felt rather as though I had been charged by a rhinoceros.

Consequently the two miles of Italy over which I crawled in the next hour and a half were the longest I ever knew. The urge to stop and rest was almost irresistible, yet prison-camp caution prevailed, and I was never quite satisfied with the cover that presented itself. It seemed an age before I reached a small but relatively dense wood, which offered not only reasonable cover but also an interesting view of a little group of squat, flaking buildings, forming the centre of a peasant smallholding, on the rising ground above. Where there are people there is food; but escape is always largely a waiting game, so I settled as comfortably as possible among the prickly bushes, watched, and waited.

So far as I had a plan at all, it was to head southward and link up with the Allied forces which had already landed in the toe of Italy. I thought I was on the road to reunion with the Allies, with the Gunners, and, perhaps, at length with my wife, Nancy, at home in Nottinghamshire. I supposed I would be posted 'missing' again, and wondered what she would think—she, to whom I had so recently written plaintively, "What an end of three years' fighting, to be captured, especially after my luck. . . ." But the road on which I had embarked so impetuously that morning did not take me either towards the front line or towards Nancy; I was on a strange road to Rome.

In the scrubby wood, with sunny shafts slanting like theatrical spotlights down through the branches on to the leggy ants that marched and counter-marched with pointless determination round where I lay, my only desires for the immediate future were food, drink, and a bottle of embrocation. To plan further ahead was useless, but I had ample time to reflect as I lay and waited for the sunlight to surrender to the dusk; escapers are creatures of the night.

As a Territorial officer in the Royal Artillery, I had gone to France with the woefully inadequate British Expeditionary Force on the outbreak of war, and, thanks to the gallantry of big men with little ships and my own good fortune, had emerged unscathed through Dunkirk. After the fall of France the only land front on which Britain remained in engagement with the enemy was North Africa, so I was not surprised to find myself a Desert Rat. In the early days, before General Rommel's Afrika Korps joined the unwarlike Italians, there was a peculiar swashbuckling charm about the way in which a little British Army fought its way up and down the narrow coastal strip that confined the ebb and flow of the desert war. But as 1941 wore on, the increasing number of Germans on the sand added a new element of grimness to the North African campaign, and at the beginning of 1942, after a misunderstanding with the infantry 'screen,' my battery was overrun, and I found myself 'in the bag.'

It was my first experience of being a prisoner, and I did not care for it, but escape proved almost too easy. Probably the Germans had never expected to make such an impressive haul of prisoners at one go, and consequently supervision of the depressed Englishmen herded together near the edge of a wadi—an ancient river gorge, long dried up—was well below the usual Nazi standards of efficiency. Since I was the officer who had chosen that site as a defence point, I had a pretty thorough knowledge of the local geography, and it seemed that if I could only get into the deep wadi there would be a sporting change of escaping.

After obliging a questioning German intelligence officer with my rank and name, I worked my way through the group of prisoners, almost inch by inch, as near as I could to the edge of the ravine, and then made a dash for it. My luck held good, and although the guards opened fire, there was enough desert scrub to provide cover, and in 200 yards I had reached the steep edge, and was over. Rolling and sliding down the slope, I reached the bottom in a flurry of sand and small stones—right beside the barely visible entrance of a tiny cave. I shot into it like a rabbit, squeezed all six-foot-three of me into its comforting darkness, and lay there panting, and feeling pretty pleased with myself. The Germans could not send vehicles down, and if they spared a few of their infantry guards there was still a good chance of evading discovery. In fact, the Germans lost interest in me with unflattering rapidity, and the spasmodic rifle-fire and shouting from above ceased almost before I had regained my breath.

I remained until dusk, and then, guided by the stars, jog-trotted along the wadi and over the desert for eighteen miles before catching up with the Allied rearguard and coming close to being shot by an alert Scottish highlander. If this is escape there is not much to it, I thought, but I was to learn that it is not always so simple. For, after a few more minor battles, I was captured again the following July, when we were overtaken by a German motorized unit while foot-slogging back to the last-ditch defence line at El Alamein. This time my luck had gone off duty, because we had seen the vehicles from afar, and had taken cover behind boulders, but the Germans had decided to camp near by for the night—and to dig their latrines right in the middle of the group.

Bundled into a captured British ambulance, I was confronted by a blue-scarfed German officer, who remarked in surprisingly good English, "I seem to have seen you before—weren't you near Derna a few months ago?" This was the sort of question often posed in an attempt to extract information, but my routine non-committal reply produced a sardonic grin of disbelief from the German.

"Oh, yes, you were," he retorted. "You are Major Derry, of the First Field Regiment."

There was no point in further denial, for five months after my first capture, 800 miles away, I had been retaken by the very same German unit, and was now being interrogated by the same intelligence officer.

We spent the rest of the time in the ambulance, chatting quite cosily, for he had spent most of his pre-war summers in the Isle of Man, as a T.T. rider for one of the German motor-cycle manufacturers.

We drove, eventually, north-west to Matruh, and hopes of making another dash for liberty declined when I was put into a strong prisoner-of-war cage, which we ourselves had built earlier, and as, stage by stage, we moved towards the west, escape chances seemed hourly to become slimmer. Finally, in an ancient transport aircraft, a number of us were flown across to the Italian mainland. We were not provided with parachutes, and it was an unnerving experience for British officers, who knew how thoroughly Royal Air Force Hurricanes and Beaufighters were sweeping the narrow sea-lane between Africa and Sicily. Ironically, at a time when hardly any of the German supply planes were getting through to the hard-pressed General Rommel, this ancient transport machine, with its load of unproductive mouths for the Axis to feed, waddled safely to Lecce, in Southern Italy. Since I had not been prepared to wager on our making landfall at all, I was happy enough to have both feet on the ground again, even on enemy soil.

On the other hand, escape now was clearly going to present considerable problems, and although I could not discover the ghost of an opportunity at the transit camp at Bari, I was delighted to discover on arrival at the enormous P.G.21 at Chieti that I need no longer be a lone wolf. The camp, the largest of its kind in Italy, contained 1200 officers, and most of them seemed to be engaged in some form of activity aimed at escape. They were linked together in a remarkable organization, which could provide anything from cash, clothing, and 'official' passes to iron rations and train timetables. The versatility of the organization sprang from the wide range of experience and interest of its vast membership, which represented a complete cross-section of British life—spiced by the inclusion of a few celebrities like Freddie Brown, the England Test captain and manager, and Tony Roncoroni, the English Rugby international, and Phillip Gardner, London's first V.C. of the war.

Eventually, I became a member of the escape committee, which co-ordinated all the getaway plans, and was assigned the task— an incongruous one for a large gunner with a civilian background of building and water-engineering—of securing the provision of rations for escapers and tunnel-builders. This work involved the construction, from condensed milk, biscuits, chocolate, and other unlikely ingredients discovered in Red Cross parcels, of small hard-tack cakes, which were as tough as teak, and tasted like sweetened sawdust, but were so high in nutriment that a man could carry food for a fortnight in one pocket. It was unfamiliar work, but it brought me into touch with many aspects of escape organization that I had never dreamed existed, and it did not take long to learn that escaping from Europe involved much more than making a dash for it, and setting a hopeful course under the stars.

I might have remained a minor and insignificant member of the organization but for an unexpected development in the spring of 1943. The entire population of the camp was turned out on parade in the middle of the night. At first nobody was much concerned, since that sort of thing had happened before, sometimes because the guards were in a panic and wanted to make a snap roll-call, and sometimes, we suspected, merely for the pure hell of it. On this occasion a disconcerting difference became clear when the Italian guard commander read out a list of the names of officers who were to be transferred from the camp in an hour's time—a list that included most of the senior officers and all the principal members of the escape committee.

Still relatively the new boy, I was not named, and immediately after roll-call the Senior British Officer, Colonel Marshall, sent for me, and commanded, "Derry, I want you to take over the escape committee as from now. You've only got an hour to find out all you need to know from the others, so you'd better get cracking."

"Very good, sir," I replied, feeling the situation was anything but that.

In a flurried fifty minutes I chased round all the members of the shattered committee as they gathered together their blankets and biscuit-tins full of the pathetic possessions that in a prison camp become a man's greatest treasures and the sole surviving indications of his individuality.

As the dust settled behind the departing lorries I was left with a nagging worry, for the membership of the escape committee was something that the Italians would have been unlikely to discover unaided : somewhere among Chieti's caged hundreds there must be a traitor. It was unwise to permit major escape activity until this leak had been checked, so I asked the new committee to direct all its immediate efforts towards the unmasking of treachery. The inquiry continued for weeks, and we were never wholly successful, although all investigations seemed to lead to the camp sick-quarters, where several non-commissioned Allied prisoners were employed.

My own suspicion fell most heavily on the small dark frame of a multi-lingual private named Joe Pollak, a Cypriot of Czech extraction, who was frequently in animated conversation with the Italian guards, and was apparently on good terms with them. Pollak, who mixed little with the other prisoners, probably knew that he was under observation, but remained always enigmatic and inscrutable—and continued to chat with the guards in his flawless Italian. Apart from that, he never put a foot wrong, so we had to treat the whole of the hospital as a potential hot-bed of spies, and issued firm instructions that no information about escape activity, however trivial, should be allowed to drift in that direction.

That done, the committee set about the complete re-organization of the camp's escape system. The basic plan was one of mass-production, and from that time there were never fewer than six escape tunnels under construction at a time. Whenever the probing guards discovered the beginnings of one, as they did occasionally, in spite of the ingenuity of sapper officers in creating concealed entrances, another was started at once.

As the work progressed I became convinced that the natural corollary to mass-production was mass-escape, for obviously the discovery of one successful tunnel after a break-out would jeopardize all the others that were near completion. So the orders went out to the sweating teams of troglodytes, who spent their days entombed, scraping at the dry earth with primitive tools or even with their hands, that work on each tunnel was to be stopped at the point where it could open up on the far side of the walls and the wire at short notice. The theory was that if half a dozen tunnels could burst through the surface simultaneously a large number of prisoners might be able to make their way to freedom before the alarm was raised.

At one stage I became hopeful that the tunnels, with all their appalling difficulties for men below and above the ground—we had to cultivate enormous vegetable gardens to dispose of the excavated earth—might never be needed at all, for over the secret radio-receiver, maintained by the organization in one of them, came the welcome news that the Allies had overrun Sicily, invaded Italy, and precipitated the fall and arrest of Mussolini, the Fascist dictator. The invading armies were still hundreds of miles south of Chieti, but it seemed quite possible that the Italian guards might desert, and leave the way open for a mass walk-out—which, in fact, is what did happen at a number of camps.

But the vital information which the secret radio did not give was that the whole area around Chieti was swarming with crack German paratroops, dropped, in an audacious plan by Hitler, to rescue Mussolini, then held by the new civil authorities in a hotel among the hills to the west of the camp. This daring raid was successful, and Mussolini was flown off to the north in a light German aircraft. But the highly trained paratroops remained— and took over control of P.G.21. Without warning, our Italian guards were suddenly replaced by humourless and grimly efficient Germans, and although escape preparations went on, there was a new, wary alertness in the air, which made men jumpy and cautious even with their friends.

We realized that the change meant we were all destined eventually for transfer to Germany. Early in September the tough new guards suddenly ordered the evacuation of 400 prisoners, but did not specify names, and the escape committee were able to select for the transfer men who were not already 'detailed' to escape.

There was barely time for us to congratulate ourselves on thus preserving the structure of the escape organization before the Germans ordered the evacuation of a second 400. That convinced me that no further time could be lost if escape preparations, already more or less complete, were to serve any useful purpose, for it was now clear that the entire camp was soon to be evacuated.

The long-planned mass-escape scheme was brought into immediate operation, and that same evening, by the time the bungalow lights went out and the machine-gun-tower searchlights started their restless probing, the five tunnels that were ready to break the surface were crammed with prisoners, all fully equipped for life in a hostile land. At the heads of the narrow tunnels five men, their hair, ears, and eyes clogged with dust, painfully scraped away the last bulwark of earth. Almost simultaneously five small holes appeared outside the walls, and all forty-six men who had been entombed got clean away into the night.

So far as we could ascertain next morning, the Germans never missed them, and had no idea of the existence of the tunnels. Probably in the first place they had not been given very precise figures for the population of the camp when they took it over from the Italians. At all events, when the rest of us were evacuated later in the day the Germans lost a few more prisoners, including some who were sealed in incomplete tunnels, and one group who spent three days hidden in the camp water-tower.

To me, the breaking up of the Chieti camp seemed tragic, for many more successful escapes could have been accomplished, including my own. I would have given much to occupy one of the escape 'billets' in which we left some of our comrades, but we had already decided, at our emergency meeting of the committee, on a firm rule of precedence, allocating all available places to the men who had done the physical work of making them. So, with the last batch of prisoners to leave, I made the journey to our new camp at Sulmona, carrying our precious secret radio rolled in my blanket. It gave it an odd, angular shape, but failed to attract unwelcome attention.

The first look around the new camp was depressing. Rocky soil ruled out tunnels and even 'hidey holes,' and, after discussing the problem from all angles, the escape committee had to advise the prisoners that only ground-level escapes seemed to have much chance of success. It was a tribute to the ingenuity and enterprise of the prisoners that two or three audacious bluffs did, in fact, succeed, though not my own, thanks to the intervention of a Senior British Officer.

I had not been long at Sulmona before I noticed that the guards were paying scant attention to the horse-drawn rubbish cart, which periodically took away the camp's refuse. One day I clambered aboard, and, reckoning myself least conspicuous if most obvious, sat comfortably on top of the mountain of rubbish, trying to look as much as possible like an Italian peasant. The cart attracted even less attention than usual as it rumbled gawkily through the gates, for the guards were fully occupied with the Senior British Officer, who was arguing vociferously with them about some small administrative technicality. My troubles were almost over, when the S.B.O., raising his eyes towards heaven in a moment of exasperation, found himself looking up at one of his own officers, seated like a ragged monarch on a mouldy throne.

He boggled. "Where the devil are you going, Derry?" he demanded.

I gave the only possible answer in broad basic English, and climbed down.

From the start, we had all realized that Sulmona was likely to be only a staging-point, and that our ultimate destination was Germany. When, therefore, the order for evacuation came it was not really a surprise. But we were not prepared for the additional order that we should march to the railway-station. This was tragic, because it meant that valuable escape equipment had to be left behind. I had to abandon practically all my personal possessions to make room in my blanket roll for the vital wireless-set on which we all depended for our news of the war's progress. Periodically, during the long march, the radio protruded inquisitively from one end or other of the blanket, but I was not unduly perturbed, because I knew that the Germans guarding us were front-line soldiers on their way home on leave. While they were no doubt formidable fighting men, they were unlikely to be very familiar with the wiles of prisoners-of-war. On the other hand, they might be inclined to be trigger happy, so that any open attempt at escape could become a short cut to eternity.

This assessment of our guards proved to be right, for while

they never gave a second glance at the guilty bundle under my
arm, they all seemed to fire at once when one of our group made
a bolt for it at Sulmona station. Captain Jock Short covered only
twenty yards, in his suicidal bid for freedom, before he crumpled
and fell, riddled with bullets. He would not have been more
efficiently shot if he had stood before a firing-squad.

Subdued, most of the prisoners were herded into closed box-
cars, and sealed in, but, with other officers of field rank, I was
thrust into a third-class compartment—a subtle class distinction,
which had the advantage of comfort and sanitation, but the
corresponding disadvantage of surveillance by an armed guard.
I would not have given much for the chances of getting out of
one of the unguarded box-cars, but escape from my compartment looked little more promising. After what had happened to
Captain Short, there was no reason to doubt that the guards were
prepared to shoot to kill.

Yet I could still think of nothing but escape. From the first
turn of the wheels towards Germany, in the small hours of the
morning, I became increasingly restless, oppressed by the conviction that getting away from the Germans was no longer merely
a personal desire, but also a matter of honour : I felt, however
irrationally, that the officers herded into the stinking, airless box-
cars would expect me, as leader of the escape committee, to make
my break, if only to avenge in some small measure the death of
their comrade.

I found myself popping up and down in my seat like a jack-in-
the-box, unable to think reasonably of anything except what the
rhythm of the wheels was thumping through my ears, I must get
away . . . I must get away . . . Once or twice I even found myself
muttering it aloud.

As the determination to escape became more and more in-
sistent, so I grew less and less capable of working out any method
of achieving it. So far as I could think constructively at all, I was
striving desperately to estimate the speed and position of the
train, as it grumbled over the Apennines into the western foothills and into daylight.

There was still no plan of any sort in my mind when at about
8.30 A.M. I asked for permission to use the toilet, and was accompanied by a burly unshaven paratrooper, carrying a carbine, to the
end of the coach. Possibly I wanted to leave the compartment

only because of sheer impatience and frustration, and certainly
I was in no way prepared for an escape attempt. I had not rested
for a moment through the interminable night, I was wearing
only a shirt, trousers, and shoes, and all my food and remaining escape equipment were still with the wireless-set and my
outer clothing in the luggage-rack.

I looked round the toilet compartment, cursing my inability
to escape from it. It had one door, outside which stood the armed
guard, and one window, boarded up, and far too small to offer
any scope to a man of my size.

Frustrated, and forced to abandon hope from that smelly
prison, I opened the door to face the guard—and in that instant
stopped thinking and started acting.

Instead of turning towards my seat, I side-stepped the German
with the sort of manœuvre that sometimes works wonders on the
Rugby field, and threw myself in the opposite direction. I was
across the carriage in a single bound, and, without stopping to
think how small were the chances of success (or even survival),
I flung open the main door, and jumped out into the sunshine.
Later, as I recalled the surprising violence with which sun-baked
Italy had come up to meet me, I knew why it was called hostile
territory.

After a long day in the woody bed of an erstwhile stream, the
multitude of sharp pains gave way to one all-pervading ache, and
although I still felt as if my whole body was held together by
rotting string, I knew, at least, I was now capable of hobbling
down to the peasant smallholding that I had kept under observation throughout the day. The only occupants seemed to be an
old man, a woman, and a couple of children, which was about
as harmless a combination as could be expected. Even so, a direct
approach to the house had its dangers. However, I had to have
food, drink, and a place to rest in reasonable security for a few
hours, before making any attempt to travel farther.

When day became dusk with the suddenness of southerly lati-
tudes I struggled to my feet, and limped slowly up the gentle
slope towards the farm, rehearsing all the way the short speech
carefully learned while still at Chieti. As I neared the house the
old man and the women emerged, and caught sight of me. They
stopped in their tracks, and stared at me with a look of incredulity
which swiftly froze into one of terror.

I was not prepared for this. While realizing that I was a bit of a giant by Italian physical standards, I had overlooked the possibility that after the battering I had received, in my leap from the train, I might appear to be a rather fearsome giant, with tattered, dusty shirt and bruised, bloodstained, and unshaven face.

Spreading out my hands to show that I concealed no weapon, I twisted my face into what I hoped was an ingratiating smile, and in halting Italian announced that I was British, and asked for food and drink.

"Buona sera, signore, signora," I stammered. "Sono inglese. Per favore, mi dia pasto, bevanda."

Their reaction frightened me. The old man's mouth and eyes opened wide, in an expression of blank horror, and the woman threw up her hands, closed her eyes, and emitted a shrill little scream. Glumly I wondered what I had said.

For a moment there was silence, and then the man and the woman faced each other, and, both talking at once, released a stream of rapid Italian, accompanied by energetic gesticulations. My tiny vocabulary of their language was not sufficient to give me even the gist of what they were shouting about, but I was becoming increasingly worried that I had blundered.

Reports from our secret radio had made it clear that the relationship between the Italians and the Germans had been strained since the fall of Mussolini's Government, and had even suggested that the majority of the Italian people were anxious to help the Allies, but the escape committee had always recommended that this assumption should be treated with reserve, and that escapers should avoid making direct approaches to Italians whenever possible. I began to wish that I had followed more closely the advice that I had helped to formulate, but it was too late now to change my tactics. I needed food and drink, and I was painfully aware that I was in no state to turn and run.

What the Italians were saying remained incomprehensible to me, but, as the noisy minutes wore on, it seemed that they were becoming distinctly calmer. Almost as abruptly as they had started, the Italians stopped shouting at each other, and turned their attention back to me—without, to my surprise and relief, any apparent hostility. Indeed, I realized that the old man was waving to a near-by straw stack, and indicating, by a mixture of gesture and monosyllable, that I should go and hide in it.

"Si, si, signore, grazie," I said, as soon as I got the gist of what he was trying to tell me.

Hobbling to the stack, I hauled myself awkwardly to the top, and lay back gratefully on the straw, but I was still by no means sure of my hosts, and after they had gone in I watched the house carefully, expecting every minute to see one or the other of them setting off to the nearest village, to report my arrival. When the two reappeared they remained together, approaching the stack, and, with a surge of anticipatory delight, I could see that they were bringing food. Gratefully I ate the dry bread and *formaggio* —a pungent cheese made from sheep's milk—which they handed up to me, and even more gratefully I observed that their expression as they watched me was sympathetic and, indeed, almost benign.

Much as I welcomed this apparent change of heart, I was taken by surprise when I realized that the old man was trying to invite me into the house for the night. I came to the conclusion that their original fear had been that I was a German agent, who, after inducing them to help, would denounce them, but I still had no particular desire to go into the house. In the first place it would put them in unnecessary peril, for while I remained outside they could always pretend they did not know I was there; secondly, and more selfishly, I realized that the chance of escape in emergency was greater from my straw stack than from within a building with only one narrow door. The escape committee had always advised, "Keep out of people's houses if there is any alternative," and, so far as I could judge, the straw stack offered a very reasonable alternative.

"No, grazie," I replied, smiling modestly, as though to suggest I could not possibly put them to so much trouble. They seemed quite satisfied, smiled, bade me "Arrivederci," and retreated to the house, bolting the door audibly behind them.

Burrowing a little into the straw, I slept. If the Italians had wished to denounce me that night my recapture would not have been difficult, for I was utterly exhausted. I was so stiff when I woke that I soon realized a continuation of my journey that day was out of the question, but I was so delighted to find myself alive and free that I did not feel inclined to complain.

My hosts, who by now seemed to accept me as unconcernedly as if I were just another addition to the livestock around the farm, brought me drink and variations of *pasta* at intervals, and for most of the remaining time throughout that day and the following night I simply relaxed on the welcoming straw and slept, trying to will myself back to fitness.

The absence of physical and even mental effort proved to be rapidly recuperative, and when I awoke the next morning I could feel at once that my strength had returned. I sat up, then stood, and for the first time really surveyed my surroundings. My vantage-point commanded a magnificent panorama, from the rolling Apennine foothills, only two or three miles away in the east, to the distant horizon of the west, flat, and unbroken save for occasional neat squares of olive-trees and——

I narrowed my eyes, to see better through the slight morning haze that broke the far horizon into a misty, shimmering line. There was no doubt about it : there, in the distance, perhaps more than fifteen miles away, only just discernible above the horizon, yet gleaming startling white in the light of the mounting sun, was a great, graceful dome. It was a dome which, I knew, although I had never seen it before, had no equal in all the world. Until this moment I had been without any clear idea of where in Italy I was, but there could be no mistaking that spectacle—it was the majestic, soaring dome of St Peter's, Rome.

From the top of a straw stack, in a remote peasant smallholding, I was getting my first glimpse of the fabulous Eternal City. I could not help grinning to myself at the incongruous thought that this might be all I should ever see of it, for I intended to go southward to war, not eastward to Rome.

Yet Fate smiled too, for within minutes she had turned my footsteps towards Rome.

2
Cabbages and Colonnades

MY first glimpse of timeless Rome, shining in the morning sunlight, gave me a thrill, yet I viewed the distant dome with mixed feelings: it was an advantage to know within a few miles where I was, but it was disturbing to be so close to the capital city of an enemy country. I felt it would be as well to put as many miles as possible between Rome and myself, and decided to set course southward as soon as the daylight faded. But scarcely had I begun to plan the excursion when there came an unexpected development.

My Italian host and hostess suddenly appeared beside the straw stack, beaming with excitement, and chattering away simultaneously, as usual, in a language of which I knew no more than a dozen stock phrases. When at last I managed to convince them that I did not understand they did what so many of us do under similar circumstances: they repeated it all over again—twice as loudly.

Gradually I began to understand, though by what means I am not sure, unless it was some form of telepathy, that they were trying to tell me there were other British prisoners-of-war in hiding among the hills only a couple of miles away, and that guides could be arranged to take me to see them. No longer suspicious about the goodwill of the two Italians, I agreed to make the trip to the hills, though not until nightfall. This meant that any journey to the south would have to be deferred for at least twenty-four hours; but the other escapers might possess more local information, and a pooling of ideas would be all to the good.

The guides, who presented themselves at dusk, turned out to be two engaging black-haired, brown-eyed, bronze-skinned boys, one about eleven and the other a couple of years older, who treated the whole enterprise as an exhilarating adventure, and were in much better physical condition for a long walk than I was.

Keeping up with them as well as I could, cursing when I fell into the ruts or tripped over stones which they nimbly and expertly side-stepped or jumped, I followed for more than an hour across the agricultural plain and into the foothills. Our walk became a climb, gradually steeper and steeper, earth gave way to rocks, the path to a barely discernible track, until suddenly I found myself among a warren of tiny caves, staring like blind, black eyes beneath the furrowed brow of the hill. But other eyes were staring too—the eyes of a dozen men standing around in the gloom. It was with a slight sense of shock that I found myself suddenly among fellow countrymen, and I lost no time in introducing myself, in case they thought I was a German or Fascist agent.

The escapers welcomed me, bombarded me with questions about the progress of the war, and then turned their interest to the young guides, who were apparently well known to them. The boys were among the helpful Italians who had been keeping them supplied with food since they made for the hills.

All the escapers came from the same prison camp, P.G.54, and had been out with farm-working-parties when Mussolini's Government fell. Their Italian guards deserted on the spot, and the prisoners, not unnaturally, did not bother to report back to camp. The fact that their food supplies were coming from the Italian families for whom they had worked had double significance: it meant that the men had made a good impression on the ordinary Italians, and that the Italians, in turn, were prepared to help against the Germans, even if it entailed considerable risk.

That all the cave-dwellers wanted to rejoin their own forces at the earliest possible moment was evident, but their plan seemed to be to remain in the foothills, waiting for the expected Allied advance. While I sympathized with this, I had secret doubts, for most of the men were clad only in ragged shirts and trousers, hardly suitable for lying around in caves as winter approached.

I realized, without much enthusiasm, that I should have to do something about it, for I was the first officer they had seen since their escape, and by any rule of military conduct I had to consider myself in command. I could not think about my own escape without doing something for them first. That, too, seemed to be the view taken by the men, who kept demanding, "How do we get back to the lines?"

The only truthful answer would have been that I had not the foggiest idea, but I replied, "I shall go back and see what can be organized. Meanwhile stay where you are. Keep out of sight during the day, and don't under any circumstances go down to people's houses. I'll be back to-morrow."

I stumbled back down the hillside to a cheerful chorus of British "Good nights," which was music after an age of un-comprehended Italian, but, much as I had enjoyed talking again in the only language which I understood, I had never felt more alone than at this moment. I had never looked forward to my own proposed journey south, but at least it was only my own skin I was risking. To bungle the escape of a dozen others was much more serious, for they had more to lose: prison-camp conditions were frequently much worse for other ranks than for officers. All my problems seemed to have been multiplied twelve-fold, and there was no one to whom I could turn for help.

Back in the peace of the straw stack, I pondered on grouping, timing, route, and rendezvous plans for a trek south. The last news I had of the war was that Naples, a mere 120 miles away, had fallen to the Allies, and I presumed that the advance was still sweeping up the long leg of Italy at good speed. The fact was that the advance had ground to a bloody standstill against stub-born resistance. The Germans held a line pivoted on the fortress-monastery of Monte Cassino, and at that moment were strengthen-ing that line with an almost ceaseless southward flow of men and arms. These conditions, had I known them, would have made any proposal to link up with our own forces out of the question.

When I went back into the hills next night, to check up on the escapers' food supplies, I was disconcerted to find that overnight the force had doubled in size—and by the next night it had doubled again. The original dozen were by no means the only prisoners to take advantage of the desertion of the Italian guards; escapers from a wide area were now gradually working their way to the relative security of the foothill caves, and, as there was no officer among them, I found myself in command of some fifty British soldiers, 120 miles behind enemy lines.

The straw stack which had been my home was now more like an operational headquarters, for, while keeping in constant touch with the men in the hills, I had decided that it was much better to remain in a position where I could maintain direct contact with the Italians. My hosts were feeding me with regularity if with monotony—for *pasta* is not only an acquired taste, but one that quickly palls on the English palate—and I had made myself comfortable by carving a small square 'room' out of the centre of the stack, with a narrow entrance which could be easily concealed in emergency. One way and another, it was a pretty satisfactory billet, and there was no good reason for leaving it.

It was, however, plain that the general situation was getting out of hand. Filtering a dozen men through a battlefield had looked difficult, but getting fifty men back to our lines was almost impossible. Yet, each day brought greater urgency to the problem of what to do with them, for the amount of food finding its way up to the hills, even at this most ample period on the farms, was not sufficient for so large a number. There was a growing need for medical supplies, and for additional clothing as winter, often surprisingly severe in the Apennines, crept closer. Already there was a distinct chill in the evenings.

All that was needed, as in most of life's little emergencies, was money—but where could a prisoner-of-war on the run lay his hands on large sums of money by honest means? One day, thinking over the problem, my eyes fell upon the dome of St Peter's, dazzling and tantalizing in the distance. Suddenly there came a shadowy recollection of having been told long ago that one of the oddities of the war was that in the middle of enemy Italy there were still some official British Government representatives, virtually prisoners in the unique neutral Vatican City. The original British Embassy had been outside the walls of the 'city within a city,' but when Italy entered the war on Germany's side it had been closed, dust-sheeted, and put under the protection of the neutral Swiss, while a skeleton staff of British diplomats had moved into the Vatican itself, knowing that they would never emerge again until the war was won.

The more I thought about this, the more convinced I became that these were the people to ask for funds. Arranging for an appeal to reach them did not seem to be a formidable problem, the obvious person to take a message being a priest. And in Italy, even in a rural area, a priest is not difficult to find.

By the language of sign and gesture, my hosts agreed to bring the village priest to see me, and he arrived the same evening. He was a genial, alert little man, in a shabby black cassock and hat. He had a calm, placid gaze, and exuded an atmosphere of homely piety which invited implicit trust, and I sensed that if he did not like my request he would reject it frankly but say no more about it to anyone.

"Father," I asked, "is it possible for you to get a message into the Vatican?"

He understood English, and seemed neither surprised nor perturbed. "Si," he nodded. "It is possible. For whom is the message?"

"Anybody English in the Vatican," I replied. His eyebrows raised a little, but he nodded again, so I handed him the brief note which I had already written. It was addressed "To whom it may concern," signed "S. I. Derry, major," and, with what might have seemed crass disregard for security, said simply that a group of escaped Allied prisoners beyond Salone were in urgent need of financial assistance and clothing.

The priest took his farewell, and disappeared into the darkness. During the next couple of days my faith wavered, and I would not have been surprised to see a posse of German soldiers, but as I knew I was remote from the main body of fellow-escapers, there was no reason why my recapture should also result in theirs.

In fact, my fears were unjustified, for on the third day the village priest returned and, with a benevolent smile, handed me a package. It contained 3000 lire in Italian notes. I was astonished, delighted, and probably effusive in thanking the little priest, but he waved aside all my protestations of gratitude, and said simply, "Please to write an acknowledgment for my superior, to say I have given you the *denaro*."

I felt that I had already committed more than enough to paper, but could hardly refuse the priest's request—so I decided that I might as well ask for some more money at the same time. Three thousand lire represented something under ten pounds, although it could buy goods worth twice as much if wisely spent in the country areas. It was a welcome surprise, but it would not go far in the provisioning of fifty men.

"Grazie," said the priest, as I handed him a scribbled note which was a compound of receipt, expression of thanks, and begging-letter. "I will take it to the Vatican myself."

I returned to the men in the foothills, and arranged with the N.C.O.'s the distribution and expenditure of some of the money, instructing them to give small sums to the farm families who had been feeding them, and to ask their Italian contacts to purchase second-hand clothing to meet urgent needs. I reckoned that with the low cost of food in the country area, there was money enough to ensure that none of the hospitable farm families would be heavily out of pocket for what they had done, and after the success of this first experiment I hoped that the financial position of our little organization would be sufficiently healthy to prevent any hardship in the near future.

Just four days after his previous visit the village priest returned to my hide-out, and handed me another 4000 lire.

"Grazie, grazie," I said delightedly. "Would you like another receipt for your superior?"

"No," replied the priest, looking me straight in the eye. "This time he would like you to go to Rome yourself."

"What?" I exclaimed.

"My superior wishes to see you personally. You will, *per favore*, go to Rome?"

"If it is possible, yes. May I ask who is your superior?" But the priest replied evasively, and instead told me that he would help me to get to the Vatican.

In fact, the prospect did not dismay me as much as it would have done a week or two earlier. When I first took up residence in the straw stack the thought of finding my way, alone and friendless, into the capital city, would have been formidable, but since then I had learned a good deal about the Italian rural scene. The peasants working smallholdings in the plain below the Apennines regularly travelled to Rome by pony cart, to sell their vegetables and fruit at the inflated prices obtainable in the city markets. Nevertheless, the idea of going voluntarily into Rome was on a par with clambering back on to the prison-train, and but for maintaining the supply of money which had now begun to flow towards the foothills fifty, I would have shied away from the suggestion. However, there was little choice in the matter, and I was grateful for the priest's offer of assistance.

He wasted no time in arranging for a smallholder named Pietro Fabri, who drove his pony cart into Rome two or three times every week, to pick me up early one November morning. Well on the chilly side of dawn we jogged off to Rome, and all I knew was that I was to be guided by my companion to a rendezvous that had been arranged. If anything went wrong I should be in a perilous position, alone in the middle of an alien city, with no idea of where I was supposed to be going, and unable to ask the way even if I had known.

Pietro Fabri, who was accompanied by one of his host of bare-footed daughters, was a gay, bucolic son of the soil. On the long journey down secondary roads he burst into song occasionally, swore frequently at the plodding pony, and chattered a good deal, apparently unperturbed by my failure to understand a word, and quite satisfied if I grinned at him, and nodded once in a while. I cannot think that he made a habit of smuggling people past the road-blocks into Rome, yet he was clearly less concerned than I was, and seemed happy to have me sitting beside him and his daughter, in front of a mountain of cabbages and in full view of any early risers who happened to be about.

Fascinated, I sat and watched the domes of Rome, dominated always by the white giant of St Peter's, creeping closer in the thin light of dawn. But before we reached the outskirts of the city Pietro motioned to me to take cover, as one of the check-points established by the Germans and their Fascist collaborators on all roads leading into Rome lay just around the next corner.

I wriggled downward through a sea of cabbages, felt Pietro and his daughter adjust the pile above me, and heard his whispered, "Silenzio, signore." Unable to see anything, and almost suffocated by the pungent smell, I felt completely cut off from the world, but as the rickety wobbling of the cart ceased, I knew that we had reached the road-block. I could hear the murmur of Pietro's voice and others, disconcertingly close to my ears, through the deafening creaking of the cabbage-leaves every time I breathed. I was nearly choking, but dared not breathe deeply for fear of causing a telltale rise and fall in the pile of cabbages, and could not pant because of the noise it would make. Every second I expected to feel the sharp prod of an inquisitive bayonet.

It was an enormous relief when at last I felt the wheels begin to turn again, with no bayonet thrusts, and no rummaging among the load—Pietro, apparently, was well known to all the guards. But I was still suffering from claustrophobia, had no idea how long I was to subsist beneath the cabbages, and prayed that it would not be too long. The cart rumbled on for an age before a whispered "Venga, venga" (Come, come) enabled me to emerge from my sweaty green confinement and take a grateful gulp of Roman air.

"Buon giorno, signore!" grinned Pietro, as I sat again upon the cabbages, which for so long had sat on me.

"And a very good morning to you," I replied in English, scraping an affectionate caterpillar from my hair.

I was rather surprised, though well pleased, that Pietro should have called me from hiding before we reached whatever was to be our destination, for I could see that we were still on the outskirts of the city. I did not know then that Rome, for its population, is a compact city. Bounded for centuries by its long, strong walls, it does not straggle out into hideous suburbs in all directions, as do so many of the capitals of the world. I was glad to be sitting out in the open again, for I did not feel that the need to avoid attracting attention justified a prolonged incarceration among the cabbages, and in my present shabby condition I was unlikely to draw a second glance so long as I remained with Pietro and the cart.

Moreover, I wanted to see as much of Rome as I could, for I presumed that this might be a once-in-a-lifetime visit, and the great white dome of St Peter's—now generally hidden behind the near buildings, and at close quarters not white at all, but a gentle, mellow grey—had been beckoning me and tantalizing me for weeks. As it happened, the Rome through which Pietro drove me was much like any other Italian town, with narrow pavements set immediately against long, flat, pastel-coloured façades studded with shuttered windows; only a fleeting glimpse of a towering gate, and part of the great stone wall of the ancient city, served as a reminder that this was the birthplace of much of what is called civilization.

Pietro Fabri halted his pony cart in a side street used as an open-air market by peasants from the surrounding country, clambered down from his perch, and, leaving his daughter to look after the pony, bade me follow him. Feeling like a lone English tourist, and trying not to look like one, I walked beside him through two or three small streets just beginning to wake up to face a new day. Passing workmen bade each other good morning, shaking hands vigorously, as though they had not met for years, although the chances were that they had caroused together in some café only the previous evening. I had not walked in the streets of any town or city for more than a year and a quarter, and everything seemed unreal.

"A destra," said Pietro suddenly, turning to the right. "Venga con me." He clumped through the open doors of a tall, drab building, led me across a deserted tiled hall, and up a stone stairway flanked by an iron balustrade. On the first floor he stopped at an apartment door, and rang the bell. The door swung open to reveal a small, greasy man of early middle age, wearing the long black cassock of a priest, who smiled toothily, stood back to allow us to enter, and closed the door behind us. We were in the hall of a small flat, and Pietro and the stranger were already engaged in rapid conversation. They obviously knew each other well, but Pietro did not treat the other man with the reverence usually accorded by Italians to priests, and although the man in the cassock kept his face turned towards Pietro, his eyes were on me. I found him difficult to assess, for there was something about him that I did not quite like; he seemed altogether too smooth, and completely devoid of the simple piety that shone like a beacon from the village priest who had sent me.

Pietro indicated that the man's name was Pasqualino Perfetti, but the latter seemed to know mine already. The rather vague introduction complete, Pietro, with a cheery "A presto," departed, leaving me without any idea of when or where I was to see him again.

Perfetti took me by the arm into a room where I was confronted by a heavier-built man of about the same age, but wearing a conventional civilian suit. Spreading an oily palm towards him, Perfetti announced, "Aldo Zambardi."

"Buon giorno, capitano," said Zambardi, gripping my hand and peering up at me, and then in good English, "I have been sent here to meet you. Did the money from the Vatican arrive all right?"

I nodded, thinking that perhaps I had come all this way, at the parish priest's request, simply to report in person the safe arrival of the 4000 lire. Nevertheless, it was difficult to believe that either of the two rather shifty-looking men with me now were the honest little priest's anonymous 'superior.' I was just beginning to feel a sense of anticlimax when, after a pause, Zambardi said something that startled me. "Now we have to go to the Vatican," he announced, in matter-of-fact tones. "It is a long way, but we shall take a tram."

I probably stared at him, and then looked down at my tattered shirt, the worn battledress trousers, dyed a streaky blue with ordinary ink, and the desert boots, which had been cut down into rough shoes.

Zambardi took my meaning, and, taking off his own overcoat, handed it over, and spoke quickly to the man in the cassock, who rummaged around to produce a pair of flannel trousers and a cloth cap.

I changed then and there, and the result was rather bizarre. The trousers flapped above my ankles, the coat did not reach my knees, and the little cap sat quaintly on top of my head. However, the two Italians seemed satisfied with the transformation, so there was no reason why I should complain, and I set off with Zambardi down the street, knowing that at least I looked nothing whatever like an English officer.

Before we left Zambardi warned me that I was not to talk to him or show any sign of recognition once we got outside, and that on the tram I should pretend to doze in order to avoid being drawn into conversation with other passengers. The two-coach tram was pretty full, but Zambardi, pushing as heartily as all the other intending passengers, elbowed me aboard, bought a couple of tickets, shoved me forcibly into a seat, sat down heavily beside me before anyone else could cut in, and stared studiously into space.

The other passengers included some in German or Fascist uniforms and jackboots, so I tried to make myself small, and in no time let my head sag in a simulated doze, as advised.

There was a droll humour in the situation: I had first seen Rome from the top of a straw stack, I had entered it covered with cabbages, and now, dressed like a music-hall comedian, I was getting my first glimpse of its eternal glories from a crowded tram —through half-closed eyes. After the drabness of the desert, the confinement of the prison camp, and the isolation of the straw stack, nothing would have been more satisfying than to stare around at the wonderfully preserved symbols of an empire of two thousand years ago. But every time I raised an eyelid I was brought sharply back to the present, for the pavements were speckled with the forbidding field-grey of German uniforms. Rome was completely dominated by the Germans, who had marched in and taken over the city, lock, stock, and barrel, after the fall of Mussolini's dictatorship.

The tram was brought to a stop a dozen times, and every time I feared it was a security check. Quite apart from my lack of Italian, I had no documents of any sort, so the chances of emerging from even the most cursory check were nil. No wonder Zambari insisted that we should pretend to be unacquainted. Eventually, as the brakes scraped on again, I felt a sharp nudge in the side, and, looking up, saw that my companion was already half-way down the car. I rose hurriedly, and followed, jumping from the tram just before it started away again.

Now, for the first time, I could see something of Rome. We had stopped beside the Ponte Vittoria Emanuele, possibly the most spectacular of Rome's seventeen bridges across the Tiber, with its three great arches, and eight triumphal pillars reaching up from the balustrades. On the far bank, just to the right of where we were walking across the bridge, was the round grey Castel Sant' Angelo, built by Hadrian as a mausoleum, but for fifteen centuries the fortress of Rome, and ahead of us, its noble façade still partly obscured by the buildings of the Via della Conciliazione, was the greatest church in Christendom. Spellbound, I crossed the northern embankment roadway behind the trotting Zambardi, and turned into Via della Conciliazione, once a solid block of shops and cafés with a narrow street on either side, but long since swept clear by Mussolini, to form a tremendous diverging avenue leading straight from the Tiber to St Peter's. It was a breathtaking sight. It is common knowledge that everything about St Peter's is on the vast scale, but until that moment, when the war seemed far away, I had never realized the colossal majesty of this church, which took the whole of the sixteenth and three-quarters of the seventeenth century to build.

As we reached the wide entrance to the enormous circular St Peter's Square, my eyes travelled down 400 feet from the top of the dome—and I came back to earth in another sense with a shock. Apart from priests and nuns, the great *piazza* was full of German soldiers, several armed and on some sort of sentry duty. Between me and the great gates of the Vatican, on either side of the cathedral façade, there was a hornets' nest.

I continued to follow the silent Zambardi, keeping my gaze firmly at ground level, careful to avoid catching the eye of the German soldiers who passed too close for my liking. Ahead of us, almost in the shadow of the noble colonnade that curved right round both sides of the *piazza*, I could see a very tall, lone figure, wearing a long black robe of a priest. He was standing with his hands folded in front of him, and his head slightly bowed, as though in prayer, yet I had the feeling that he was watching our approach.

Zambardi went straight towards the tall priest, who flashed a quick glance at me, and turned on his heel. In that momentary glance I caught an impression of piercing blue eyes behind simple steel spectacles, and of a strong, humorous mouth. And, as he turned abruptly away, I heard him speak in a delightful lilting brogue, but in unmistakable English. "Follow me—a short distance behind," was all he said.

It was all so rapid that Zambardi and I had barely slowed our stride; we kept on walking as though we had no connexion with the tall cleric, who now strode before us. I followed obediently, but noticed with a twinge of alarm that we turned, not towards the great gates of the Vatican, but through the colonnade itself, and walked away from the *piazza* and into a narrow side street.

After covering a couple of hundred yards, the priest turned into a wide arched entrance, which appeared to be some sort of porter's lodge. From the shadow of the archway we passed into the intimate sunlight of a small, secluded square, flanked by solemn stone buildings, and crossed to a massive doorway on the far side.

As we passed through the portico I glanced casually upward at the inscription over the door, and as I read it I felt myself go cold. I knew little enough Italian, but there was no mistaking the meaning of that inscription : *Collegio Teutonicum*—the German College.

3

Two Tall Monsignors

THE last thing I could have foreseen, when setting off from the straw stack in the morning, was that I should walk voluntarily into some sort of German establishment. But there was little I could do except follow the tall priest dumbly, with a mixture of resignation and curiosity gaining the upper hand over fear and suspicion.

The priest led the way into a small, sparsely-furnished ground-floor office, next to a porter's room, and, after a quick grin at me, he opened a lengthy exchange of Italian with Zambardi.

"Now, me boy," he said, turning to me at last, "we'll go up to my room—but we're leaving Aldo now, so you had better give him his coat back."

I did so, and thanked Zambardi warmly, though with the suspicion that I was thanking him for leading me into a trap. Then, still bewildered, I accompanied the priest up two steep flights of stairs, along a dim corridor, and into a small study, one end of which was concealed completely behind two long curtains. The rest of the room contained a wash-basin, a desk, with a couple of well-filled golf-bags propped casually behind it, a radio-set in one corner, a sofa, and a couple of easy chairs. There appeared to be nobody else in it.

"Now you'll be all right—you can talk here," said the priest, and promptly plied me with some biscuits, which I accepted gratefully, but which made talking difficult, rather to my relief because I wanted him to make the opening gambit.

"I got your receipt for the money," he said, as I munched. "Did you get the second lot all right? But, of course, you must have done, or you wouldn't be here."

"So it was you who sent it, Father?" I asked.

He nodded, and asked me about the men I had left in the hills. I answered fairly cagily at first, but my host made up for my reticence by his own frank willingness to talk—and within minutes any illusion that most of the escaped Britons in Italy were in my care was shattered.

"There are a good many groups like yours around here," he

said. "Hundreds and hundreds of prisoners simply walked out when the Italian guards deserted, and now they are in hiding all over the countryside, most in pretty bad need of more food and clothing. As a matter of fact, we even have some chaps here in Rome itself."

I wanted to know what he meant by "we," and a dozen questions occurred to me, but, sensing my thoughts, he said, "It is a long story, and you will pick it all up soon enough. Meanwhile how about a nice warm bath?"

As I had not so much as seen a bath since on leave in Cairo, nearly a year and a half previously, I accepted with relish. My host, who had observed our similarity in size and build, rummaged around, produced a handful of his own clothing, and escorted me to a bathroom a short distance down the deserted corridor. "Take your time, me boy," he said, as he closed the door. "Come back to my room when you're ready—and don't get lost on the way."

In a glow of heavenly cleanliness, dressed in the priest's underclothes and smoking-jacket, Perfetti's trousers and my own shirt, I listened cautiously at the door before I ventured into the corridor again, but everything was wrapped in a calm ecclesiastical silence. I made my way along the corridor, and knocked softly at the priest's door. There was no reply. I knocked again, a little more loudly, and then, fearful of attracting unwelcome attention, tried the handle gently. The door opened smoothly, and I slipped inside. There seemed to be nothing to do except wait and see, but still half fearful that I had been led into a Nazi trap, I took a peep to see what lay behind the curtains at the end of the room. There was nothing but a simple narrow bed. Keeping well back in the room, I tried to see what lay outside; the view from the single large window behind the desk was almost filled with the vast bulk of St Peter's, but to the left, extending from the college in which I was either guest or prisoner, was a series of elegant stone buildings, squares and gardens, enclosing and disappearing behind the great sacristy, which projected from the southern wall of the cathedral. All these were part of the Vatican, and linked with the building in which I stood, yet it was puzzling that I had entered here from an ordinary street in German-occupied Rome, without challenge from either military sentries or Vatican guards. It did not add up.

I was still pondering when the sound of a hand on the latch caused me to swing round sharply to face the door. It opened softly, but not secretively, to reveal a stocky, dark-haired man of early middle age, wearing a neat black coat and pin-striped trousers, and carrying a small black-leather brief-case under one arm.

"Major Derry, I believe?" he said, with a charming smile, and offered his hand. He was completely English in appearance, and his accent carried a trace of the Londoner.

"Yes," I replied doubtfully, taking his hand. "And you?" He grinned, and instead of answering, he opened his brief-case to produce a large packet of cigarettes and a welcome bottle.

"We've been expecting you," he said. "I thought you would be glad of these to celebrate your safe arrival."

I tried to express my gratitude, and decided I should have to accept, for the time being, the situation in which everybody knew me and I knew nobody. He asked a good many questions about myself and the party in the hills, and I answered with some reserve, uncertain how this obvious Englishman could fit into the picture. Most of my own questions, however innocuously worded, were adroitly side-stepped, and I was no nearer an explanation of my surroundings when the door opened again, and the tall priest strode in.

"Oh, good—John's here!" he exclaimed, and, turning to me, he beamed. "This is John May. He is the man who will look after you, and tell you everything." For a few minutes the three of us spoke together, but only in the most general terms about the war. Then the priest asked to be excused, and, as suddenly as he reappeared, strode out through the door again. I looked blankly at the man named John May, and asked, "Does this go on all the time?"

"Pretty nearly," he laughed. "He's an official of the Holy Office, and he has a little office downstairs, where people are in and out to see him all the time. Never seems to rest—but I expect you'll get used to that, eventually. A wonderful character, the monsignor."

"The what?"

"Our Irish friend—the Right Reverend Monsignor Hugh O'Flaherty."

"Oh, dear," I said. "That sounds damned important—and I've been calling him 'Father' all this time."

"Never mind," said John May. "The monsignor would be the last person in the world to worry about that. But you're quite right—he is an important chap, and you really ought to call him 'monsignor.' He's been at the Vatican since 1922, and seems to know everybody in Rome. Everybody knows Monsignor O'Flaherty—and, what's more important, they all adore him."

I was beginning to understand why. And since my companion seemed more prepared to accept me, and not parry questions, I wondered if he knew what sort of British organization remained in existence behind the walls of the Vatican.

Nodding towards the window, I asked if there was still a British Ambassador in there.

"Not quite," said John May. "We no longer have an Ambassador in Rome, but there is a British Minister to the Holy See, with a small legation inside the city walls—which reminds me, I must get back to my duties. As a matter of fact, I am the Minister's butler."

With that he was gone, and all I now knew was that I was the guest of an Irish monsignor and an English butler in a German college.

The fact that the name over the portico was no mere archaic title was brought home to me when the monsignor returned with an invitation to join him at his desk for lunch. The meal was brought in and served by two nuns, who were obviously German, and spoke in the language that I associated with jack-booted guards. However, they were very subdued in the presence of the monsignor, speaking only when spoken to, and the barley soup and spaghetti they served, though plain and simple, was the best I had eaten for many months. The monsignor watched my enjoyment of the meal with sympathy and delight, and it was only with difficulty that I was able to persuade him to eat his own meal instead of giving it to me. After the nuns had left I asked point-blank, "Monsignor, are we in the Vatican?"

The monsignor leaned back in his chair, and emitted a great, rich laugh. "Has that been bothering you?" he chuckled. "I suppose the only accurate answer is 'yes and no.' This college, like a good many other places, is extra-territorial property: it belongs to the Holy See, and forms no part of the Italian State, but it is outside the Vatican City, and, as you know, it leads out on to the streets of Rome. The military authorities have left us alone so far, though I wouldn't put it past them to raid us one day. You are pretty safe here, but not as secure, of course, as a few of your friends who got into the Vatican City itself early on—they are interned for the duration. The Vatican is a neutral State, you know."

"But this place—it's German, isn't it?"

"Yes, so it is," he grinned. "Almost everybody in it is German, but don't let that worry you, me boy—this is not part of the Wehrmacht. All the same, I don't think we should advertise too extensively that you are an English officer."

Before I had time to find out more he excused himself, and dashed off again to his office, but, in view of his last remark, I was startled on his return, half an hour later, by his next words. "Blon, I thought you would like to meet this British major."

Disconcerted and slightly embarrassed, I found myself looking into the dark eyes of a staggeringly attractive brunette about nineteen years old. "Miss Blon Kiernan—Major Derry," the monsignor beamed. "I thought it would be nice if you two met."

The girl greeted me charmingly in English, and although I was quickly becoming accustomed to the unexpected visitors to this remarkable room, I was still surprised enough to ask, "How do you happen to be here?"

"Coming from you, that's rich," she laughed. "Don't you know there's a war on? As a matter of fact, I'm neutral—my father is the Irish Ambassador."

Blon Kiernan and the monsignor chatted about mutual acquaintances, and it was clear that the monsignor was a frequent visitor to the Irish Embassy. They both tried, graciously and charmingly, to keep me abreast of the conversation, but I was content to sit and listen, uncomprehendingly; I could not remember when I had last heard casual English small talk, and had the feeling that I had drifted right out of the war into the gay, peaceful, social life of some never-never land.

When the dark Irish girl went out of the room, and, so I presumed, out of my life, the monsignor went with her, and I sat alone again, thinking it would be rather fun to have a sweepstake on who would come through the door next. It turned out to be John May, which was not particularly surprising, but what he said took me off balance.

"I have had a talk with the Minister about you," he said chattily, "and he would like you and the monsignor to join him for dinner at the Legation to-night."

Fortunately, Monsignor O'Flaherty reappeared through the door, and, learning of the Minister's invitation, at once accepted. He and John May sorted out the timing and other details before turning any attention to what I considered the principal problem —namely, getting me into the Vatican.

"It is easy enough to get into the Vatican without being captured by the Germans," confided the monsignor, "but the difficulty is we want to get you out again. If you are caught by the Vatican Guards or gendarmes you will either be interned for the duration or immediately expelled into the arms of the Germans."

"You know," said John May, looking from one to the other thoughtfully, "it is surprising how alike you two are in size and shape."

The monsignor's face wreathed into a cherubic smile, and, with a hand on John May's shoulder, he bade him farewell with the words, "We'll be there."

Early that evening two figures, each topping six feet, stood and surveyed each other across the little room. "Not at all bad, me boy," said the monsignor approvingly. "You look more like a monsignor than I do."

He had changed into the dress worn by monsignors only on formal social occasions: low-crowned black hat, long black cloak, with scarlet buttons all the way down the front, a vivid scarlet sash and silver-buckled black shoes. As he inspected me, he might almost have been looking into a full-length mirror, for I was dressed identically, the monsignor having produced a duplicate of every garment.

"Now, leave everything to me," he said. "Walk beside me, but don't speak or look about you at all. Walk slowly, keep your head bowed, and mumble constantly in prayer. If you don't know any prayers keep your lips moving anyway."

Together we walked slowly down the stairs, out into the courtyard, through the archway, and along the street towards the colonnade, where we turned left towards the great church. Although I was obediently keeping my head down and my eyes low, I was acutely aware of the majesty of the great columns, each ten feet across, soaring more than sixty feet up to a vaulted roof, and set so far apart that a couple of coaches could have driven abreast down any of the curving avenues. I was also aware of the grey-uniformed German soldiers hovering about the vast square, and in my unfamiliar clothing I felt that all their eyes must have been upon me; to walk slowly, and apparently placidly, along the colonnade was a test of self-discipline.

The colossal columns crawled past, and I sensed, rather than observed, the Swiss Guards, now no longer in their picturesque costumes of yellow slashed with blue and red, but in forbidding war-service uniforms. Quivering inside my cassock, I concentrated on praying, and at that moment my prayers were fervent and sincere.

As we passed through the gate the guards looked at us, but with no more than casual interest. No doubt monsignors lost in their devotions were a familiar sight to them, and in any case they probably recognized at once the long-familiar figure of my companion.

The first hurdle was crossed, but I still kept my head well down as we crossed the square, where once part of Nero's circus had stood, and where the first Christian martyrs, including St Peter himself, had sacrificed their lives. We passed the lofty walls of the sacristry, visible from the monsignor's window, and reached the limit beyond which no ordinary pilgrim to Rome is ever allowed.

As we approached the dangerous corner where the Vatican gendarmerie maintained their vigil night and day, I wondered how the audacious impersonation could possibly succeed. Luck was with us, however, for as we passed within a couple of feet or so, the formidable gendarmerie snapped to attention, and saluted. I pretended to be lost in my prayers, but I noticed that the real monsignor acknowledged the salute with a slight nod of the head.

We walked slowly on through little squares and passages, and I realized that although we were still separated by the great edifice of the church from the main palace of the Vatican, this really was a city within a city; everywhere the yellow-and-white flag, with its insignia of tiara and crossed keys, reminded me that in the midst of war I was now on neutral soil. Silently we walked into an austere four-storey building, crossed the hall, and entered a small passenger-lift. Monsignor O'Flaherty pressed the button for the topmost floor, and, as the lift started to climb, turned to me and smiled.

"That wasn't so difficult, was it, me boy?" he asked. "This is the place we want. The Vatican still uses the ground floor for offices, but the refugee legations from Poland, France, and England have the rest of the building now."

At the top we emerged into a small passage, and the monsignor guided me to a door at the end. He pressed the bell, and the door was opened by an Italian footman, who bowed and admitted us into a lofty and immensely long corridor, along which I could see approaching the familiar figure of John May. Grinning at the sight of me, he ushered us into the first room on the right, which was comfortably furnished as a drawing-room, and pressed a White Lady cocktail into my hand before he went off to appraise the Minister of the arrival of his guests. The genuine monsignor refused a cocktail; he never drank, and, in fact, despite the tasteful smoking-jacket he had lent me, he never smoked either, although he was completely tolerant of the indulgence of others.

The British Minister turned out to be so like my preconceived idea of the perfect English diplomat that the impression of theatrical unreality, which had pervaded all my experiences that day, was heightened. Sir Francis D'Arcy Godolphin Osborne, calm and quietly courteous, left me at once with the feeling that there was no crisis in the world which could shake, even momentarily, his unruffled poise, no series of calamities through which he could not walk steadily, smoothing chaos into orderliness. Seldom have I met any man in whom I had such immediate confidence. He welcomed us warmly, yet I found it impossible to behave with anything but strict formality. Apart from the restraining influence of my clothing, I was almost overwhelmed by an atmosphere of old-world English courtliness and grace, which I had thought belonged only to the country-house parties of long ago. Sir D'Arcy was spry, trim, a young sixty, but he had spent years enough in the diplomatic service to develop an astonishing aptitude for creating around himself an aura of all that was most civilized in English life. I felt as though I had returned home after long travels, to find that royalty had come to dinner, and I had to be on my best behaviour.

If a monarch had descended on the dinner party that night

he would have found little to criticize. A large circular table,
set with fine linen, gleaming silver, and glistening glass, seemed to
my prison-camp jaded eyes a picture from a world of fantasy.
A footman prepared the dishes at a sideboard, and John
May served us with grapefruit, a tender steak, with mushrooms,
grilled tomatoes, and more trimmings than I remembered existed,
and a delicious, unidentifiable, creamy sweet, and cheese. The
Minister and the monsignor spoke inconsequentially to each other,
mainly about people known to them both, but, with immense
tact, refrained from involving me in long discussions likely to dis-
tract me from the full enjoyment of a meal which at any time
I should have considered extremely good, and which at that particular moment seemed like something out of the kitchens of
Paradise.

As we dawdled over the cheese the Minister asked me how the
fall of Mussolini had been received by our men in the prison
camps, and in turn told me how the Germans, with a couple of
divisions, had managed to take over Rome, which the new Italian
'republic' had claimed to be defending with very considerable
forces. From Sir D'Arcy, I learned that Rome was now, to all
intents and purposes, just another German-occupied capital, with
the only difference that there was still a residual Italian Fascist
element actively co-operating with the Military Government.

Over the coffee and cigarettes in the drawing-room, many of
the questions which had been buzzing around in my brain all
day found their answers. As I had begun to suspect, there was
already in existence the shadow of an underground organization
working for the welfare of Allied escapers and evaders, and it
was intended that I should be brought into it. Many of the details I was not to learn until several weeks later, but as we talked
late into the night I began to secure a grasp of the immensity and
complexity of the problem. Most of the story of what had already
been done was not revealed until after Monsignor O'Flaherty had
left us, promising to return for me the next day, for it transpired
that it was this remarkable cleric who had done the greater part
of it.

The monsignor, I gathered, first came into contact with Allied
prisoners-of-war as early as 1941, when he was appointed secre-
tary-interpreter to the Papal Nuncio, whom he accompanied on
tours of camps all over northern Italy. The Papal Nuncio

travelled in fairly leisurely fashion by car, visiting one camp a day, but Monsignor O'Flaherty soon found himself travelling by train between camp and Rome every night, because he quickly formed the view that one of the duties of the Church was to ensure that information should be sent to the next of kin of newly captured prisoners as soon as possible. His incessant train journeys enabled up-to-date lists of names to be broadcast promptly by Vatican Radio, and he also took upon himself the task of speeding up the delivery of Red Cross parcels to the prisoners, apart from personally collecting more than ten thousand books, which he distributed around the camps.

His persistent championing of the cause of prisoners-of-war eventually proved irksome to the Italian Government, and around Christmas 1942 he was asked for his resignation, as the result of Fascist pressure. Back in Rome he became a sort of rallying-point for the underdog; Jews and anti-Fascists who were in danger turned to him for help, and he found places for them to hide, secreting one or two—including a glamorous Italian princess— in the German College itself.

The Vatican City authorities, saddled for the duration with half a dozen Allied escaped prisoners-of-war, who had got past the guards, sensed the danger of becoming a Mecca for escapers, and gave orders that all would-be internees should be forcibly expelled at the gates. The first fourteen to suffer this fate all avoided recapture—and had the good fortune to be put in touch with the monsignor. He arranged for them to be housed, under the care of a friendly carabiniere, actually in the Italian police barracks, but when the Germans marched into Rome on September 14, 1943, the Italians fled, and all the escapers except one were recaptured.

Meanwhile the desertion of the Italian guards at camps all around the city had enabled hundreds of prisoners to get away, and many were now beginning to arrive in Rome, mostly in the hope of getting into the neutral Vatican. Some had been directed by friendly priests to the monsignor's office, some turned up at the neutral Swiss Legation, and some contacted Secundo Constantini, the Swiss caretaker at the dust-sheeted British Embassy. The monsignor, bombarded from all sides by calls for assistance, mobilized the help of many Vatican priests, including Irishmen, New Zealanders, and Maltese, in organizing lodgings for the

escapers, but his financial difficulties would have been considerable except for an unexpected gift of money from an anti-Fascist
nobleman, Prince Doria Pamphili. There were plenty of risks,
and even picking up the money proved something of a problem,
for the Prince's house was raided by the S.S. while the monsignor
was there. He had to make his escape disguised as a coalman,
his face blackened, and his clerical robes in a sack over his
shoulder, but fortunately the Germans never thought to ask themselves why a coalman should be carrying a full sack out of the
palace.

As the number of escapers seeking help steadily increased,
Monsignor O'Flaherty realized that some sort of organization had
to be established, and thus it was that a Council of Three came
into being. It consisted of the monsignor, with contacts through
innumerable priests, who brought the escapers in, and found
paces for them to stay; Count Sarsfield Salazar, who was with
the Swiss Legation, and knew of approaches for help made to the
Swiss or to Secundo Constantini at the closed British Embassy;
and John May, who not only provided a direct link with the
British Minister, but had contacts all over Rome, and always
knew where the black-market supplies of food or clothing could
be purchased.

The Council of Three decided to find somewhere for the
accommodation of escapers as soon as they arrived in Rome, for
the men were usually conspicuous because of their tattered clothes,
and were often in poor physical condition. One of the monsignor's
priests found the answer to the immediate problem at 12 Via
Impera, the home of a vivacious, motherly Maltese widow, Mrs
Henrietta Chevalier. In her small flat she lived with her six
daughters and one son, but she was delighted with the idea of
looking after a few of 'our boys' as well. With the best will in the
world, however, she could not accommodate many, and, with
the influx of escapers still expanding, Monsignor O'Flaherty decided that he would have to rent a flat of his own, where reasonably large numbers could stay until permanent billets were found
for them. It delighted his sense of humour when he found what
he wanted in the Via Firenze, for it was in a block backing on the
hotel used as the S.S. headquarters, and was consequently well
within the S.S. curfew cordon; however, he realized that this
might have a practical advantage, since the Germans, if they be-

came suspicious that escaped prisoners were being hidden in Rome, would scarcely begin searching so close to their own premises.

Still the demands on the resources of the Council of Three increased as more and more escapers found their way into the city, often guided by well-meaning priests. Unfortunately, many of these did not realize that it was now impossible for the men to give themselves up for internment at the Vatican, and that the Germans had imposed the death penalty for the harbouring of escapers and evaders—a development of which the German-controlled Rome Radio was daily reminding the inhabitants of the city.

Monsignor O'Flaherty rented another flat, this time in the fashionable Via Chelini, about a mile away from Via Firenze, and obtained supplies of money from the British Minister in the Vatican. But it was clear that the organization was a snowball that threatened to engulf the monsignor. More and more escapers were pouring into Rome, Count Salazar's 'country branch' was developing with alarming speed, and new requests for help were being brought in daily by village priests, from groups scattered about the rural area.

The monsignor kept in close touch with the British Minister, and both agreed that a complete underground military organization was required, but the difficulty was that among all the escapers with whom they were in contact there was no senior British officer who could take command, and the Minister himself, virtually a prisoner in his legation, and in any case in a delicate diplomatic situation, could give little direct help.

"Your note signed 'S. I. Derry, major,' was the first contact we had made with a senior British officer," Sir D'Arcy told me. "When the monsignor saw that in one breath you had thanked him for the money and asked him for more he was highly amused, and decided on the spot that you were the man to take control of the organization. That is why we sent for you.

"I must tell you that I consider the monsignor's efforts have been absolutely wonderful, but he feels, and I agree, that the time has come now when we must appoint somebody to co-ordinate all the work. It will not be easy, and I am afraid it is likely to get more difficult as time goes on. Now that you know what it is all about, are you prepared to take command?"

There was only one possible answer. In the ordinary way I might have been overwhelmed by a sense of inadequacy for the task, but after the stagnation of prison-camp life the chance to do something active again was irresistible.

"Of course, sir," I replied. "But you realize I don't speak any Italian? Won't that complicate things a bit?"

"Very probably, major," said the Minister, "but I am sure you will find a way round that difficulty—and if you don't the monsignor will. You will need to lean on him rather heavily, I'm afraid, particularly in the early stages, but you have no doubt already come to the conclusion that he is a pretty remarkable man. I imagine you will not come across many problems that you and he together cannot solve."

I was still not at all clear about exactly what I was supposed to do, but the Minister brushed aside questions of detail, and said that all specific plans could be worked out later. I asked him when he wanted me to start, and told him that I felt I ought to return first to my own group near Salone, so that they would not be left with the impression that I had simply gone away on my own, and let them down.

"That is what I hoped you would do," said Sir D'Arcy. He told me he would arrange with the monsignor for me to be taken back for a day or two, during which time I was to place the most reliable N.C.O. in charge, and organize the distribution and expenditure of some money that he would give me.

That night, in a proper bed for the first time in eighteen months, I should have gone to sleep as soon as my head touched the pillow, but for an hour or more I lay revelling in the unaccustomed comfort, and musing on my good fortune. When I awoke next morning I still felt as though I was in a dream, for there was a smiling John May beside the bed, with an appetizing breakfast on a tray. All this, I thought, and breakfast in bed too. I felt in the lap of luxury as I ate my boiled egg, toast, and marmalade, as I relaxed comfortably in another hot bath, and as I tried on some stylish clothes of the Minister's, which John May had laid out for me. The Minister was slightly shorter, and a good deal more slender in build, than I, but I found to my delight that I could wear the shirts, socks, pullover, smart blue suit, and shoes which he had provided, without discomfort or apparent absurdity; I also noticed with ironic amusement that the excellent shoes came from a shop in Unter den Linden, Berlin. I kept one pair of socks and one of the cream-coloured shirts with the outer clothing I had worn the day before, and John May said he would take the rest of my new wardrobe to the monsignor's room, where it would be available for me on my return from my trip to the country.

Most of the rest of the day at the legation I spent catching up with the latest war news, and committing it to memory so that I could pass on as much up-to-date information as possible to the men in the foothills, but it was still only mid-afternoon when the monsignor arrived at the legation to take me back to the Collegio Teutonicum.

I put on my clerical robes again, and descended with him into the sunlight, but, in spite of the success of our adventure the previous night, I found it unnerving to repeat the pose in broad daylight. There were many more people about, and it seemed to me, so far as I could see through my lowered eyes, that a higher proportion of them were gendarmes and guards; however, none of them gave us a second look, and it occurred to me afterwards that generally they were all more concerned with keeping people out of the Vatican than with keeping them in. The position in the great *piazza*, with Germans much in evidence, was rather different, but the monsignor walked slowly on through the massive colonnade without apparent concern, and I walked with him, hoping for the best. At the entrance to the college I was startled to see a porter on duty, but he greeted the monsignor reverently, and paid no particular attention to me.

Back in the security of Monsignor O'Flaherty's room, I took off my heavy black robes thankfully, and drew deeply on a cigarette. As I relaxed I allowed my gaze to wander idly over the buildings that could be seen through the window, and suddenly I realized there was something familiar about one of the closest of them.

"Monsignor!" I exclaimed, pointing. "Surely that's the place we have just left?"

"That's right, me boy," he said, joining me to look through the window. "That's the Ospizio di Santa Marta."

"Then didn't we go rather a long way round?" I asked, wondering if it had all been some sort of elaborate joke.

"We did so," he agreed, "but the important thing is we got you there and we got you back. There is a much shorter way, but it means going through two or three gendarmerie posts, where they are used to seeing me alone, and would have been suspicious of you at once. So many people go in and out of the big gates that there is far less risk of being questioned. John May has his own ways through, of course, but he is well known to all the guards, and I think they are mostly beholden to him in a good many little ways."

"You think of everything," I said admiringly.

"Thinking of everything," he replied, "is going to be your job in future."

I stayed the night in the monsignor's room, sleeping on the long sofa. He had arranged for me to return to the foothills next morning with Pietro Fabri, the smallholder who had brought me to Rome, and at dawn he wakened me, and introduced me to a smiling little priest, who was to be my guide.

Through the routine of walking and tram-dozing, to which Zambardi had introduced me, I followed the priest back to the flat of Pasqualino Perfetti, whose greasy appearance depressed me less now that I knew he was associated with the British rather than the Gestapo. My guide departed, and after I had changed back into the old rags which I now considered my country suit, Perfetti led me to the street market, where Pietro Fabri and a daughter—he had too many for me to be sure if it was the same one—were just selling the last of their vegetables.

I looked at the cart, now bare save for one or two empty lettuce boxes, with sudden alarm. In changing into my ragged old clothes, principally because I did not want any of my new outfit to suffer through mingling with the cabbages while I hid at the road-block, I had completely overlooked the fact that on the return journey there would be no cabbages under which to hide, unless Pietro had experienced an unexpectedly disastrous morning. But Perfetti had gone, and there was little hope of making Pietro understand my concern at the lack of cover.

Sitting up, where he had indicated, beside him on the box, and in full view of everybody, I felt sure the end had come when I saw one of the guards at the road-block ahead waving us to a halt. I sat petrified as the guard approached, but so far from demanding to see all our identity documents, he glanced into the back of the cart with sour disinterest, stepped back, and waved us on.

Pietro had not seemed concerned at being stopped, and did

not now appear to be surprised at being allowed to continue on his way instead of being carted off to be shot for helping escaped prisoners; but what I could not know was that Pietro, for all his happy illiteracy, had a much sounder knowledge of the Roman law than I. There were obscure regulations about what sort of wares could be taken into, and out of, Rome, but the only rules affecting people were designed to prevent Italian provincials from moving in, and taking up residence in a city, when there was a general food shortage; thus the road-blocks at every access tended, like the Vatican guard, to be a one-way business, concerned more with what went into the city than with what came out of it.

Half-way home we wobbled to a halt again, but this time it was Pietro's own idea. We stopped outside a little wine-parlour, and I gathered it was his custom to pull up there every time he returned from Rome, the length of his stay being dictated chiefly by the degree of success of his operations on the street market. Although after my early start I welcomed the idea of a glass of red wine, I was somewhat embarrassed—not because I could not pay for my share, but for precisely the opposite reason.

I was carrying in my trousers pocket no less than fifty thousand lire, given to me by the Minister to help my group of escapers, but the notes were all rolled together in a tight wad, and I knew that to produce that amount of money in such a place as this crowded little wine-parlour would probably cause comment. Nevertheless, I could not let Pietro, who had certainly taken his life into his hands to be of service to me, pay for my refreshment. Carefully, a fraction of an inch at a time, I gradually managed to separate just one note from the rest, and produced it from my pocket. It turned out to be a 1000-lire note, and that was more than enough to cause eyebrows to lift.

Pietro welcomed this windfall with ebullience, and was slightly tipsy by the time we mounted the cart again at about three in the afternoon. He had also become rather talkative, and I was not sorry when the wheels started turning, for, apart from consideration of the risks he was taking, I was anxious to get back to my headquarters as quickly as possible. It was not going to be easy to explain my impending departure to the men in the foothills, for the Minister had made it clear to me that I must not tell them where I was going, although I could assure them that they would

continue to be looked after. Equally, explanations would be
difficult with my own hosts and other Italian families in the
vicinity, who had come to look on me as a sort of local British
chargé d'affaires.

In fact, I did not get back to my headquarters at all that night.
When we reached Pietro's farm, which was still a couple of miles
short of my destination, he cheerfully insisted that I should spend
the night with his family. I did so, and found conditions rather
different from those I had experienced in the last two nights—in
the tiny house were fourteen people, sleeping anywhere and everywhere in their clothes.

Early next morning I returned to my own billet, where I was
greeted by my hosts with warmth that turned to rapture when I
presented them with 4000 lire. To me, it seemed a small price to
pay in return for their loyalty and help at the risk of their own
lives. I knew that whatever gratitude there was should be on my
side, but to them it was clearly a fortune, and for an awful moment
I thought they were going to fall on their knees.

That evening I went up to the foothills, briefed the N.C.O.'s
about the disposal of the money I gave them, and told the escapers
what I had learned about the general war situation. From their
point of view, it was not altogether cheerful news. The front line
had become static, and there was practically no hope of making
a successful link-up with our forces until the position became
more fluid, which might well be not before the spring.

"Any of you who want to make an attempt to get south are
at liberty to have a go," I told them. "You will be given all the
help possible—but I can't advise you to try. Your best plan is to
make yourselves as comfortable as possible here, and await developments. Don't take any chances, and don't be tempted to
head for Rome; above all, don't accept invitations to sleep in the
houses around here—the Italians may not all realize that they
would be risking their lives. I must go away from here now, but
I can assure you that you won't be forgotten."

Feeling rather mean, I parried their questions about where
I was going, and after bidding them farewell and wishing them
luck, I returned to sleep for the last time in the straw stack which
had given me such splendid service as hospital, headquarters, and
home.

Next morning Pietro had more cabbages for Rome.

4

Underground Army

QUITE suddenly I realized that I was being interrogated. Sir D'Arcy Osborne was not talking about escape and evasion at all, but was plying me with questions about England and my home town of Newark, about my regiment, about people, and places.

Having been often interrogated by German intelligence officers, I knew the form well enough, but it was a new experience to be subjected to it by somebody who was unquestionably on our side, and it came like a cold anticlimax at the end of a day in which I had looked forward, with excited anticipation, to learning exactly what I was supposed to do in Rome.

I had returned to the Eternal City without incident, the mixture being as before; by Pietro's pony cart to the street market, with a brief sojourn under the cabbages while we went through the road-block, a change of clothes at Perfetti's flat, an escorted tramride to the Collegio Teutonicum, and another successful masquerade as a prayerful monsignor to get into the Vatican. It had seemed almost too easy, and now, in the Minister's blue suit and in the Minister's study, I waited only for my final instructions.

The Minister seemed to be in no hurry to give them, and I became increasingly impatient with his apparent trivial small talk until, suddenly, I realized what lay behind it.

"Sir," I said, when he asked whether I found it more convenient to go through Nottingham when travelling from Newark to London, "you are obviously checking on me. But as I want to help all I can, I hope you will soon be convinced I am who I say I am."

Sir D'Arcy leaned back, and looked at me directly, his sensitive features mingling gravity with mild amusement, in an expression with which I was to become very familiar, but which I never saw on any other man. "Quite so, major," he said, "but you will understand that I have to be very careful. The monsignor never checks up on anybody; he simply accepts at face value every one who asks him for assistance, and immediately gives all the help he can, whatever the risk. I worry about him sometimes, but there seems to be no way of convincing him that his own life is well worth preserving. I imagine he made no attempt to check up on you?"

I realized with a pang how easy it would have been for the enemy to infiltrate an agent into the line through which I had passed, and had to admit that the monsignor had taken me completely on trust, although John May had been rather more cautious. The British Minister had been still more careful, and although I did not know it at the time, he had taken no chances from the start. The courtly knight had been the perfect host at our first meeting, but had not neglected to send off an urgent demand for full information about his guest. His coded message had found its way by devious means from the Vatican to the Foreign Office, in London, then to the War Office, then to Scotland Yard, and finally to Newark Borough Police Force. In Newark Police Inspector Morley called on my father, to give him the information that his son, once again reported missing, was alive and well, though he knew no more information than that. Such, at any rate, was the ostensible reason for his visit, but he spent some time chatting with my father, and, by the time he left, had a good many personal details about me to add to the growing dossier in London.

Consequently, by the time I returned to the Vatican, Sir D'Arcy Osborne knew a good deal about the background of Major S. I. Derry, and in his quiet, apparently casual, conversation he elicited insignificant details which even the most accomplished pretender or agent could scarcely have acquired.

My answers apparently satisfied him, and with that the official British Organization in Rome for Assisting Allied Escaped Prisoners of War was born: a unique military unit, the like of which may never be seen again. The Minister's studied reticence vanished, and I, previously in possession of only a general outline, was soon flooded with details. The aim was straightforward if not simple—namely, to build up, on the foundations laid by Monsignor O'Flaherty and the Council of Three, an organization capable of keeping the constantly growing numbers of escapers converging on the Rome area out of enemy hands. That meant finding places for the men to live, ensuring that they regularly received food, clothing, and medical supplies, and, where possible, concentrating them in relatively 'safe' coastal areas for evacuation by British 'cloak and dagger' forces.

Sir D'Arcy made it quite clear that because of his delicate diplomatic position he would be able to give little direct assistance beyond arranging a supply of funds from British Government sources, for, although Pope Pius XII had been fearless in his outspoken denunciation of Fascist excesses, there was little doubt that the Vatican Secretariat of State would jealously preserve its neutrality, even to the extent of withdrawing its hospitality to the British Legation if it had any suspicion of abuse.

"I think I may be able to help you in one way, though," said the Minister. "There is no reason why we should not arrange for some of the British officers interned in the Vatican to do whatever clerical work you may find necessary, so that you are not cluttered up with administrative detail. They have plenty of time on their hands, and your paper work will be safer inside the Vatican, although you must still be very careful about what you put in writing : the fact that the Vatican has never been raided does not mean that it never will be, particularly when our advance gets near Rome."

This offer of administrative staff was welcome for it had already occurred to me that there would be a mammoth piece of paper-work involved. There were more than a thousand escapers in contact with the organization, but, apart from those actually in Rome and a few others, we did not know who they were. At home they would have been posted as missing, and until we knew their names there would be no way of attempting to get reassurances through to their relatives.

Together the Minister and I discussed the general war situation, and pored over maps of Italy. We could see that there was no reasonable chance of a rapid Allied advance northward, and we realized that any plan to keep escapers out of enemy hands would have to be on a long-term basis. On the other hand, Sir D'Arcy pointed out that in Rome food supplies had to be channelled largely through the black market, that they were already scant, and would probably become much scarcer when winter settled in. So we decided that, so far as possible, escapers should be kept out of Rome, where the risks were greatest, but as it was certain that men would still drift into the city, we decided to work on the principle of providing accommodation temporarily, while continuously filtering them out into groups in the country-side. We could then direct them at the right times either to the coastline or somewhere reasonably close to the front line. A study of the maps revealed a number of places where it seemed unlikely that the Germans would stand and fight, and these I earmarked as areas on which to concentrate.

By the time I had returned with Monsignor O'Flaherty I had a profound realization that little could be achieved without his help, and I told him, "It's a good thing you're pro-British, monsignor."

"What makes you think I am?" he asked sharply.

His reply took me by surprise, but while I was still fumbling for a coherent reply he went on, "I've no reason to be fond of the English, you know. Have you ever heard of the Irish Troubles? The Black and Tans? Well, I saw it all—I was there. It didn't leave me with any vast feeling of affection for your countrymen."

Confused, I stammered, "Then why . . . ?"

"Why am I helping you now? Well, I'll tell you, me boy. When this war started I used to listen to the broadcasts from both sides. All propaganda, of course, and both making the same terrible charges against the other. I frankly didn't know which side to be-lieve—until they started rounding up the Jews in Rome. They treated them like beasts, making old men and respectable women get down on their knees and scrub the roads. You know the sort of thing that happened after that; it got worse and worse, and I knew then which side I had to believe."

In the monsignor's little room I made my headquarters and my home, sleeping on the sofa, and having all my meals brought to me by the German sisters, to whom I was passed off by my host as a friend of his, one Patrick Derry, an Irish writer employed in the Vatican. At first I did not go out at all because, although I now had a reasonable civilian wardrobe, the monsignor advised against it until he was able to equip me with some sort of identity document.

The document produced for me was no rough forgery: it was a genuine Vatican card, bearing a genuine photograph of me in my too tight blue suit. But it named me as Patrick Derry, a Vatican writer, native of Dublin, and son of Isidore Derry and Mary O'Connell; it gave the date of my birth as December 4,

1903, which added eleven years to my real age of twenty-nine, making me too old for national service, and its date of issue was stamped as January 15, 1943, at which time I had actually been firmly incarcerated at Chieti. The protection which it gave was, in fact, slight, since a simple inquiry to the Vatican authorities, or even to the neutral Irish Embassy, would have established very quickly that there was no such Irishman in the place as Patrick Derry, but, on the other hand, it gave me the opportunity of satisfying casual checks or inquiries in the streets of Rome.

That I should have to pound the Roman pavements pretty thoroughly was clear, for while the greater number of escapers remained outside the city, the biggest problem by far was in Rome itself. As I saw it, the concentration and supply of the 'country branch members' was a relatively simple administrative matter, but the lone-wolf stragglers who continued to make their way into Rome would be a permanent headache.

I decided to see for myself all the hiding-places which had so far been arranged in Rome, and with this plan the monsignor was in wholehearted agreement, but for different reasons. He felt it would be a good thing if the escapers were shown that they were once again under direct military command, and he thought it might give a boost to the morale of the Italian helpers if they saw something 'official' was being done.

The first place I wanted to see was the Via Firenze flat, and Monsignor O'Flaherty arranged for one of his priests, Father Owen Snedden, a New Zealander, to act as guide. There was little chance of finding my way about alone, but nevertheless I arranged to follow him at a distance, rather than accompany him, for I had already decided that the priests must remain uncompromised at all costs.

We went by tram to the Via Firenze, which leads off from Via Venti Settembre, the wide road running straight from Rome's Buckingham Palace, the Quirinale, to its most famous gate, the high arched Porta Pia, and housing along its noble sides most of the great Ministry buildings. This is the Whitehall of Rome, but, unlike Downing Street, Via Firenze is not a dead-end. It opens out on to a great opera house, beyond which lay the forbidding Ministry of the Interior. Only a few blocks away was the great railway terminus, which could be guaranteed to contain more German soldiers to the square yard than any other part of

Rome. It would have been hard to think of a less healthy site for an escape centre, but I could see the monsignor's point that it was unlikely to be a suspect area, and it had the further advantage of being close to the dust-sheeted British Embassy, in Via Venti Settembre, where individual escapers were still regularly establishing contact with the caretaker, Secundo Constantini.

The flat contained two or three English soldiers, who had walked out of their camps when the Italians deserted, a fiery Jugoslav Communist, a couple of Jugoslav girls, and a British officer who was not an escaper for the simple reason that he had never been taken prisoner. Lieutenant R. 'Tug' Wilson, R.A., already the holder of the D.S.O., as the result of some brilliant sabotage work behind enemy lines, had been landed on the Adriatic coast prior to the Allied invasion of Italy, and had let off a series of interesting explosions on railway lines and docks before a submarine, which was due to pick him up, failed to keep its rendezvous. He made his way to Rome, and tried to get into the Vatican, but arrived just after the Secretariat's ruling that all would-be internees were to be forcibly excluded. He was picked up bodily by the guards at the gate, and dumped unceremoniously in St Peter's Square, where, luckily, he failed to attract German attention. He was fortunate enough to be directed to Monsignor O'Flaherty, who took him to the Via Firenze flat—and brought away a letter addressed to the Pope himself, in which Wilson complained angrily of the treatment he had received at the Vatican. It says much for the monsignor's sense of humour that he actually delivered this expression of injured feelings to the Secretariat, and in due course returned with an official acknowledgment, enclosing a personal invitation to visit the Vatican at some more propitious time.

Because of the difficulty of getting back to my 'headquarters' on the right side of the curfew, I had arranged with the monsignor to spend the night at Via Firenze, and I found the experience somewhat disturbing: we were well within the S.S. security cordon, and after the streets had been cleared for the night I had great difficulty in getting used to the German motor-cycles and patrol-cars, which howled past the windows continuously.

The other occupants of the flat treated the noise of German activity with complete indifference, and the Jugoslav Communist kept me up for most of the night in animated argument. Bruno Büchner was a man of strong views, and he treated the idea of an organization to help Allied escapers with derision. "Why spend money on them?" he demanded. "What use are they to the war effort? We all ought to be killing Germans, and blowing things up."

Patiently I tried to explain that the numbers of men at large would eventually represent a very considerable addition to the war effort, if we could keep them well and free, quite apart from the even more important humanitarian aspect. Büchner thought little of the first point, and nothing at all of the second. The farthest he would go was to suggest that all the men should be given food, and sent blundering southward. The Jugoslav's arguments gave me an interesting new outlook on Communist philosophy, but I could not foresee then what I learned later: that his passion for blowing things up could be a tragically back-firing weapon.

Next morning Graziella, one of the Jugoslav girls, guided me back to St Peter's Square, where, as arranged, I found another priest waiting for me under the colonnades. Father John Claffey led me a little way down the great avenue away from St Peter's, then right into Via dei Penitenzieri, where he shared an apartment with another Irish priest, Father Vincent Treacy, of the Congregation of St Mary. Because they lived so close to the monsignor's office, they frequently accommodated his latest protégés, and I met three new escapers there.

Father Claffey then took me to my next guide, a cheerful little Maltese named Brother Robert Pace, who was to lead me to the home of his gallant countrywoman, Mrs Chevalier, the first to provide accommodation for the monsignor's escapers. Brother Robert, whose black cassock was ornamented by the little white bows of his Order, led me back to the tramstop on the far side of the river Tiber. We had, of course, agreed not to sit together, but the tram was unexpectedly full, and I found myself completely separated from my guide by a crowd of Italians. I wondered, as I 'dozed' on the tram, how I should manage if I lost him altogether, but I was not unduly alarmed. I had memorized the address to which we were going, and I could manage enough Italian to ask, "D'ove la Via Impera?" I should probably have failed to make much of a voluble reply, but I was prepared to

take a chance on interpreting the gestures which would undoubtedly go with it. In any case, I was pretty sure I could find
my way back to St Peter's and the Collegio Teutonicum, although
it might mean a long walk through dangerous streets instead of a
tramride. By the merest chance, my more pessimistic plans did
not have to be put to the test; at one stop something seemed to
compel me to 'wake up' and take the risk of staring round behind me—and there was my guide with one foot already on the
road. I leapt up, pushed my way past the other passengers, and
jumped off with the tram already moving away.

Brother Robert led me through a couple of streets, which, like
so many in Rome, seemed to be a mixture of the seedy and the
spectacular—overcrowded apartments with peeling plaster rub-
bing lintels with palatial buildings, in a curious classlessness. We
turned into an entrance between two shops, climbed endless
stairs, and rang the bell at an apartment door, which was opened
by a vivacious and voluble little woman with bright dark eyes and
a kind, motherly face.

Mrs Chevalier was expecting us, and she welcomed me as
though I were a long-lost son. She ushered us in, and introduced
me to the four British soldiers who were billeted with her. Looking round the tiny flat, I could not imagine how they all managed to live there at once, and I was amazed at the thought that
the little widow also had seven of her own offspring in residence.
It was not surprising that there were mattresses to be seen everywhere, on the floor, all along the corridor, and propped against
the walls.

My intention had been to thank Mrs Chevalier on behalf of
the British Army for all she had done and was doing, but her
idea was clearly to have some sort of party. She fussed around,
setting out food and drink, laughing, and chattering continuously
to the effect that everything was wonderful. When at last I was
able to edge a word into the cheerful torrent, and asked if the
escapers were giving any problems, she replied, "They are absolutely grand, these boys. They are just like my own children. It
is all so marvellous."

If Mrs Chevalier realized that her life was in danger every
minute she had a single escaper, let alone four, in her care, she
gave no signs of it. With the same spirit of stoic gallantry that
earned for her island home a George Cross, she accepted her

rôle in the war as a personal duty, and then proceeded to make a pleasure of it. I was embarrassed by the realization that she looked upon my visit as an honour bestowed upon her, whereas I had, in fact, come to thank her humbly and gratefully. But every time I tried she thanked me for letting her have 'her boys,' and plied me with pastries and wine. I decided that if I could not express my thanks I would at least take the practical step of ensuring, so far as lay within my power, that no harm ever befell her, and, as a start, I impressed firmly on the four escapers that they were in a position of great responsibility, and would be held personally answerable if she should find herself in trouble through any carelessness or indiscretion of theirs. I was glad to observe that they accepted this burden willingly: it was obvious that they would gladly have given their own lives to save hers.

Before I left we also worked out a rudimentary escape drill, the cardinal principle of which was that in emergency they should get as far away from Via Impera as possible, and thereafter refrain from divulging, even to other escapers, where they had been living, for the use of Mrs Chevalier's flat as an unofficial transit camp meant that already more than enough people knew of her work. Needless to say, my visit to Mrs Chevalier lasted a good deal longer than I had expected, and I returned to the Collegio Teutonicum only just in time to beat the curfew.

The course of the next few days followed the same pattern of scurrying about Rome under the noses of the enemy, but although I felt conspicuous in daylight, I knew that to be found on the streets after curfew would invite searching, and possibly a disastrous interrogation. I never became quite used to the sudden shock of finding myself walking among a group of German soldiers, or face to face with a couple of S.S. men as they emerged from a café, their jack-boots gleaming, and the skull-and-cross-bones insignia leering hideously from their lapels; nor did I ever conquer the sense of loneliness that walked with me on the streets of Rome—for if the stranger in a strange land is always lonely he is never more so than when he dare not speak, even in his own language.

Then followed a period of reconnaissance rather than action, but at every billet I visited I put the senior man in command, and instituted a form of evacuation drill, the foundation of which was that the escaper should rapidly remove all traces of his occupation before he left. There was not much point in preserving the freedom of the escaper if it cost the lives of three or four loyal Italians.

I visited all the other billets in Rome, usually with Monsignor O'Flaherty as my guide. If the distance was reasonable we walked, partly because I needed the exercise, but chiefly because the monsignor liked walking. In any case, tram journeys were always worrying, because sometimes a voluble Italian wanted to talk, and my 'dozing' act was not invariably successful.

On one occasion the talkative passenger beside me was not a Roman at all but a grey-uniformed German soldier, who decided that I was just the person on whom to practise his Italian. He asked me a question, in what was obviously intended to be Italian, but was so mangled by guttural Teutonic intonation that I doubt if any Roman citizen could have understood it, let alone me. I dared no more than grunt a reply, but the German was persistent, and spoke again. Making a show of annoyance at being disturbed, I settled more deeply into my 'doze,' but realizing as I turned an expressive back to the soldier that this was not the sort of behaviour that Germans expected or generally tolerated from Italians, I decided not to press my luck too far, and as the tram ground to its next stop, I 'awoke' with a start, pushed past the soldier, jumped off, and walked quickly down the street. I was still far short of my destination, but fortunately the priest who was guiding me had noticed what was happening, and got off in time to overtake me, and, without speaking, lead me back to my proper course.

I was paying fairly frequent visits to the British Minister to report progress, and the monsignor's soutane now sat less uncomfortably on my shoulders; indeed, the gendarmes never made any effort to challenge me, and the guards around the Collegio Teutonicum became so accustomed to the new 'Vatican writer' in the tight blue suit that they even acknowledged me with salutes. I was becoming quite adept at behaving with priestly calm and dignity on my visits as a monsignor to the Vatican, but it was always a relief to get back into the rôle of the Irish Patrick Derry, which called for no acting ability.

On one call at the Vatican Sir D'Arcy Osborne introduced me to Captain Henry Judson Byrnes, a Royal Canadian Army Service Corps officer, who had been interned in the Vatican since

September. With Major John Munroe Sym, of the Seaforth Highlanders, and Sub-Lieutenant Roy Charlton Elliott, a young submarine officer, he had broken away from a prison-camp party being marched through the back streets of Rome, and they were lucky enough to contact a friendly Italian doctor, who drove them in his car to the Vatican. There they were promptly taken over by the Pontifical Gendarmerie, and lodged in the barracks as internees, shortly before the Vatican made its unequivocal 'no admittance' rule. They were living in the barracks, furiously impatient, and annoyed with themselves for having voluntarily become internees in the mistaken hope that they would be freed within a few weeks by a rapid Allied advance. However, they had a certain amount of freedom during the day, and were able to visit the British Legation, where eventually the long-suffering secretary to the Legation, Mr Hugh Montgomery, surrendered his own office for use by them as a sort of clubroom—a typical gesture by a generous man, whose work for the organization was in due course to place escapers all over northern Italy permanently in his debt.

Captain 'Barny' Byrnes was to be my promised administrative assistant, and it was pleasing to learn that he and Elliott had already begun card-indexing all escapers so far known to be at large in Italy. Although records were reasonably secure with Byrnes, we agreed that all documents relating to the day-to-day work of the organization for escapers should be placed in tins, and buried each night in the Vatican gardens, to which he assured me he could gain access after dark. These records, showing how the Government's money had been spent, would be available for the ultimate day of reckoning with the War Office, but could remain safely undisturbed in the meantime. Byrnes tackled his mammoth task with enthusiasm, and it was largely through his work that we were able, not only to ensure that the assistance we were giving went into the right channels, but also to set at rest the minds of worried relatives of missing men much sooner than might otherwise have been possible.

On the same day I was introduced to Count Sarsfield Salazar, the only member of the original Council of Three whom I had not previously met. He told me that the Swiss Embassy was still being inundated with requests for help from escapers in the surrounding countryside, and we arranged that he should continue to send out assistance, with the aid of funds which I would pass to him. Unfortunately, his work was interrupted only a few days later, when, learning that he had been denounced, he went into hiding. It was a timely warning, for two days later the S.S. burst into his vacant apartments, and carried out a search so thorough that all his valuable furniture was wrecked and most of his personal possessions destroyed. The Count remained under cover, and his efforts for the organization were naturally restricted, although he continued to do much good work in the purchase of clothing, food, and medical supplies.

A more spectacular meeting put me in contact, for the first time, with our own forces on the other side of the line. Unaware of what was being done in Rome, the British 'cloak and dagger' force headquarters in the south of Italy had decided to send an agent north with 20,000 lire, to help any Allied escapers or invaders he might meet. The man chosen was a small dark Italian named Peter Tumiati, who had for several years been a political prisoner of the Fascists. Tumiati, knowing Rome, naturally knew Monsignor O'Flaherty, to whom he sent a message immediately upon arriving in the city. The monsignor replied, asking him to a rendezvous with me, and so we met in the usual place, under the colonnade of St Peter's Square.

Tumiati told me that he was returning to Bari, on our side of the lines, and asked me if there was anything he could do to help. My difficulty was that one can scarcely ask an M.I. 9 man for his credentials. The monsignor, in whatever way my questions were phrased, simply said, "Why, me boy, I know him well," and changed the subject.

There was method as well as madness in the monsignor's outlook, for in the 'underground' business one had to have a certain amount of faith. However, I thought I had better ask for something pretty harmless, and then wait and see whether Tumiati came back with it or with a couple of Teutonic friends, so I asked him if he could possibly find me a few street-maps of Rome. This was an innocuous request, because although maps were physically difficult to come by, possession of them was not viewed with any suspicion by the authorities, and Tumiati looked faintly surprised that I should need assistance in such a simple direction.

"That," he said, "I can do at once." And he did, picking up

a sizeable supply from the back room of a local printer, who was known to him.

Although not inclined to entrust much information to the agent, I decided that the most useful and least dangerous thing to do was to send back to Bari a list of all the ex-prisoners known to be at large. If it fell into enemy hands it would probably tell them little they did not already know, since it could be assumed that the Germans had by now discovered the loss of several hundreds of prisoners; but, on the other hand, it would be of immense value to our own side, and would indicate to Military Intelligence that some sort of organization in Rome was looking after escapers.

"If we are to do this," I said to Monsignor O'Flaherty and John May, "and the Germans catch Tumiati with it, he will certainly be shot. We have to find a way of giving him a sporting chance of smuggling it through the country."

"Microfilm the lot," said John May thoughtfully. "I can arrange it," he grinned, giving the broadest possible wink, which I took as a recommendation not to inquire too deeply into his methods.

The tiny microfilm, which John May produced a few hours later, was so small that it was hard to believe that it could contain in legible form perfect copies of all the lists prepared by 'Barney' Byrnes, running now to nearly 2000 names, numbers, and ranks.

"Where do we go from here?" I mused.

Again it was the ingenuity of John May that produced the answer. He took the film away, and later returned with a number of small loaves of the type the Italians were always seen carrying. He had put the film into the dough and baked it.

"There!" said John May happily, "and a better bit of bread you won't find in Italy, though I say it myself."

Peter Tumiati was delighted with the ruse, and promised that if he got through to Bari a particular phrase at the end of a B.B.C. broadcast from London would give us the news in due course.

"Don't eat the wrong one!" I grinned as he departed.

I listened to the B.B.C. broadcasts, and, sure enough, one night some weeks later a single phrase told me that Tumiati had been as good as his word. The British were now in possession of a list of the escapers in our care, and in nearly two thousand homes missing had become 'Missing—but known to be safe.' Unfortunately, the list was now far out of date.

In the meantime I had made another unexpected contact. Umberto Losena had been a major in the Italian paratroop corps, but after the German occupation of Rome he had volunteered to work against the Germans, and had been trained by the British as a radio-operator. He had arrived in Rome to find out whatever he could about the enemy, and report back by means of a tiny British transmitter in a suitcase.

The monsignor brought the ex-major to me, and I liked him on sight: he was a handsome man, and there was a burning integrity in his dark eyes. He had the singular, calculated courage of all underground radio-operators—for the man who was caught with a secret radio knew that he could expect only torture until he talked, and only death when he talked. Losena had a glowing loathing of the Nazis, and his eagerness to help the organization extended far beyond sending the occasional message to Bari. "I am an Italian," he smiled, spreading his hands, "I can go anywhere for you."

He was the first free-lance agent, able to travel with relative freedom anywhere in the country, to come my way, and he soon became one of my most valuable contacts. He would visit me two or three times every week, and take supplies to the escapers and evaders all over the provinces of Lazio and Umbria.

But I did not forget that Umberto Losena was in Rome for the purpose of relaying information about the Germans. The men I visited in the billets often saw troop and other movements, and I made a point of noting details, like the unit badges worn by German soldiers I saw. It was satisfying to be playing an attacking rôle again, though in but a small way, and in any case I felt that the military side of the organization ought, if possible, to provide some return for the British taxpayer's money being expended on it. We comprised two thousand potential agents behind enemy lines, and it was a natural duty to keep our eyes open for anything useful to the intelligence people. But I think I got the better of the bargain. Apart from his direct assistance to the organization, Losena enabled me to put into operation a plan for the supply and evacuation of some of our escapers.

Messages to Bari arranged successful supply-drops from Royal Air Force planes to two of our largest country groups, at Montorio Romano and Nerola, some miles north of Rome, and four separate drops of parachute canisters not only relieved the strained resources of the organization but also overcame, for a time, the problem of transporting vast quantities of stores out of Rome.

With Losena's radio it was also possible to arrange for three successful evacuations of escapers concentrated near the Adriatic beaches. In each case the 'cloak and dagger' boys sent in field teams, who arranged for the escapers to be on the right spot at the right time, and in each case the remarkable nearly independent force known as 'Popski's Private Army' landed a tough detachment to form a bridgehead, and, if necessary, engage the Germans while the ex-prisoners were loaded on to the waiting troop landing craft.

The 'cloak and dagger' boys were prepared for trouble on any scale, but the remarkable fact is that several hundred escapers were moved to the beaches, and spirited into the night without attracting any attention at all from the Germans; not a single shot was fired.

These three operations, despite their audacity, must have been among the cheapest of the war—but not for Umberto Losena, whose little wireless-set had made them possible. He always made his transmissions from the same place, and gradually the Gestapo net tightened around him, as direction-finding equipment took new bearings on each successive signal. He was arrested, and my gloomy foreboding that we should never see him again was fulfilled.

The lesson of the gallant Italian was taken to heart, and thereafter secret radio-operators working in Rome—in time there were four—sent each message from a different place, often working from park benches while apparently making love to a girl. Rome has many parks and public gardens, and it was never necessary for an operator to send his messages from a building. The continuous changes of location defeated the Gestapo direction-finders, who possibly believed that there were a hundred secret transmitters in Rome, but so far as I am aware no other Allied operator was ever arrested.

Security ruses such as these were beyond me during my first week or two in command of the new organization, for most of my early thoughts about security were directed against Monsignor O'Flaherty's extraordinary habit of introducing all sorts of characters, some of whom I viewed dubiously. Sometimes he sent a message asking me to come down to the Holy Office to meet some one, but often, without any warning, he would throw open the door of his room, in which he was harbouring an escaped British officer without the approval of his superiors, and usher in a complete stranger.

It was in this disconcerting manner that I met two immaculate Frenchmen, Jean de Blesson and François de Val, whom the monsignor gaily introduced as first and second secretaries at the Ambassade de France—unaware, I presumed, that French embassies were units of the Vichy Government, which was actively collaborating with the Germans.

The two Frenchmen welcomed me almost passionately, and lost no time in pointing out that the French Ambassador was, indeed, a Vichy man, hand in glove with the German Military Government. His embassy, on the other hand, was the headquarters of the Free French movement in Rome, which De Vial and De Blesson were spending almost all their time organizing. I had now had several meetings with Blon Kiernan, and had become used to the idea of an Irish Embassy headed by a strict neutral with a wholly pro-British family, but I was surprised by this even more extreme division in the French Embassy.

De Vial and De Blesson were not merely pro-British: they wanted to work positively against the Germans straight away. Volubly and enthusiastically they offered me the use of all the resources of their organization. Embarrassingly they made it clear that they looked to me, as the only British commander in Rome, for instruction on all matters of war policy. Although I could not see myself in the rôle of a sort of underground elderly statesman, I accepted their offer of help gratefully.

An astonishing number of underground organizations seemed to be operating in Rome. Apart from the Free French and ourselves, there were the Royal Jugoslavs and the Jugoslav Communists, the organization of Roman noble families and the Italian Communists—all with remarkable 'grape-vines,' which soon told them of me and my hopes. In normal times the people making up these groups would have been at each other's throats, but now they all wanted the same thing—the defeat of Germany. One by one, their representatives contacted me, all offering help, though some were more concerned with active subversion and sabotage than with the maintenance of escaped prisoners. I was the first British commander they had met, and most of them assumed, quite wrongly, that I was in direct touch with the armies in the field. Consequently, like the French secretaries, they started looking to me for policy decisions, and I found myself, rather to my surprise, the mandatory leader of a unique underground army—or, as I preferred to think of it, the honorary president of a sort of United Nations conglomeration of 'kindred societies.'

The most swashbuckling, although one of the smallest, of the underground movements was that of the Greeks, and my first introduction to them rather took my breath away. Presented to me by the monsignor, Evangelo Averoff and Theodore Meletiou immediately announced that the latter, on a trip to the north of Italy, had discovered a spectacular group of British escapers : three generals, an air vice-marshal, and four brigadiers.

Averoff, a former Prefect of Corfu, who was later to become his country's foreign minister at a time when relations with England were far less amicable, did most of the talking. He said that Meletiou had been taken prisoner, while fighting in the Greek army, and subsequently escaped. He had been travelling about the country looking for other Greek escapers who were in need of assistance, was just about to head north again, and his services were at my disposal.

I was not sure what to do for the best, for while it was clearly desirable for me to establish contact with the impressive addition to the 'country branch,' I certainly did not consider Rome at the present time to be a secure place in which to hide eight very senior British officers. Finally, I gave Meletiou, who used the code name 'Mario,' 10,000 lire for the officers, and suggested he might lead one of them—but not more—back to Rome if he could manage it. Mario did not seem to consider this a formidable assignment, and set off happily on his travels, but I confess that I never really expected to see him again, let alone one of the generals. However, I was to learn, like the Trojans and the Italian Fascists before me, that it is unwise to underestimate the Greeks.

The generals would have been an embarrassing addition to my company of underground Romans, but apart from that, the whole object of my strategy at that time was to keep the traffic flowing in the opposite direction—from Rome into the country. With the help of rural priests and villagers, we had, in fact, managed to move a good number of billetees from Rome out to the greater

safety of the country groups, but as soon as we laboriously evacuated a few, others drifted in to the city. From all over northern
Italy Allied escapers were still making a bee-line for Rome, mostly
with the out-dated idea of surrendering for internment at the
Vatican. Not only the escapers themselves, but the Italians who
helped them, thought this was the right thing to do. As soon,
therefore, as we stopped a trickle from one direction, a stream
started coming in from another.

I decided that we should have to provide a reception centre,
so that large numbers could be lodged at short notice if necessary,
while alternative billets were found. So we cleared the flats at
Via Firenze and Via Chelini.

There was a risk in keeping large groups of escapers in one
place, even for a short time. Too many eggs were in one basket.
But there were advantages, for it gave us time to interrogate new
arrivals, check their stories, and so reduce the growing danger of
admitting a stool-pigeon into the line. Moreover, the flats gave
us a certain amount of breathing-space, since finding 'lodgings'
with Italian families could not be done on the spur of the moment,
and the number of men who could be accommodated in any one
'cell'—as the billets became known—was restricted; often just a
couple, and sometimes only one.

By the beginning of December the number of escapers and
evaders on the organization's books had passed well beyond the
2000 mark, and there were eighty precariously hidden in Rome
itself. Even with the two flats, finding accommodation for this
number was a serious problem, and the supply of food was becoming daily more difficult. The most severe winter for many
years had begun, and, one way and another, the Rome organization was stretched to its limits. Once again, the only solution
seemed to be an increase of staff. Monsignor O'Flaherty's priests
were working wonders, but I considered they were already carrying too heavy a burden, and they could not become involved in
the expanding intelligence work now becoming an important part
of the military side of the organization. We needed a couple more
officers, confident, yet with a sound sense of security, and pre-
ferably able to speak Italian with some fluency. So I began to
size men up for reasons other than mere caution as I interviewed
the new arrivals. Most of those interviews took place in Monsignor O'Flaherty's office on the ground floor at the Holy Office,

to which escapers were directed in a steady stream by a host of agencies, and to which I was constantly being invited over the internal telephone.

The monsignor, needless to say, welcomed every new arrival with cheerful enthusiasm, and paid no attention to my repeated protests that he was putting himself in danger. "Don't worry, me boy," was always his reply. Nevertheless, I could not help worrying for the safety of this great and generous man. I broke into a cold sweat every time I contemplated how readily he might help some reasonably competent Gestapo agent to uncover all his activities, and how easy it would be for the Germans to get a stool-pigeon into the organization's headquarters.

On December 8, beaming all over his face, Monsignor O'Flaherty flung open the door of his room, and announced, in a resonant boom that echoed all the way down the corridor, "Another new arrival for you, Patrick." Turning, I caught my breath. I recognized at once the dark, inscrutable face and the small sallow frame of the multi-lingual Cypriot, whom I believed responsible for the treacherous denunciation of the escape committee at Chieti prison camp. It was Joe Pollak. And, for all I knew, the monsignor had already given away enough to get himself shot.

5

No Red Tabs

EVER since I started working for the organization, I had been looking out for people from Chieti, particularly now I was seeking potential assistants, but I had never given a thought to Joe Pollak, who was certainly the last man from P.G.21 I wanted to see in Rome. Yet here he was, and losing my head would only add to whatever trouble we were in already, so I steeled myself to greet him politely. I decided that the best way of preventing him from finding out any more was to do the asking myself.

"It's a hell of a surprise to see you here," I told him truthfully. "How did you manage it?" Pollak, who seemed quite at his ease, said he had been underground with a large number of escapers and evaders in Sulmona, eighty miles to the east. This, at least, I knew could be true, because a good deal of financial assistance had been going there through an Italian girl.

"Things got a bit hot at Sulmona," Pollak continued. "The Jerries were raiding everywhere, and our Italian 'padrones' started to lose their nerve. Most of the chaps decided to get away until things calmed down a bit, and some of us thought we would make for Rome. I've left the others in a hotel here. I came with six others, apart from a couple of Italian girls."

This seemed to be the obvious way for an agent to infiltrate himself into the organization, and the fact that it was difficult to get people into the city only increased my suspicions. Quite apart from that, even if all were genuine escapers, it meant seven additional mouths for the organization to feed at a time when our strategy was to get people out into the country. I must lose either way. If his six companions did not exist Pollak was certainly working for the enemy; if they did, and were genuine, it was still possible that he was an agent who had infiltrated with them.

Playing for time, I asked for the names of those he had brought with him, and he started his catalogue. "Well, there's Lieutenant Furman, Lieutenant Simpson . . ."

This was better news indeed, for John Furman and Bill Simpson, both Gunner lieutenants, had been close friends of mine at Chieti, and I knew that they were men who could be trusted implicitly. Both had made escapes in the Sulmona area some time before my own jump from the train.

Simpson, tall and thin, with a slow, calm smile, and sensitive hands that had managed to coax music from an unfriendly double bass in the Chieti camp orchestra, had, in fact, contrived to avoid the Sulmona camp altogether. On the way there in a lorry, with about thirty other prisoners, he had jumped over the side as the vehicle turned into the lane leading to the camp. His timing was impeccable, for the turn diverted the attention of the German guards, and also brought the lorry sufficiently close to the hedge at the side of the road to enable him to plunge clean over it into a field, where, shaken but unharmed, he lay low for a while, and then got away while the Germans at the camp were still trying to work out how and where they had lost him.

Furman, a complete contrast in temperament and appearance, was short, wiry, red-headed and dynamic, a master of the theory of escape, and endowed with more initiative than any other prisoner I had known. No troglodyte, he confessed that tunnels took too long to produce results for his tastes. Always during our discussion of various schemes at Chieti, he favoured the use of subterfuge, although many of his ideas were impracticable for anybody without his fluency in both German and Italian. Unlike Simpson, his close friend, Furman was transported to Sulmona camp by the Germans, but he did not condescend to stay for very long before bamboozling them into letting him walk out again, unhindered, and in broad daylight. He persuaded the Germans to allow prisoners to go, under armed escort, out of camp, and down the road to a village horse-trough, where they could wash. This, he pointed out to the hygiene-conscious Germans, would reduce the danger of lice infestation in a camp that suffered from a chronic shortage of water. He enjoyed his first wash, although he and his companions startled the Italian peasants by stripping naked, and plunging bodily into the trough. But his principal aim in going out with the first party was to survey the geography beyond the double wire, and an opportunity to put his new knowledge to good use came only a day or two later. He saw another column heading through the gates towards the trough, so, on the spur of the moment, he grabbed a towel, and rushed after them, explaining in breathless German to the sentry who stopped him at the gate, "I'm with that party. I'm a bit late." Curtly commanded to hurry after them, Furman made every pretence of doing so, trotting diligently, but carefully refraining from closing the fifty-yard gap between him and the two armed guards at the rear of the marching column. He was still fifty yards behind when he followed them round a bend in the lane, where a hedge obscured the view of the sentry at the gates, and, bending suddenly double, he charged straight through the hedge, and into the very field from which Bill Simpson had begun his escape.

I had heard nothing of either since their rejection of further German hospitality, and their arrival in Rome seemed to me too good to be true. It was clear that the only way to find out if Pollak was telling the truth was to see them for myself.

"Would you feel happy about going back now, and returning here again to-morrow?"

"Certainly," he said.

"Very well, then. Come back in the morning, and bring Lieutenant Furman with you, will you?"

I was watching Pollak keenly as I spoke, but he remained impassive, and seemed not at all perturbed. After he had gone, I was alternately depressed, as I thought of the danger to which the whole organization seemed exposed, and elated, at the prospect of a reunion with John Furman. If Furman really was in Rome I knew that he would jump at the chance of helping with the work, and no one was more suited to the task.

Reckoning that sufficient risks had already been taken, I arranged to be told of Pollak's arrival at the inquiry office next morning, and to go down there instead of allowing him and whoever he brought to be shown up. When the messenger came I made my way with mixed feelings to the porter's office. Two visitors were already facing the door when I opened it, and with delight I recognized the unmistakable diminutive form of John Furman, thinner than I remembered him, but still wiry, and obviously bursting with suppressed energy.

"Sam!" he shouted, and then looked round him guiltily, as though remembering he was not in a British officers' club. I knew that we were safe enough, and that the one or two guards pottering about the room were friends.

"John, you old beggar! It's damned good to see you!" I exclaimed, and there followed a welter of hand-shaking and back-slapping.

As I led Furman and Pollak through the courtyard to the Collegio Teutonicum, I learned that they had arrived at the Vatican in style, Pollak, with his supremely confident command of the language, having engaged a *carrozza*, or horse-drawn cab, so that Furman should see something of the glories of Rome on the way.

Outside the college I collected a salute from a guard to whom I had by now become a familiar figure.

"You seem to be pretty well known around here," said Furman, wide-eyed.

"I know most of the guards in this part," I admitted. "They are all first-class chaps. But be careful—don't jump to the conclusion that all the guards at the Vatican will be so friendly."

At the door of the room which I shared with the monsignor we paused, and I told Furman to go in while I took Pollak to an empty room at the end of the corridor, where I asked him to wait. I was determined to get Furman alone, and find out how they had come in contact with each other.

Remembering the warm hospitality that had made my own first visit to the monsignor's room such a delight, I did not immediately broach the subject with Furman, but told him to make himself comfortable, and offered him a drink.

"Well, just one, as this is a bit of an occasion," he replied, "but, by and large, I have to keep off the stuff. They tell me it is no good for dysentery."

I assured him that could be put right, because by now the escapers in Rome had their own underground health service, supplied by a couple of R.A.M.C. officers—a doctor and a dentist.

"I expect you are wondering where Pollak is," I said, as we set our glasses down, and Furman nodded. "Well, John, before I take him into my confidence, I want you to tell me everything you know about him. We were not at all sure about him at Chieti —thought he might be the stool-pigeon. We couldn't prove anything, but the stories he told about his capture in Greece and transfer to Italy never seemed to add up. What do you think?"

"I think," said Furman slowly, "that Joe Pollak is one of the most terrific chaps I've ever met."

This was unexpected, but I began to understand what he meant as he gave me an outline of what had happened to him since he walked out of the prison camp at Sulmona. After bursting through the hedge, Furman had lain low in his field for seven hours before judging it safe to proceed, and even then he had difficulty in keeping out of the way of the searchlights, which continuously swept the surrounding countryside from towers set along the barbed-wire perimeter of the camp. His aim was to walk south, and join up with the Allied forces, but first he had to skirt the town of Sulmona. This took all night, crawling through streams and bogs, but at dawn he found to his disgust he was back where he had started. He hid in a hut, where he was discovered by some Italian boys, who fortunately turned out to be friendly, and took him to a family just outside the town. There the son of the house, a former lieutenant in the Italian artillery, agreed to help him on his way south.

But first, the Italian said, Furman must stay long enough to meet a friend of his. He rummaged through a pile of books, and brought out a small photograph. It was of Joe Pollak. After a couple of wearying days, Pollak arrived at the house, well dressed in civilian clothes, and looking prosperous. He explained that he had been one of a large group of prisoners who had escaped when their guards deserted, and had taken to the mountains near Sulmona. There, because of his knowledge of the language, he had been appointed liaison officer with the Italians. Eventually, he obtained forged identity papers as a 'medical student,' and was moving quite freely about the town, where he had formed a number of anti-Fascist families into a loose organization aimed at helping Allied escapers. Furman was delighted to learn that the officer who was engaged in organizing the escapers into billets was none other than his old friend, Lieutenant Bill Simpson, and was all in favour of meeting him at once, but Pollak advised against attempting to wander around Sulmona looking like the least prosperous sort of tramp, and suggested that he should wait until he was re-kitted.

Several days later Furman and Simpson were reunited, and they shared the growing work of organizing the escaped prisoners. Between them they arranged the audacious escape by sheet-ladder of seven prisoners from the local hospital—and the Italian woman doctor, who had been looking after them, went too, deciding that she could do more for her own patients if she set up headquarters in the hills than if she remained under close German supervision.

The Germans, in fact, had a tight hold on Sulmona, and round-ups were frequent. When the usual accompaniment of shouting, door-battering, and hysterics announced another raid, one night in October, Furman hid in a bush in the garden, and was just congratulating himself on a narrow escape when he got up to find himself face to face with a German soldier. It would be difficult to say which was the more surprised, but the Briton was the quicker to react: he gave the German a hearty shove in the chest with both hands, sprinted away, and leapt at a three-foot fence. Unfortunately, Furman was never designed for hurdling, and he picked himself up painfully on the other side, to find that he was surrounded by menacing Germans. He was added to a growing group of captives, but, on looking round, recognized hardly any of them, and when the explanation dawned on him he was not sure whether to be amused or horrified. This was not a round-up of escaped prisoners-of-war and their helpers, but a routine collection of Italians for forced labour.

The idea of becoming a slave labourer for Hitler's Reich did not greatly appeal to Furman, but he spent a fortnight digging vehicle pits under German supervision at a site some miles from Sulmona. He put little effort into his spade-work, but devoted a good deal of energy to investigating the possibility of bribing his way out of the labour camp. At length it paid dividends, for with the connivance of a disgruntled Austrian guard, he slipped through the gate, and walked back to Sulmona.

He revelled in the welcome he received from Simpson and Pollak, but in Sulmona food, clothing, medical supplies, and accommodation were all becoming more difficult to obtain in the absence of money. After a long discussion, they hit upon the idea of trying to get an appeal to the British diplomats in the Vatican, and Iride, a Sulmona girl, who regularly thumbed her way to Rome and back on German vehicles, in connexion with her successful black-market activities, undertook to deliver the message.

Her success astonished the group, for she returned with 40,000 lire, as well as an unsigned note (from me), warning the escapers not to attempt to make their way to Rome at the present time. Thereafter, as I knew well enough at the Vatican end, Iride's

journeys—which the Sulmona escapers suspected were facilitated
by the provision of some personal satisfaction for the German
drivers—became a regular supply line. Iride used some of the
money she received for the purchase in Rome of pullovers, socks,
and other essential supplies, and at Sulmona Bill Simpson organized the distribution of cash, food, and clothing to the various
houses where escapers were accommodated.

In other respects, however, the Sulmona situation was deteriorating, and when one entire Italian family was arrested and
shot for harbouring an escaper the whole town became jittery.
One night the Germans raided an area in which Simpson, Furman, and a dozen others were living, searching every house, with
one exception. In the one house they overlooked all the escapers
were having a birthday party. Minutes before the clatter of German jack-boots and the thudding of rifle-butts on the doors had
shaken the houses on either side, the escapers had been happily
singing *Roll out the Barrel*.

After that raid, which could so easily have cost the lives of a
dozen Italian families, since the German death penalty was more
than an idle threat, the escapers evacuated their billets. Most
went back to the hills, unwillingly enough in the face of approaching winter, and a few tried to make their way south to the lines,
but soon returned. With the front now static, that avenue, they
reported, was firmly blocked.

Simpson, Furman, Pollak and four others took up residence
in the church tower, and they decided, in spite of the anonymous
advice they had received, that their best hope lay in Rome. The
journey was organized by Pollak, who almost alone still dared to
be seen abroad in Sulmona, and although he was frequently
stopped, he always managed to talk his way out of trouble. When
the morning train puffed out of Sulmona on December 8 it contained about a hundred Germans, a handful of Italians, and seven
Allied escapers, accompanied by two Italian girls—Iride and her
sister, Maria. Their tickets had been obtained by Pollak and the
girls, each of whom had purchased three at the booking-office,
but during the journey Iride, in conversation with the conductor,
discovered that because of the number of refugees flooding into
Rome, an order had been made forbidding entrance to anybody
without a permit signed by the German military governor. The
party decided that a couple of guards on a country road would

be a less formidable obstacle than half a dozen at a station barrier, and luck was with them, for the train halted, quite unaccountably, in the middle of nowhere, while still ten kilometres short of Rome. Seven men and two girls, all carrying suitcases, jumped down, and made off across the tracks—and, without interest, the Germans on the train watched them go.

It was Joe Pollak again who got them through the road-block: his smooth line of talk, backed up by hysterical demonstrations by the girls, convinced the Italian guard that they were all members of one family, bombed out of Sulmona, and now making their way to their only surviving relative in Rome. The German guard at the post, contemptuous of the whole affair, left everything to the Italian, who eventually let all nine pass, with only a glance at their false identity cards.

Iride led them to a small hotel in Via Cavour, the wide road running from the main railway station to the Foro Romano, centre of the fantastic ruins of ancient Rome. Ironically, this took them right past the station which they had been at such pains to avoid, but the hotel itself was quiet, and kept by a proprietor not fussy about the identity of his guests. The two girls collected some food from a near-by restaurant, and after the meal Pollak and Iride set off for the Vatican, where it was assumed that he was going to contact a British diplomat.

"You can't imagine what it was like when he got back yesterday evening," said Furman. "He was in a state of obvious excitement, and told us we would never guess who he had been with. Everybody demanded to know at once, and I imagine Bill's face and mine must have been a picture when he said 'Major Derry.' He practically went through the third-degree treatment, but he wouldn't tell us anything except that you wanted to see me."

I hurried off down the corridor to collect the waiting Pollak. "I owe you an apology," I said, as soon as we got back to the monsignor's room. "The reason I separated you was because I thought you might be a stool-pigeon. From what John has told me, I now know I couldn't have been more wrong. You have done a wonderful job of work, and I apologize for having doubted you."

Pollak showed no signs of concern at the discovery that I had been treating him as a traitor, and I realized that the inscrutability, which had no doubt stood him in good stead in many dangerous situations at Sulmona, was likely to be a valuable asset to the escape organization in Rome. I had already earmarked Furman for a place in the organization, and I now knew that Pollak, with his even greater command of languages, would be no less of an acquisition. I took both men completely into my confidence, and outlined what was being done for escapers in and around Rome.

They were both captivated by the exploits of the monsignor, and Furman, who had yet to meet him, was so intrigued by the idea of a Scarlet Pimpernel of the Vatican that he kept asking me questions about his character. I was always learning new things about him myself, and was able to give a glittering illustration. Rummaging around the untidy papers on the desk, I found a heavy gold chain, something like those worn by English mayors. "Every link is of solid gold," I explained. "It was given to the monsignor by a Jew just before he set off south to try to join our people on the other side of the lines. I don't know whether he got through or not, but I do know that his family are well looked after. He had the foresight to put them in the care of the monsignor—and each single link in that chain will keep them fully provided for a month."

I told them that they, too, were worth their weight in gold, and could be gifts from heaven to the organization.

I explained that we were seated inside the Vatican's protective wall, but were not actually inside the Vatican City; we were on what is called extra-territorial property. "All the same," I said, "I can easily show you how to get inside and have yourselves comfortably interned for the duration. All you have to do is to turn left instead of right as you leave here, and walk through the back gate. If you tried to get in through the main gates you would certainly be turned back, but from here you can walk straight through to the gendarmerie, give yourself up, and spend a nice quiet time until our troops reach Rome. Any takers?"

Both scorned the idea of a peaceful internment, and instead demanded to know when they could get down to a job of work.

"Then consider yourselves on the staff as from now," I beamed. "Sorry about one thing, though—I can't offer you any red tabs to sew on your uniforms. Only a cup of tea to celebrate."

"Fine," said Furman, "but before we start the bun-fight I should tell you that just as we were leaving the hotel Bill Simpson said, 'If there's a job of work to be done put in a word for me.' Is this the right time to do it?"

"When you get back tell Bill he's joined. And now let's have that brew up—I don't suppose either of you has had a decent cup of tea for months."

As I put on the kettle I felt enormously elated: I had started the day with a faint hope that I might be able to enrol one military assistant, had later acquired two, and had ended up with three, all of whom spoke Italian with some fluency. All would be able to find their way about Rome, and each would be a distinct acquisition.

As we sipped our tea, and talked about some of the problems of keeping hundreds of men at large in enemy territory, John Furman asked why we did not get more men inside the Vatican. This question was put in different forms by others later, and my explanation was put this way.

"There is a hell of an inquiry when anybody does get in, and you can bet your boots that if we started pushing people through it would soon be traced back to one person, which would put him and us all in a very tricky position. But there is another reason. The Germans have been reasonably tolerant about the neutrality of the Vatican up to now, but if we start filling the place up with escapers they will simply march in, put all our chaps back in the bag, and close the legation. That would mean sacrificing the welfare of all the hundreds we are maintaining outside Rome for the sake of the few, at best, that we could get into the Vatican."

"In other words," said John, "at the point where your organization comes in, the escaper can consider the Vatican ruled out?"

That was the position in a nutshell.

Pollak's forged identity documents were excellent in every respect, and we could not do much to improve them beyond the addition of some papers basing him in Rome, but the photograph on John Furman's Italian identity card showed him as a rather seedy tramp, with a scarf wound tightly round his neck. I gazed at it sadly, and sighed, "What is the Royal Artillery coming to?"

"I couldn't help it," said Furman ruefully, "I hadn't got a collar and tie."

The kindred societies soon came into action to help the newcomers. The French secretary, De Vial, took money from me to them at their hotel, and two Jugoslavs took the escapers in pairs to a warehouse, where they were fitted out with fresh clothing from the stocks of a relief organization run by Capuchin monks. Monsignor O'Flaherty organized social calls by several of his priests on the hotel-bound group, and I arranged for the Italian girls, Iride and Maria, to return to Sulmona with fresh supplies of money for the ex-prisoners still hiding there.

It was more difficult to fix billets for the three men I wanted in action in the city, but the Free French undertook to find a temporary home for the new staff, while I arranged for the others to go "up the hill" to our safest hiding-place. That was the only description used for the Collegio Americano. Situated on the top of a high hill on the western outskirts of the city, it had been brought into use by a former corporal in the Pope's bodyguard, one Antonio Call, who rounded up a few Allied escapers on his own, and ensconced himself there to look after them. Small adaptions to the outbuildings had created the perfect hide, for, if necessary, a pretty large number of men, but to preserve its security we ruled that those who went there did so on the understanding that they did not move again until our troops occupied Rome. They had pleasant surroundings, reasonable comfort, above average safety, and perhaps the best meals of any of our larger groups, but against these advantages "the hill" was in the nature of an internment camp.

Such a billet was, of course, useless for Furman, Simpson, and Pollak, but De Vial managed to find temporary accommodation for them with a family in a working-class flat at Tor Pignatara, a suburb in the south-east—although this, apparently, entailed the eviction of a Frenchman who had been lodging there.

Pasqualino Perfetti, the greasy pseudo-priest, my first contact in Rome, was now spending most of his time as a sort of billeting agent for the French—who, unlike Monsignor O'Flaherty, were able to pay him sizeably for his services—and he was sent by De Vial to guide my three 'staff officers' to their temporary quarters, where they discovered that the evicted Frenchman was still in possession of the smaller of the only two beds.

Next day they reported for duty, having come in from their suburb by train and trolley-bus, during the rush hour. This taught them, the hard way, a new aspect of the lesson that in Rome it was necessary to do as the Romans do, for strong shoulders and sharp elbows were essential to find a place on the crowded public transport. The porters had been warned of their impending arrival, and they were shown straight up to Monsignor O'Flaherty's room, where I was waiting for them with the monsignor and John May.

Introductions were scarcely complete before John May busied himself in the unexpected task of cooking porridge. "I heard you had dystentery," he told Furman, setting before him the steaming dish and a jug of cream. "This is the best thing in the world for it." It was also, Furman told me later, the best porridge he ever ate; and I, who had sampled John May's cooking on several occasions, could believe it.

Together the five of us mapped out the division of duties. Broadly, we should still rely on the priests to do most of the finding of new billets, but Furman, Simpson, and Pollak would take over much of the dangerous work of guiding escapers, issuing money, and delivering supplies. In her overcrowded little flat Mrs Chevalier was building up a sort of cache of food, from which came supplies for the Via Firenze and Via Chelini flats. This, and food for other 'cells,' had to be collected from her, and carted about Rome in suitcases, so I decided that my three new assistants should spend the rest of their first day familiarizing themselves with the routes and the tram services. After lunch with the monsignor, they set off in the company of two Maltese priests to call on Mrs Chevalier, with whom they left money and requests for further purchases from the various black-market contacts she had developed, and then went on to visit the flat in Via Firenze, and the more luxurious apartment at Via Chelini.

Pollak was completely at home in the false identity described on the papers he had obtained at Sulmona, and the documents I had given Furman and Simpson invested them with identities of genuine Italians. The cards were based on Naples, which was now safely in British hands, and therefore beyond the reach of any really thorough check by the Germans, but we had gone to great pains, by the use of Italian directories and with the aid of local knowledge of some of the priests, to ensure that the names and addresses were capable of standing up to any ordinary investigaton. There were plenty of false identity documents floating about Rome at that time, but I imagine ours were among the best. Sometimes they were virtually perfect, as in the case of one escaper who took over, in its entirety, the identity of an Irishman

who had died early in the war, but whose documents, including
the invaluable Irish passport, had been thoughtfully preserved by
one of the priests.

With their new identities and their new suits, Furman, Simpson, and Pollak found they could move about Rome with reasonable freedom, and their understanding of Italian gave them confidence. Not only could they ask for obvious things, but they had
a comfortable awareness of what people around them were saying.

The secret agent who does not understand the language of the
country in which he is operating is like a deaf man trying to cross
a busy road : the only dangers of which he is aware are those he
can see. Pollak, with the advantage of latin appearance added to
linguistic accomplishment, could pass as an Italian even among
Italians, and the willowy Simpson could certainly count on fool-
ing most Germans, while John Furman, with reasonable knowledge of both enemy languages, had a system of his own which
he said could not fail. If he was engaged in conversation by
Italian Fascists he would pretend to be German, and in the
presence of Germans he would be a swaggering Italian Fascist.

The three 'billeting officers,' as they came to be known, went
into action straight away, and they had been at work for only
about three days when I received from them, through one of the
priests, a plaintive SOS pleading for permission to use *carrozze*
to convey provisions from Mrs Chevalier's to the flats. They had
apparently been fighting a losing battle, encumbered with heavy
suitcases, against the determined tram-travelling populace of
Rome. Although they would be more conspicuous in an open
cab, I knew from experience of the risk of detection on a tram,
so I considered the small extra cost justified.

As they became accustomed to the work they split up the billets
among themselves, to avoid duplication and reduce unnecessary
travelling, and Furman and Simpson, always close friends, discovered that it was not impossible to enjoy a measure of social
life. They usually had to meet during the day to sort out details of
their work, and decided they might as well combine business with
pleasure by arranging a rendezvous in some pleasant place, where
they could either eat or drink.

They lunched at some of the better restaurants, often close to
German officers or leading Fascists, and found a fashionable bar
where, apart from other attractions, there was an attendant who

was no lover of Germans. The barman, Felix, who had once worked in London, quickly sensed that his new customers were engaged on some sort of activity likely to engender official disapproval, although he may have thought no more than that they were black-market operators—which, after all, was not so far from the truth. At all events, he accepted them as friends, and could always be relied on to reach up towards one particular bottle of little-used liqueur on the high shelf behind him whenever danger threatened. This hint enabled Furman and Simpson to take their leave with reasonable speed.

Their social circle did not really expand, however, until they were introduced to an Italian film director named Renzo Lucidi, and his wife, Adrienne, who had been among Monsignor O'Flaherty's staunchest allies from the start. Renzo was by birth half Danish and by inclination wholly anti-Fascist, while his wife was French, and there was never any doubt about where her sympathies lay. They had a son of twelve, and Adrienne had also a son of eighteen, born in France by a former marriage, and the four of them lived in a pleasant and well-appointed apartment. When they suggested that all three of the billeting officers should take up residence with them I approved, because the Lucidi home in Via Scialoia was much closer to Mrs Chevalier's and the two flats, and was also much better placed than suburban lodgings for the organization of billets in the city. The billeting officers themselves approved, of course.

Although the Lucidis' flat shared a block with the home of a leading Fascist family, it was the accepted meeting-place of many of the principal anti-Fascists in Rome, including a number of curvaceous young film stars, who brought a new glamour into the life of the ex-prisoners-of-war.

Renzo and Adrienne were keen opera-goers, and Simpson, the erstwhile double-bass player, and his companions welcomed with joy the suggestion that they should go along as well. In time their visits became quite frequent, and Pollak went so far as to introduce some of the other escapers under his care to the delights of the opera.

One evening, at the head of a long and somewhat restive queue at the booking-office, Pollak was questioning the clerk and then turning to interpret to the two escapers who were with him, and who could not make up their minds which seats to have. As Pollak turned once again to the booking-office he noticed that the man standing right beside him was a tall German officer, who, in pointed, perfect English, demanded, "Are you going to be much longer?"

"No," replied Pollak, also in English. "We're leaving now." And they did, with alacrity.

For Simpson and Furman, their first visit to the opera remained the most memorable, for they emerged from it with a remarkable trophy. They shared a box with Renzo and Adrienne Lucidi, and had scarcely taken their places when into the adjoining box stalked a heavily decorated German general and what appeared to be his entire personal staff. During the first act Furman and Simpson noticed that the attention of one of the general's A.D.C.'s, a stiff-backed Prussian of early middle-age, strayed constantly from the energetically vocal Italians on the stage to the handsome profile of Adrienne a yard away. Adrienne, who had outgrown youthful prettiness only to replace it with a mature, statuesque beauty, softened by the ageless charm which is the most appealing feature of women of her race, noticed the German's admiration too, and leaned across to borrow his opera-glasses, which he readily and gallantly surrendered.

The two Britons exchanged a wink, and when the interval came they chaffed Adrienne. "You've made a conquest," they told her. "Why don't you ask him for his autograph?"

Adrienne arched her delicate eyebrows, and raised her shoulders in an almost imperceptible shrug. "But of course," she replied.

At the end of the performance she pushed her programme across the ledge between the two boxes, and, in French, asked her Teutonic admirer if he would sign it.

"I will do better than that," said the German, beaming with flattered pleasure, "I will get the general to autograph it for you."

Furman and Simpson watched, fascinated, as the German general scrawled his name across the programme, which the A.D.C. handed back to Adrienne with a bow. "Which of you is to have it?" she asked them later, and when they tossed up for it the memento went to Simpson. The two British officers studied the signature with mounting delight: it was that of General Maelzer himself—the Military Governor of Rome.

It would have made a perfect postscript to this anecdote if I had been able to record that the signature was received with delirious joy at headquarters and rushed off to the printing-presses for the production of hundreds of forged passes for escapers, and, indeed, such a story has been circulated since the war, but there is no truth in it. In point of fact, I gained some comfort from the knowledge that the autograph was available for use, should we ever need it, but, as the man responsible for the security of the organization, I could not look upon this sort of adventure with official approval, much as I was amused.

The truth was that the organization's documentation service was now so good that we did not need to rely on blatant forgeries of that sort. Furman, Simpson, and I were in possession of rare passes, made out specially for us, and signed by the German Minister in Rome himself; and who would want a forgery when he was equipped with the real thing? I obtained ours through an experiment about which I felt rather guilty, because it was the only time I ever really took advantage of the Vatican Secretariat.

Through the inexhaustible ingenuity of John May and the transfer of a little money among minor clerks, documents made out in the names which the three of us were using came to be inserted into a pile of others being sent from the Secretariat to the German Ministry for the issue of passes, mainly for officials who had to travel during the hours of the German-imposed curfew. The trick worked perfectly. Passes for three British officers were made out, signed by the German Minister, imposingly stamped with the swastika surmounted by an eagle, and then, by more sleight of hand, returned to John May, and eventually to me. I never compromised the incalculable value of these three passes by attempting to repeat the experiment, but it always gave me singular satisfaction to realize that in a city of forgeries each of the principal officers of our organization held an unmistakably genuine German pass.

The success was all the more surprising in view of the growing signs that the Germans were aware that British escaped prisoners were in their midst. Indeed, they could scarcely fail to be aware of it, since the editor of a leading Fascist newspaper had printed a scathing article about fashionable restaurants in which escaped British officers were to be seen brazenly eating expensive meals, while the poor of Rome had difficulty in finding enough food.

The only result of this, so far as I could see, was that some of the best eating-houses in Rome were promptly closed down by order of the Military Government, to the chagrin of the German officers, who were their principal patrons.

Security of the organization had become my major concern, for apart from the hundreds of escapers in the country, we now had men billeted in more than forty different places in Rome itself, and it was difficult to plan the continuous fetching and carrying of supplies so that there was no regular pattern of visits which might attract attention. In the interrogation of new arrivals, to which much of my time was devoted, I began to pay particular regard to the temperament of the escapers, and earmarked those unlikely to endure the frustration of lying low for several weeks as priority cases for sending to the country areas, where they could expect to move about rather more freely.

The never-ending growth of the organization presented many problems beyond that of security, and the finding of sufficient food and other supplies was a constant headache. Provisioning arrangements might have broken down altogether, had it not been for the ubiquitous John May, who, although confined to the Vatican, contrived to maintain contacts all over the city, and knew at once when any stock of food or cheap clothing found its way to the black market anywhere in Rome. Even when supplies were unearthed, delivery remained a problem; the rationing system meant that Italian families were unable to obtain food through the ordinary channels for any escapers in their care, so bulky items, including meat and bread, had to be transported physically to the individual 'cells' as well as to the two flats. But fortunately a growing number of the Italian 'padrones' established their own black-market contacts, and in these cases I was able to send money, which was much simpler to deliver.

The amount of money I was spending on behalf of H.M. Government was beginning to reach impressive proportions. At first the British Minister had been able to supply odd thousands of lire through normal financial channels, but as the number of escapers sky-rocketed, demand outpaced supply, and it took strenuous efforts on the part of Sir D'Arcy Osborne to evolve a system for the conversion of Foreign Office pound notes in London into lire notes in Rome.

We were not extravagant, paying out only 120 lire a day for

the keep of each prisoner in Rome, and substantially less in the country. In purchasing terms 120 lire represented about four shillings, and few of the 'padrones' could make anything out of that. In the first six weeks up to December 9, 1943, the organization distributed 69,000 lire, but in the next four weeks the million mark was topped. I was now collecting from Sir D'Arcy Osborne sums of up to 400,000 lire at a time, and I was also extracting, though with rather more difficulty, various contributions from the American Minister, Mr Harold Tittman, towards the cost of maintaining United States servicemen who had entered the escape line. In the main these were men who had baled out of crippled bomber aircraft.

I had a shrewd suspicion that in the long run I should be expected to account for these sums, and bought a cheap school exercise-book. It was the simplest form of ledger, with income on one side and outgoings on the other, and I doubt if ever in the history of field accountancy were such vast transactions recorded in so crude a form. I also asked, wherever possible, for plain and not too revealing receipt chits, to relate to the entries in the 'ledger,' and these were dutifully buried by Captain Byrnes each night in the Vatican gardens, where they would be safe even if the Germans decided on a raid.

To make sure that the 'ledger' would be of little value to the enemy, each entry consisted of nothing more than a date, a code name, and an amount of money. Everybody in the organization was given a code name, by which alone they were known for all purposes of conversation and communication, and, as a further protection, I ruled that the code names of "Mount" (the British Minister), and "Till" (the Secretary to the Legation, Mr Hugh Montgomery), were never to be committed to paper at all.

Many of the code names gave a strong clue to the individuals. Thus, Monsignor O'Flaherty became "Golf," in recognition of his passion for the game, which he had frequently played—with the most modest of handicaps—with Count Ciano, Mussolini's son-in-law and foreign minister. I was "Patrick," and the three military assistants were simply "John," "Bill," and "Joe"—an arrangement of which they approved heartily. The Irish Father Claffey was "Eyerish," dear old Father Thomas Lenan was "Uncle Tom," the Dutch Father Anselmo Musters was "Dutch-pa," the Maltese Mrs Chevalier was "Mrs M.," and Brother

Robert Pace was "Whitebows," in recognition of the most distinctive feature of the habit worn by his Order. The Maltese Father Borg found his name reversed, and became "Grobb," and the name of the Swiss caretaker at the British Embassy, Secundo Constantini, was abbreviated to "Sek." Some of the code names were chosen with no logical reason, as with Owen Snedden ("Horace"), Father John Buckley ("Spike"), and the unfortunate Count Sarsfield Salazar ("Emma"), while others were more obvious, as in the case of Father Flanagan ("Fanny"), Father Galea ("Sailor"), and, of course, poor Renzo Lucidi, who inevitably became "Rinso."

By Christmas we were looking after more than 2000 escapers in the country areas and about eighty in Rome, and I decided that things looked bright enough to justify a modicum of Christmas cheer: small sums of extra cash, to enable the men to buy additional food and comforts—usually cigarettes, which were scarce and very expensive—and among the men in Rome we distributed a few bottles of wine, and such small luxuries as the black market could produce.

My own Christmas began impressively with a midnight service in the chapel that occupied most of the ground floor of the college. The monsignor had invited me diffidently, for in all the weeks that I lived under his care he never once tried to sell religion to me. Right at the beginning of our acquaintanceship he had said, "I realize you are an Anglican, but you need not be afraid that I am going to spend all my time talking to you about the Catholic faith. Any time you feel like talking religion, I shall be happy to join in, but if you don't I shall never preach at you." He never did, but I frequently took advantage of his offer of discussion, and learned much from him, and from his tolerance and restraint. Religion was not only his vocation but his over-riding academic interest, and among his three doctorates were those of Divinity and Canon Law.

He always ate frugally, and Christmas dinner, served by the German sisters, who now accepted me with something like affection as the Irish Patrick Derry, was no great gastronomic experience, but at a time when meat was very scarce, even a slice of mutton was most welcome, if hardly festive. Certainly, there was nothing sparse about the cheerful goodwill that flowed about the monsignor's room throughout that day, and it seemed to me that visitors were in and out in a never-ending procession. There were priests of half a dozen different nationalities, who were all helping in the organization's work, diplomats and their families from the French, Polish, Jugoslav and other legations, Mrs Kiernan and her two daughters from the Irish Embassy, and a large number of unusual characters, who had been in hiding in various parts of the college since before my arrival.

Among these was an Austrian ex-mayor, with whom I had struck up a firm friendship. He was anti-Nazi from the earliest days, and had fled to Italy when Hitler's troops marched into Austria. When Italy went to war at the side of Germany he took refuge in the Collegio Teutonicum. From him I received my most valuable Christmas present, a gold pencil, which I still treasure, and with it a Christmas card on which was a message, in which he described me as "the finest English officer I have met." I should have been embarrassed, had I not realized that he had probably never met any other English officers. However, I was moved by his kindness.

Looking back over the previous few weeks, it seemed to me that the Rome Organization was developing well. Two thousand escapers and evaders were adequately clothed and fed as part of an organized force. They regularly received information and instructions from British officers, while their welfare was watched by more than twenty priests.

It might have seemed that the organization was playing no really useful part in the Allied war effort, and this point of view was certainly widely held and frequently aired among the Communist organizations with which we were in touch. This overlooked three important factors: first, escapers who were recaptured would have been sent to Germany, where camp conditions were deteriorating, and where, as it turned out, they would have been incarcerated for another soul-destroying year and a half; secondly, all the food and other materials consumed by escapers were, in fact, enemy resources, and our men were indirectly helping the Allied war effort by absorbing a good deal of the enemy's productive effort; thirdly, our troops would reach Rome long before the Allies began to batter on the walls of Hitler's Germany, and would find a couple of thousand men, in reasonably good physical condition, ready to rejoin our forces. Additionally, a proportion of the bill could reasonably be set against the intelligence service it was providing, and the goodwill it was developing among thousands of ordinary Italian people. Although it was impossible to convince the Communist associates, such thoughts as these comforted me as I totted up the staggering figures in the schoolbook ledger.

But any complacency I may have been developing was shaken by three unexpected developments which caused concern. The first was the decision of the German Military Government to change the curfew hour from 11 P.M. to 7 P.M. This, the penalty of some not very worthwhile sabotage attempts by the Jugoslavs and Italian Communists, meant that helpers who were already hard pressed were forced to rearrange the system of visits and supply deliveries that we had built up.

A second, and in some ways more serious, development was the closing of the street door through which we literally kept in touch with the world outside. The Vatican authorities, possibly with the aid of a hint from German military sources, had apparently become aware of the volume of this traffic, and at a single stroke had made it impossible for anyone to reach our headquarters without going through some kind of check-point.

It happened shortly before Joe Pollak was due to call, and he did, in fact, arrive to find the way barred. Unaware of what had happened, he hammered so persistently on the gate that a Roman gendarme walked up, and demanded to know what he was doing. "Nothing," replied Joe meekly, and inexplicably the gendarme allowed him to walk away.

John Furman was also due to arrive that morning, but we were able to arrange for "Horace" (Father Snedden) to go out and intercept him. "Horace" showed him the only remaining way of getting into contact with headquarters, through the Porta Santa Marta, a gate behind the colonnades on the left of St Peter's, to a post of the Swiss Guard, where he had to produce his Italian identity card and state who he wished to see. He could not, of course, ask for the mythical "Mr Derry," and if he asked for the monsignor it was still a matter of chance whether the guard would give him a chit to enter or merely put through a message on the internal telephone. The immediate effect of this change was that we had to cut down visits to a minimum, and rely more and more on notes.

The third ill omen was a report, brought back by Lieutenant

Ristic Cedomir, a Royalist Jugoslav officer, on his return from distributing funds in the Arda Valley, where there had originally been about 600 Allied escapers, about half of whom made their way to Switzerland or warmer parts of Italy. He reported that "owing to the imprudence of prisoners rather than unreliable Italian inhabitants," the police had arrested eighteen Italians, and had offered rewards for information about the source of supply of money for escaped prisoners-of-war.

This meant disaster for the Italian helpers through the lack of caution of the men they were helping, and I had to think up immediate and drastic steps to tighten security. As I worked out my plans, I could not foresee that I was on the threshold of a New Year nightmare which threatened to bring down the whole organization. Worse was about to befall.

6

New Year Nightmare

IN underground work in war-time it is generally a mistake to abandon the interests of security for the sake of expediency. If I had not weakened in my decision to clear the Via Firenze and Via Chelini flats of escapers by December 31, the worst part of the January disaster would have been averted. But the billeting officers, who were the first to express doubts about keeping such large numbers of people in one place, had been having great difficulty in finding other accommodation, so I gave a ten-day postponement for the 'eviction order.'

Despite the inconvenience of the early curfew and the firmly closed street door, there was nothing in the early days of January to cause concern about the general situation in Rome, and I was concentrating on a tidying up of the organization's finances.

I was, in fact, constantly worried by the thought that the supply of money, the source of which was not known to any of my assistants, might suddenly dry up.

Both Furman and Simpson regularly put forward the request that the hidden soldiers, who at home were piling up substantial sums in army pay, should be allowed to draw some money for extra comforts against their swelling 'credits,' and both also urged that officer-escapers should be paid money against 'cheques' on their bank accounts. I imagine they considered me unreasonable in turning them down flat, but I had no alternative: it was not that I had any moral objection to the escapers spending their own idle money; it was simply that the physical supply of lire did not exist.

The only ways in which additional currency notes could be obtained were by stealing them or borrowing them, so I suggested to Furman and Simpson that they might be able to raise a loan privately, repayable after the Allies reached Rome, from which they could at least cash officers' cheques. Furman thought this a splendid possibility, and, through a friend of Renzo Lucidi, began discussions for a sizeable loan.

The suggestion also arose that Joe Pollak should revisit Sulmona, where all was not as it should be. Iride was still taking money to the escapers, but the distribution system was breaking down. As Pollak's identity documents were based on Sulmona, and Pollak himself was prepared, and even anxious, to go, I thought it would be a good thing, but as it turned out he was not to have the chance. Neither did Furman finish his negotiations with Lucidi's friend.

On January 6 Furman, Simpson, and Pollak arrived together at Porta Santa Marta in a state of considerable concern, and were fortunate enough to make contact with Monsignor O'Flaherty, who brought them all up to his room. "It looks like trouble," said Furman solemnly, as they entered.

The previous evening, quite by chance, Furman and Renzo Lucidi had met in the street a French officer, Henri Payonne, who had come into Rome with Iride. They had no more than a few minutes because the curfew was almost on them, but Furman gave Payonne the telephone number of Lucidi's flat, and told him to ring through later, warning him not to reveal the number to Iride. He gave this warning because it was obviously inadvisable that she should learn where he was staying.

Early that morning the telephone rang at the flat, and the voice that spoke was that of Iride, who somehow or other had got hold of the number which Furman had tried to keep from her. She asked to speak to "Giuseppe," the name by which Joe Pollak had been known at Sulmona, and told him she must see him at once. "It is vital," she said.

Pollak said he would go to her as soon as he could, and, after hanging up, discussed the situation with Furman and Simpson, but within a few minutes Iride was on the telephone again, pleading with Pollak to go to her at once. They were now all suspicious and worried, and when the telephone rang again for the third time Renzo picked it up. There was no one, he said, by the name of Giuseppe in the house.

"There must be! I have just spoken to him," shouted Iride.

"You must be mistaken," said Renzo coolly, and replaced the receiver.

They were in a bedroom, debating the best course to take, when the telephone rang yet again. This time the call was taken by Adrienne Lucidi. Bursting into the bedroom, she almost screamed at them, "Quick! You must escape! They're coming here!"

The caller had been the Frenchman, Payonne, who in urgent tone had told her that they were all in danger, and she must get the escapers out of her flat as quickly as possible. Furman, Simpson, and Pollak, immediately connecting this call with the mysterious three from Iride, packed immediately, removed all traces of their occupation, and left. They decided that it would be better if even Lucidi did not know their whereabouts, and they agreed to stay temporarily at the Via Chelini flat. After dumping their luggage, they came straight to me with the news.

I had been aware for some time that Iride was a potential danger, for clearly she resented the way that the escapers had grown away from her after she had helped them to reach Rome. My impression was that she was of the unstable type of character, in which a little jealousy could easily turn affection and loyalty into indifference and treachery.

"It looks like a damned trap," I said. "Joe, I don't think we dare let you keep that date with Iride."

"But supposing it really is something vital to our people at Sulmona," said Pollak. "We can't just ignore it—we might be letting them all down."

"There's another thing," said Pollak slowly. "That girl knows practically everything about the Sulmona organization. And she knows all about 'Patrick,' too."

I agreed that if she started talking there would be a hell of a mess, but the risk of letting Pollak walk straight into a trap seemed very real, for it looked as though she was already in contact with the enemy.

We talked round and round the problem, and I could see that the others, while agreeing that both possibilities were dangerous, did not share my view. Finally, I decided to permit Pollak to go to Iride, chiefly because that was what he himself wanted to do.

"It's the only possible way of finding out what all the mystery is about," he said, and I had to agree.

We took such security measures as were possible. Pollak emptied his pockets, leaving his documents and personal valuables, including his wrist-watch, and we agreed that if he were not back by three o'clock we would assume he had walked into a trap.

Pollak left at noon, and shortly afterwards Bill Simpson went out to continue the routine work, leaving the monsignor, John Furman, and myself in the growing tenseness of the little room. Three o'clock struck, and we looked at each other. Silence, pregnant with foreboding, filled the room until shortly before four o'clock, when it was suddenly shattered by the shrill ringing of the internal telephone.

Monsignor O'Flaherty was up from his chair and across the room in a stride, his face alight with expectancy. But, as he listened, I could see that this was not the hoped for message, and when he put down the receiver he was obviously worried.

"That was the man at the gate," he told us. "He says there is an Italian laddie down there who says he will give his message to no one but the man called Patrick. Do you think it might be a trap to identify you?"

"Sounds possible," I agreed. "In any case, there is no point in my going down there because I can't speak Italian, and certainly you mustn't be mixed up in this. John, it looks like you: make sure no one is watching you, and try to find out what you can from the young Ite."

Furman was back in a few minutes with a letter in his hand. "It was the son of the proprietor of Iride's boarding-house," he said. "All he knew was that he had been told to hand this to Patrick, but I persuaded him to give it to me."

"It's from Iride, but the damn thing's in Italian," I said as I opened the note. "Here, John—tell us what it's all about."

Dearest Patrick [Furman read]. Yesterday at midday I was arrested, and I got the news that my mother, sister, and my baby, as well as Flora and her family and Dino, had also been arrested, and were in the hands of the German command. We were betrayed by Captain "Dick," who is not a captain but a simple Red Cross orderly who has divulged everything. They are here looking for Giuseppe [the name by which she knew Pollak], and at all costs must take him. I begged Giuseppe to come to me because I am very sick, but I am guarded. I think the arrest of Giuseppe will be the saving of us all. I won't talk unless threatened that I endanger the life of my baby by not doing so, in which case I shall poison myself. I beg you, however, to save the lives of my baby and my poor mother. You must not believe if they take Giuseppe that it is a betrayal. He is of no interest to them—they only want to know who supplies the money, and I repeat they will never know from me—I prefer death. I am only afraid that Giuseppe may talk if he believes himself betrayed.

IRIDE

Pollak had, indeed, been betrayed. He was, of course, already on his guard when he reached Iride's room at the boarding-house, and suddenly he noticed the shape of a man silhouetted against the glass panel of a door opposite. In a flash he turned on his heel, but two plain-clothes men pounced after him. He dashed out of the building, along the street, and into the entrance to a big block of flats, only to find himself trapped. Behind the main door there was another door, closed and locked, and for Pollak there was no possibility of escape from the tiny vestibule as the two Gestapo men entered, their revolvers drawn.

I cursed myself for having permitted Pollak to be recaptured, but I was not the only person filled with remorse. When the French officer, Payonne, had told Adrienne Lucidi to get the escapers out of her flat he had also warned her that under no circumstances was Pollak to keep his appointment with Iride. If we had been told of that message we should have known for certain that the appointment was a trap, but in her panic over the first warning Adrienne overlooked the second, and did nothing about it. When she realized the importance of that small omission, and its cost, she broke down completely.

As soon as we knew that Pollak was in German hands I sent agents out in all directions to find out what had happened to him. I learned that Pollak had been arrested by men sent from Sulmona, and both he and Iride were taken back there that night. There were thus no signs that the Germans had yet found out anything of importance about the Rome Organization, and I was certain that the Italian families who had been arrested at Sulmona would not even be aware that it existed.

On the other hand, there was Iride. Her promise not to talk had been pretty thoroughly qualified, and, in any case, I could not place much reliance on it after the events of the last few hours, so I had to work on the assumption that everything known to Iride would in due course become known to the Germans.

The Lucidis' flat was already in the clear, and the Free French had put Payonne out of the way, but there was little I could do about my own position, and nothing at all that I could do for

Pollak. Although, so far as I knew, Iride was not aware of the monsignor's part in the organization, it was obvious that if she put the Gestapo on to me he would inevitably become involved, but he brushed this point aside unconcernedly, and told me I worried too much about the unnecessary details.

I decided that the Via Chelini apartment, which was now housing twelve people, must be cleared as soon as possible, and devoted most of the day after Pollak's arrest to organizing alternative accommodation. New billets were found for Lieutenants Furman and Simpson, and it was arranged that they and the other occupants of the flat should move out the following day, but before any changes could be put into operation I was stopped in my tracks by a blow from another direction—a blow which was all the more unexpected in its impact because it was not aimed at the Rome Organization at all.

Like the Western farmer who drills for water, fails to find it, but strikes oil, the Gestapo were digging for Italian Communists and unearthed escaped prisoners-of-war. In their more or less constant struggle against the Communists, whom they blamed (not unjustifiably) for much of their discomfiture in Rome, they had hatched a typically cunning scheme.

During the morning of Saturday, January 8, two men in raincoats and trilby hats called on an Italian widow in no way connected with the organization, whose son, a Communist, was held prisoner in the grotesquely named Regina Coeli (Queen of Heaven), a great, grim mountain of a prison on the north bank of the Tiber, only a few hundred yards from my headquarters at the Collegio Teutonicum. They told her that they had just been released from the gaol, where they had arranged a plan for the escape of her son, who was being constantly tortured, and who would pretend to break down and offer to lead the Germans to the hide-out of his Communist friends. His friends would, in fact, be ready, and in the ambush the Germans would be killed, and their prisoner would escape. The widow's part in this ingenious scheme was to get all her son's Communist friends together and arrange the ambush, and she readily agreed to do so.

She took her two visitors to the flat of a man named Nebolante, a leader of the Italian underground, who questioned them, and, satisfied with their replies, invited them to stay for the midday meal.

There was something grotesque about this meal, for it was shared by an Italian resistance leader, two German Gestapo agents, and two highly decorated British officers. Nebolante was, in fact, 'padrone' to a couple of the most colourful characters on the organization's roll—Lieutenant "Tug" Wilson, D.S.O., the 'cloak and dagger' saboteur I had met on my first visit to the Via Firenze flat, and Captain "Pip" Gardner, V.C., M.C., who had been among the prisoners at Chieti. I had arranged for Gardner to be brought into Rome, where he teamed up with Wilson, and eventually they arranged their own billet at the house of Nebolante. They went about Rome a good deal, were very much at home, and on one occasion found themselves face to face with John Furman and Joe Pollak during an interval at the opera.

Neither Wilson, the past-master at the art of operating behind enemy lines, nor the gallant Gardner, had any enthusiasm for the idea of lunching with two complete strangers whom they distrusted, and after the men had gone they took Nebolante to task for being so dangerously trusting. He was scoffing at their pessimism when the strangers returned—accompanied by a squad of armed and uniformed S.S. men.

With their host, the two officers were bundled off, fuming, to the Regina Coeli, leaving the Gestapo agents in the flat with Nebolante's cook. The cook was an old man, not difficult to frighten, and by some awful mischance he knew of the existence of both our flats, at Via Firenze and Via Chelini. The breach in our security went even further, for Nebolante's cook knew also the secret signal that had to be given on the doorbells of the flats to gain admission. Furman, Simpson, and I were unaware of this, and my two lieutenants had agreed to meet at their temporary billet in the Via Chelini flat at 2.30 P.M. to collect their baggage.

Simpson was first to arrive, and found there a disconcerting newcomer—a man who said he was Adolf Hitler. In fact, he was an American Air Force sergeant, who had cracked his head when he baled out of a crippled bomber, and in due course had been led, as a temporary measure, to the Via Chelini flat. He had a form of concussion manifesting itself in a sequence of wild delusions. He had an alarming habit of suddenly deciding that he was either Hitler or the German air chief, Hermann Goering, and plunging into noisy and delirious arguments with the entire German General Staff.

Faced with this problem, somewhat unsympathetically outlined by the laconic Jugoslav, Bruno Büchner, who was more or
less in charge of the flat, Bill Simpson decided that the sergeant
would have to be got into a hospital. There were several small
hospitals run by various religious orders, where such a case could
be kept without too much risk, for clearly the unfortunate sergeant could not be inflicted on any Italian helpers already facing
dangers enough.

Simpson had just left the flat to try and arrange something
when, in Via Chelini itself, he bumped into Lieutenant John Furman, trotting nonchalantly to the flat as arranged.

"Hallo," he said, "what's up?"

"Plenty," said Simpson, and, after explaining briefly, told
him, "Go ahead as planned. I'll meet you at the billet as soon as
I've arranged for some one to shift this character."

"No," replied Furman. "One of us ought to stay in the flat
until he is moved, in case there is trouble. I'll wait until you get
back."

It was a logical but fateful decision.

Furman went into the apartment, where our R.A.M.C. doctor,
Captain Macauley, had already arrived, and was very concerned
about the American. They talked with the sergeant, who was
lucid for long enough to tell them, "If you want to know, I feel
lousy," before embarking upon a creditable, if unconscious,
imitation of the Führer.

They were all impatient for Simpson's return, but it was fully
half an hour before the doorbell rang, the proper signal being
given. Bruno Büchner answered it, and Furman, hearing voices
in the hall, went out to join him a minute later, expecting to see
Simpson. Instead he saw at the doorway a small white-haired
Italian and two rather thin men, who kept their hats on.

"This is Nebolante's cook," said the Jugoslav, indicating the
old man. "He says he has bad news."

Furman, who had never seen the man before and did not like
the look of his companions, demanded, "Well, what is it?"

Before the cook could answer, one of the thin men cut in,
"Nebolante's flat has been raided, and the Gestapo have got him
and Gardner and Wilson. We thought we should let you know."

Furman thanked the two men for calling, but said pointedly
he could not see why they had bothered to accompany the cook,

who could quite easily have delivered the message on his own. This remark seemed to annoy the thin men, but as they turned away, Furman asked quietly, "Before you go, would you mind showing me your identity cards?"

For answer the two men swung round, and pulled from their pockets, not identity cards, but vicious squat revolvers. Simultaneously, there was a clatter in the passage outside, and half a dozen S.S. men, armed with sub-machine-guns and pistols, burst into the flat in a roar of shouted German commands.

They fanned out through the apartment, and within seconds the two escapers, Büchner, the Jugoslav, and Herta, the Austrian girl, who looked after them, were all lined up against a wall, hands high above their heads.

"So! We were too clever for you!" boasted one of the sleek plain-clothes agents, who seemed to be in command of the operation. "Well, we shall have some more of your friends to keep you company, besides Wilson and Gardner."

There was no knowing whether this meant the discovery of other billets or even a raid on our headquarters at the Collegio Teutonicum, and Furman's first thought was how to get a message of warning to me and also keep Simpson away. There was nothing he could do about it himself, but he had noted that the prisoners lined up against the wall did not include two soldiers who had been billeted in the basement—Lance-Corporal T. W. Dale and Gunner E. C. Jones. He hoped they had been able to slip out through the back windows and get away; and that the Germans had arrived by car and left it outside the building, for this would alert Simpson to trouble. Desperately anxious to know if they had, and hoping vaguely that he might be able to give some sort of signal, Furman tried to edge his way towards the window, but was roughly thrust back by a pistol in his ribs.

Meanwhile Simpson hurried back to the flat, strode across the vestibule, and gave the secret signal on the doorbell. Furman's heart sank as he heard the bell stutter, but there must have been a fault in the circuit, for it failed to ring properly. One of the S.S. men asked if the bell had rung, and when one of his companions said he thought it had the soldier walked quite slowly across the hall to the door.

Meanwhile Simpson, his finger still on the bell-push, had caught sight of the Italian porter, frantically signalling to him to get out of sight. Without stopping to ask questions, he turned, and even as the S.S. man was moving to the door, Simpson was racing up the main stairs. As the German opened the door, Simpson dropped full length along the first-floor landing. Furman, watching warily from inside, saw the S.S. man open the door to an empty vestibule, and breathed again. Simpson, peering through the banisters, saw a uniformed German emerge, look along the vestibule, and testily jab the doorbell, which failed to emit any sound at all, and realized that a providential electrical fault had saved him.

Undetected, he slipped out of the building by the back way, and hurried straight to the Vatican, where he burst in on me, white-faced, and reported shortly, "Via Chelini's fallen."

I already knew, for Corporal Dale and Gunner Jones had indeed got clean away from the basement as the S.S. burst in above them, and had made their way at once to the Swiss Legation, where they left the all important message with one of the organization's many friends. This message reached me almost immediately, but after Dale and Jones left the legation they walked straight into a police check, and were immediately arrested.

Simpson, of course, could add little to the scanty knowledge I already had about the raid, except by confirming that Furman was among those captured. It was obvious that the flat would be kept under guard, and that any residents out at the time of the raid would be taken as they returned. This is exactly what happened to Major D'Arcy Mander, of the Green Howards, who was due to spend only one more night at the flat. He returned to find himself grabbed by a couple of armed Germans. They bundled him into a room by himself, and locked the door but forgot the window. Mander promptly climbed out, found a billet for himself, and was never recaptured.

The immediate task was to find out exactly how many billets had fallen, and to warn the occupants of any which survived to remain indoors, in readiness for immediate evacuation if necessary, for I had no way of knowing whether the Via Chelini raid was an isolated lucky stroke by the Gestapo or a symptom of the breakdown of the entire organization. One by one, with the aid of Monsignor O'Flaherty, the priests were contacted, and asked to find out what they could about the billets for which they were responsible without exposing themselves to risk.

In general the billets were with private families, and a visit from a priest would not therefore be suspicious. Even if a billet had been detected by the Germans, a priest who called would not necessarily be compromised. On the other hand, if a large number of billets was under observation, and the Gestapo reported that they were all visited by priests during one afternoon, the Germans could scarcely fail to put two and two together and arrive at Monsignor O'Flaherty. Thus, all the priests were warned that they should not enter any billet until they had made reasonably sure that it was not being watched.

I was particularly concerned about "Horace" (the New Zealand priest, Father Owen Snedden), for he had the dangerous task of checking up on the other flat at Via Firenze, where a routine pastoral call would be much more difficult to explain. However, as he approached the block, Father Snedden slowed his pace, walking contemplatively, and just before he reached the main door he saw a silent but expressive warning signal from the waiting Italian porter. Without faltering, Father Snedden walked slowly on past the block, and, a short distance along Via Firenze, was caught up by the porter, who walked beside him, and, in a brief, urgent whisper, gave him the news.

"Bad news, I'm afraid," the priest told me on his return.

Assuming that the rot had started with Iride, the Sulmona girl whose treachery had cost us Pollak, I cursed myself for having failed to press ahead earlier with my plans to empty the two flats. When I learned that Nebolante's flat had been the first billet to fall that day I realized that I was probably blaming Iride unjustly, and my second thoughts were confirmed when reports came that Nebolante's cook had been seen cruising around Rome in a car with Gestapo agents.

In a way this was reassuring, since the cook's knowledge of the organization must be very limited, and I began to relax as, one after the other, couriers returned with the information that their groups of 'cells' were still secure.

In particular I was glad to hear that nothing disquieting had happened down Mrs Chevalier's way. Nevertheless, the disaster could not be minimized. We had lost both 'clearing house' flats and one 'cell,' the Germans had captured John Furman, Dr Macauley, eleven other escapers, Büchner, Herta, and Nebolante, the Italian 'padrone.' Two days earlier we had lost Joe

Pollak, Iride and her family, and at least a dozen escapers, and probably as many entire families in Sulmona itself.

The only consolation was that none of those captured knew much about the organization except Furman, and none of the priests had been compromised.

For Furman I felt particular concern, because the only hope of preserving his life lay in his ability to establish his prisoner-of-war status, and in any case his only way of avoiding rough handling and, probably, torture was by convincing the Germans that he was an ordinary escaped prisoner and not a member of some sort of underground organization. Here there would be difficulties because, apart from his smart civilian clothes and false documents, Furman would probably have coded notes and receipts collected that day, and I knew, too, that he was in possession of an incriminatingly large sum of money, given to him that morning. I confided my fears to Lieutenant Simpson.

"Thank heaven, John gave me 10,000 lire for my chaps when we met this afternoon," he replied, "and I know that he had already been round to 'Mrs M.,' and given her 10,000 too, so he can't have much left."

"Anything up to 15,000 lire," I corrected him.

Simpson whistled. "Too much!" he said quietly.

"Far too much," I agreed. "The Germans will never believe that an ordinary escaper could have that sort of money. Let's hope he managed to dump it."

"Well, after all, John has got dysentery," said Simpson. "Maybe he has managed to dump it down a lavatory by now."

In point of fact, Simpson was not far from the truth: Furman got as far as obtaining permission to use the lavatory while still at Via Chelini, but the armed guard who accompanied him insisted on keeping the door wide open, and stood facing him with a fixed, disconcerting stare. They were, indeed, still in this unorthodox situation when Simpson pressed the doorbell, but the diversion was insufficient to allow Furman to dispose of all his documents.

Nevertheless, he did get rid of them eventually, setting a weird paper trail through Rome, when carted off to the Regina Coeli prison. Under the cover of a blanket on his lap, he tore all his papers into little pieces, and pushed them, at intervals, out through the gap between the canvas hood and the side of the van. Bit by bit, his two identity cards, his notebook of coded addresses and telephone numbers, a statement of accounts, which he had intended to deliver to me later in the day, and two or three receipts fluttered out into the slipstream.

His money, however—he actually still had 12,000 lire—remained securely in his raincoat pocket. Furman, the master of subterfuge and bribery, had already come to the conclusion that if he had to go back to prison, money was likely to be useful, but he also knew that the sum he carried was too large for comfort, and before he was interrogated he managed to stuff most of it into a bread roll, which passed German inspection without arousing suspicion.

The success of this ruse meant that Rome Organization money was providing black-market cigarettes and other minor luxuries for the recaptured prisoners in the Regina Coeli prison before I even knew where they were. Furman achieved this through a 'trusty' prisoner, a crafty Italian, who ran many profitable sidelines in addition to that of being prison barber, and who must have combined serving a sentence with making a fortune.

It took a day or two to establish where the men had been lodged, but as soon as I was able to confirm that at least some of them were in the dreaded Regina Coeli, I decided that we ought to try to make use of the services of our 'Protecting Power,' to find out what was happening.

Accordingly, I sent a memorandum to the British Minister, saying:

As we know that at least three of the prisoners-of-war recaptured on January 8 were taken to the Regina Coeli, could the Swiss Legation send a representative to visit them? The fact that these men were taken there presents an excellent opportunity for the Swiss to inquire into the conditions of any other British prisoners-of-war detained in the Regina Coeli.

Actually, it is a very delicate situation regarding the other Britishers in there, because we do not know what stories they have told the prison authorities. Their lives, even, might be endangered if the Swiss were to interfere directly. For example, we know that (a) Captain John Armstrong has been detained there for nearly four months; (b) a Britisher named Cunningham has been there for a considerable time; (c) there are three Britishers in there whom the records show to be Italians. We believe that in the case of Cunningham and these three, they were dressed in civilian clothes when captured, so the authorities may still not know that they are British. If it had been the authorities' intention to shoot the three men shown as Italians the sentence would, I think, have been carried out before now, but if the authorities got the idea that these men were British they might be able to charge them with new offences resulting in the death penalty.

In terms of diplomacy I was somewhat naïve, for Sir D'Arcy Osborne discussed the matter with the Swiss Legation, but then informed me that they did not feel they could visit the prisoners in the Regina Coeli at once, because the Germans would want to know where they got their information about them. They would suspect that it came from the British Legation, which would immediately indicate the existence of an organization assisting escapers from within the neutral Vatican.

However, the Minister told me, one of the Swiss had asked for an interview with the German officer in charge of all matters connected with prisoners-of-war, and hoped to see him shortly. He would ask if there were any British prisoners-of-war detained in Rome, and perhaps suggest the Regina Coeli.

I had to leave it at that, and turned my thoughts to the welfare of the 2000 escapers still at large.

As an immediate step, we decided to evacuate all billets known to the Italian helpers who were captured, and to reorganize the whole system of supply and distribution so that each helper was responsible for a small group of three or four 'cells,' and had no connexion with any others. The actual groups of 'cells' were known only to Monsignor O'Flaherty, Lieutenant Simpson, and me.

The new system, put into operation at once, placed a very heavy burden on Lieutenant Simpson, who was now my only military assistant on the operational side, for more and more escapers were coming in all the time. After the New Year raids and the Sulmona breakdown, the need to guard against infiltration of informers was greater than it had ever been; but greater also, alas, was the difficulty of achieving protection.

At first the home of two Irish priests, always game for anything, had to be used as a sort of reception centre for newcomers, but within a few days we were able to establish a transit camp in the basement of a block of flats near the Vatican. The flats were used by Vatican officials, but the basement was the province of a tiny Italian porter, Paolino, who cheerfully gave up accommodation which was none too extensive for his own family, in order to provide overnight lodging for up to half a dozen escapers at a time. The position was still further improved when we arranged for a small shop, close to the Vatican, to be used as an interrogation centre, where I could meet newcomers. Then came two more blows aimed at the nerve centre of the whole organization.

The first came in the form of an innocuous invitation to Monsignor O'Flaherty to attend a reception at the Hungarian Embassy, and the monsignor, well aware that the Hungarian Embassy was a favourite choice by the Germans for much demi-official diplomacy, accepted it with the resignation of a man answering a summons. He had not been long at the reception before the German Ambassador himself approached him, and said, "I would like a word with you, Monsignor, if you don't mind."

The Ambassador drew the monsignor aside, and quietly but firmly told him that the German Military Government of Rome was fully aware of what was going on in the way of aid to escaped prisoners-of-war.

"It has gone on too long, and it has got to stop," said the Ambassador. "In future you will stay where you belong. If you leave the area of the Vatican you will be arrested on sight. This is a final warning," concluded the Ambassador gruffly. "Think carefully about what I have said."

"Oh, to be sure I will," replied Monsignor O'Flaherty. "Sometimes."

He was irrepressible, and told me about the warning with evident glee, but almost immediately afterwards he received some sort of official caution from the Vatican Secretariat. This, of course, he had to treat seriously, and he delegated all his outside visits to priests who, so far as was known, were not under suspicion, but he continued to direct their operations as energetically as ever from his office.

The second blow, which affected me directly, was not long in arriving. The monsignor entered the office, looking unfamiliarly grave. "It's more trouble we're in," he sighed. "This time it's marching orders for you, me boy."

"You mean I have to leave here?"

"Aye, that's about the size of it. Would you believe it, now, the rector has just informed me that he has reason to believe the gentleman who is a guest in my room is not a neutral Irishman at all, and he would therefore be very much obliged if the gentleman would leave at once."

The rector, who was in charge of the college, was a German, but I knew that he was no Nazi, so I guessed that he, too, must have received some sort of warning from the Military Government or the Vatican Secretariat.

With sudden affection, I gazed round the little room which had seen so much drama and so much simple conviviality in the last few weeks: at the sofa, which had been my bed, at the littered desk, which had been our dining-table, at the little radio, which had brought the English news to good men of half a dozen races. The small room had become home to me in a very real sense, and I could not bear the thought of leaving it, quite apart from my growing realization that a change of address was bound to bring forth a bumper harvest of problems if the work was to continue.

"I suppose it couldn't last," I said with resignation. "Well, I had better set about organizing myself a place in one of the billets straight away. Damned nuisance we haven't even got the flats now."

"One moment," said the monsignor solemnly. "It's not quite as straightforward as that. I haven't told you everything yet."

"Not more trouble?" I asked without optimism.

"Afraid so, me boy. It seems the Germans now know that Patrick Derry is the lad who has been issuing all the help to escaped prisoners. If you stay here they may pay you an unwelcome call within hours, but if you go to a billet you'll have to make up your mind to remain there. They'll pounce as soon as you show your face anywhere round here."

"But that's impossible, Monsignor!" I protested. "How can we keep the work going if I can't remain in touch? God knows it's tricky enough already, with Furman and Pollak in the bag, and you confined to barracks."

"Things are seldom so black as they look at first sight," said the monsignor comfortingly, "but, I agree, it is rather a problem."

"A problem," I replied thoughtfully, "that merits solution at Ministerial level. Monsignor, I'm going to have to ask you to lend me your second-best soutane again. . . ."

7

Ghost of the Vatican

THOUGHTFULLY and deliberately, like an assize-court judge summing up a peculiarly technical case, the British Minister pinpointed all the arguments for and against my establishment in a billet in Rome, and then propounded a surprising solution.

"You will have to stay inside the Vatican," he announced.

"You mean I must be interned, sir?" I asked, startled and worried.

"That," he replied, leaning back and fixing me with his slow, calm smile, "is just what I do not mean."

He explained that would never do. Now that the Germans knew all about Patrick, they would be watching with considerable interest to see where he turned up, and if they discovered a sudden addition to the internees they would not take long to put two and two together. He imagined they had already discovered that Patrick was a British officer of some seniority, and suspected that the legation was mixed up in it. They must be kept guessing: Patrick must disappear altogether.

"Well, I have already decided to change my code name to 'Toni,'" I said, "but surely everything you have said only proves that I must go out into Rome and find myself a billet?"

"On the contrary," he said.

The force of his subsequent arguments was irresistible, and much as I disliked the prospect of cutting myself off from all my friends, and from the interest and excitement of the work in Rome, I had to admit that the organization of assistance for our enormous 'country branch,' representing more than 90 per cent. of all the escapers, could be continued from within the legation, whereas it might prove impossible from a secret billet somewhere in the city.

So I 'disappeared,' and became the only Allied serviceman ever to live, without being interned, within the Vatican City while Rome was in enemy hands. With a twinge of regret, I handed my Irish and German documents to Captain Byrnes, and told him to bury them, for I wanted to know that they were still available, in case a German raid on the Vatican forced me to make a run for it. Patrick Derry ceased to exist, and I was flattered to learn that Monsignor O'Flaherty had some difficulty in accounting for my sudden departure to the German nuns, who had become quite attached to the tall 'Irish' writer.

Sam Derry also ceased to exist, for no reference to my name appeared on paper in the legation or elsewhere in the Vatican. I became a man utterly without identity—not even a false one. I was the ghost of the Vatican: a ghost known only as "Toni."

The Minister, observing my lack of enthusiasm for anonymous incarceration, had tried, in his kindly way, to comfort me by suggesting that it might now be only a matter of days before the Allied advance swept up the long leg of Italy and liberated the Eternal City. But from all the information that he himself had given me, apart from what I had learned through the wireless, I could not be optimistic. With snow reported from places that had never seen it, and the prospect of seas of mud as soon as the rapid Italian spring began, it was clear that the conditions for a winter advance could not be less propitious. In any case, we had no reason to believe that the Germans would not stand and fight at Rome, allowing the city to be laid waste, and making our own position completely untenable.

Thus, throwing off the monsignor's soutane for the last time, I took up residence in the legation, with a feeling of gloom which was not dispelled by John May's skill in preparing food, nor even by nights in a proper bed.

Indeed, my frustration was only heightened when, on my first full day in the legation, I found myself unable to meet the organization's most distinguished 'client.' In a crowded four weeks there had been no news of the Greek agent, "Mario" (Theodore Meletiou), since he set off northward in mid-December, with instructions to bring back, if possible, one of the senior officers in the group he claimed to have contacted at Arezzo, 120 miles from Rome. I had not really expected ever to hear of him again, but on January 13, while I was glumly establishing myself in my new headquarters, he suddenly reappeared in Rome. With him were Major-General M. D. Gambier-Parry, M.C., captured during the North African campaign, and Mrs Mary Boyd, an Englishwoman who had been under partial internment in the

Arezzo area, but who had placed herself in great danger because of the help she had given to Allied escapers.

The three of them had been travelling since January 9, when Mario led them on a five-hour trek on foot to a place called Badia Prataglia. There they caught a bus to Bibbiena, and completed the journey to Rome, audaciously, by train. The Greeks found temporary billets for them, and their arrival was announced in a letter brought to the monsignor's office by Mario.

> The bearer of this, who is known to you [wrote General Gambier-Parry], will tell you of my arrival here this morning, effected through his magnificent efforts on my behalf. Is there any chance of my getting into the Vatican, either (*a*) with the knowledge and approval of H.M. Ambassador; (*b*) without it; (*c*) with it—but 'winked' at. I left five brigadiers and three other officers in the area I have come from. They have hopes of another plan, which may or may not come off. To come to Rome, if our friend can arrange it as he did for me, may be an alternative, and in any case three of them would like to come at once, or as soon as it can be arranged. Will you discuss it with our mutual friend, and send me back word by him also saying what are the possibilities of getting them into the Vatican.
>
> *Postscript:* Mrs Boyd and I are without money, and if we cannot get into the Vatican the question of how we are to live will arise very shortly. Have you any funds at your disposal from which to help us? I have also got to buy a complete outfit of clothes.

By now I already had a number of officers of my own rank in the care of the organization, but the presence of a major-general was a new experience, so I called on the British Minister—now a very simple thing to do—and he agreed to investigate the chances of getting the general into the Vatican, since he was now the senior Allied escaper in Italy. Lieutenant-Generals P. Neame, V.C., C.B., D.S.O., and Sir Richard O'Connor, K.C.B., D.S.O., M.C., and Air Vice-Marshal O. T. Boyd, C.B., O.B.E., M.C., A.F.C., who walked out of their castle prison at the time of the Italian Government's collapse, had succeeded in getting out of the country.

While the Minister was making discreet inquiries, I sent "Whitebows" (Brother Robert Pace), to the general's temporary billet with a letter.

I strongly advise against your friends coming to Rome. Our organization has recently been denounced, and seven officers and several other ranks and helpers were retaken. We consider the country to be far safer. Chances of getting your friends into the Vatican are very small.

I also enclosed 20,000 lire in notes, and told him :

If you are unable to buy clothes please let me know your requirements and rough sizes, and I will endeavour to get them.

But the Greeks, apparently, had good black-market contacts of their own, and in his next note the general wrote :

Many thanks for the 20,000 lire, with which I have been able to fit myself out most successfully, with the help of our friends.

Within a day or two I was able to get a message from the general through to his wife, whom he had not seen for five-and-a-half years, though because his name was so well-known, I could not use what I had to look upon as 'normal channels'—channels which had still better not be disclosed. For this the general was particularly grateful, although his message could not exceed ten words.

Meanwhile I had asked the monsignor if he could arrange a billet of more than average security, as I did not want the Germans to recapture such a valuable prize as the general. It so happened that the monsignor had been keeping a very special billet in reserve for just such an emergency, and told me of a secret room made, not without foresight, in the home of Signora dio Rienzo, in Via Roggero Bonghi. The signora was English by birth, the daughter of Lord Strickland's brother. On the fourth floor the door of an end room had been walled up, and from inside the house there was no indication that the room existed at all; the only entrance was through the window, and even that, in turn, could be reached only when a plank was put out at night from the window of a passage at right angles to the secret room—a hazardous 'draw-bridge,' forty feet above the ground.

It was the perfect hiding-place, so we arranged for the general to be guided there forthwith. Once I knew that he was safe I breathed freely, for now, apart from his host and hostess, nobody knew of the general's whereabouts except Monsignor O'Flaherty, his guide, and myself.

The general wrote:

The new billet is all that could possibly be desired, and far exceeds everything I ever dreamed of when I set out on this venture a fortnight ago. My host and hostess are quite charming, and spoil me dreadfully. I am revelling in every comfort after what was a pretty rough life in the part of the world I have come from, and the conditions under which we were still living there; and you can perhaps imagine how I enjoyed my first hot bath for four-and-a-half months.

I certainly could, having gone eighteen months without one.

The secret room [the general continued] is a wonderful hiding-place, and while it has its drawback in the way of not being able to get out into the air, or take any exercise, I certainly don't feel disposed to complain, for in that respect I am probably no worse off than yourself and a great many others, and in many ways probably better off than anyone.

I greatly wish that we could meet, and have a good talk, but I realize it is impossible at the moment. . . . I am still very much in the dark as to the exact nature of your organization, and the various parts which you and others play in it. But I do realize that you are doing splendid work, and I only wish that there was something I could do myself, instead of sitting here in comfort and complete idleness.

I could scarcely contemplate putting a general to work as a billeting officer, even though my sole representative in that field was now seriously overburdened, but, on the other hand, he was the senior British officer in Rome, so, through "Whitebows," I asked him if he would like to take over command of the organization. With characteristic diffidence, he declined, and instead said some very flattering things about what the organization had done for him; I decided not to point out that he was only in Rome at all as the result of a flamboyant Greek venture in which I personally had never had any faith, but thereafter we corresponded regularly, and I kept him in touch so far as possible with all major developments. He wrote long and frequent letters, and showed great interest in all who were helping in our work.

On one occasion he wrote direct to Monsignor O'Flaherty, with a suggestion about the future of the brigadiers he had left in the north, but almost immediately afterwards sent me a letter saying:

Thinking it over, I am not sure that I should not have written to you direct instead of to our mutual friend, but I had to write to him in any case, and as I have already explained, I am more than a little hazy about the chain of command as between yourself and others. I am sure, therefore, that you will acquit me of any intention of going behind your back.

In fact, the general's letter brought home to me—I think, for the first time—the strangeness of this organization, in which soldiers and priests, diplomats and Communists, noblemen and humble working-folk, were all operating in concord with a single aim, yet without any clearly defined pyramid of authority. On reflection, I could only write to the general :

Regarding "chain of command," although I have tried to keep the show on military lines for the ex-prisoners-of-war (on the whole discipline has been good, though one or two of the boys have gone a little wild from time to time), we have no real chain of command between "Golf" and his party and myself. Consequently, "Golf" sent me your letter to read, and he will see your letter to me; he sends me daily an account of his activities, and I keep him informed of everything I do.

With so much correspondence floating about, I was beginning to feel as though I was engaged, not so much in an escape organization, as in some sort of big business enterprise; even with my key contact with the outside world, Lieutenant Bill Simpson, communication was limited to paper, although, fortunately, it never had to pass outside the precincts of the Vatican. Simpson could always get to the guardroom at the Porta Santa Marta, and usually without much difficulty to the monsignor's office, while John May, working from the opposite direction, could reach either place by a complex route which took him through one of the Pontifical Guards' barrack rooms. During his long sojourn in the Vatican he had maintained the friendliest of relationships with the Swiss Guards, and his persuasive charm even succeeded in inducing them to part with their boots, when he was unable to obtain supplies for escapers from other sources.

How much footwear John May himself wore out in the service of our organization I cannot guess, but he seemed to be almost constantly ferrying messages between Monsignor O'Flaherty, the visiting Lieutenant Simpson, and me. In one respect this cumbersome system had an advantage.

One of the weaker links in our security was now strengthened because Simpson read, memorized, and then destroyed all written instructions from me before he left the Vatican, and did not write any reports to me until he reached the guardroom.

Simpson was spending his whole time on the organization of billets and the distribution of money and supplies, always keeping room available for new arrivals in Rome, but he too must have felt that he had become involved in big business, for he was saddled with the loan negotiations which Lieutenant Furman had initiated.

In his first written report Simpson enclosed cheques made out by four hopeful officers, and asked, "Could you cash them? If you can't they'll kill me." The officers all knew that cheques were being paid each month into their idle bank accounts at home, while the other ranks knew that they were piling up "credits." I realized as well as anybody that freedom to spend just a little of their involuntary savings would have made a great difference to their rather bleak lives, but that did not alter the inescapable fact that I just did not possess the funds. Indeed, I would have been as glad as any officer to be able to cash my own cheques. I had no alternative to telling Simpson that the money I sent him was strictly and solely for the essential maintenance of escapers, albeit at subsistence level. But I pointed out that there were apparently sufficient officers asking to cash cheques to justify the raising of a private loan of lire, as John Furman had planned. So far as the other ranks were concerned, similar facilities could not be provided, since the War Office payments were not normally made into bank accounts, but I authorized the payment of twenty lire a day for extra comforts to each man—with the exception of those staying with the bountiful Mrs Chevalier.

Simpson picked up the underground loan negotiations where Furman had suddenly left off, and soon reported that he had been able to arrange an advance of lire at "a goodish rate," if I and a couple of other officers would sign an agreement for the repayment. I agreed, and Simpson drew up a simple agreement in Italian to refund the money in pounds sterling immediately after the occupation of Rome by the Allies or the end of the war, whichever was the sooner.

A week later Simpson reported that he had been able to collect 100,000 lire at the rate of 650 to the pound, which struck me as a noble effort, since the normal rate was about 450. "Not bad, eh?" asked Bill, with some jubilation, reporting that he had given a temporary receipt, and enclosing a final agreement for signature. So I signed, hoping for the best, and supporting signatures were added by Major Fane-Harvey and Simpson himself. In the middle of a war Simpson had, in fact, succeeded in pulling off a financial coup. He had converted 154 pounds worth of British bank credit into enemy currency. He encashed the officers' cheques at the rate of 525 lire to the pound, and gave the profit of 3750 lire to the Italian who had acted as go-between in arranging the loan on such favourable terms. -

Now that the officers had a little money of their own, and the other escapers were receiving a small personal allowance, it seemed to me that most of the difficulties of their confinement in Rome were overcome, but I could not help wondering how many laws I had broken in authorizing this unique transaction. In a letter to General Gambier-Parry I commented:

> There are a few small points for the future like an odd 100,000 lire borrowed on the promise of £154 sterling immediately after the liberation of Rome. Although I hold officers' cheques on Cox and King's for the full £154, I cannot help doubting if the field cashier will cash them for me. And will snags crop up like "trading with the enemy," etc.? The point was that we had to have cash, and I didn't much care how we obtained it; now that we have the cash, I don't feel inclined to ask the good persons who lent me the money to accept practically worthless lire back. Still, all this will wait.

Even with 'the firm's money,' I was meeting continuous problems, a good many of which seemed to revolve around Mrs Chevalier, who by nature was generous rather than provident. For Simpson, "Mrs M." was a new experience. The responsibility of paying for the five escapers billeted in her crowded flat now rested with him, and at the end of his first survey, after the January disaster, he reported to me, "She is quite content to carry on as before with her family of boys, and I think it is O.K. too. She has to buy a stock of potatoes and would like some more money." I could not help smiling; I had already spent a good deal of time curbing Furman's enthusiasm for pouring Government funds into the gallant widow's household, and now, apparently, I had to go to work all over again for Simpson's benefit, for, if I did not tighten the rein, her escapers would end up the five best-fed men in Rome.

To Bill I wrote:

> This lady has done excellent work all the time. However, as John possibly told you, she is inclined to spend too much money, and feed her boys too well; great tact is required on this subject, but from time to time we tell her she is spending too much, and should cut out the eggs, etc. The great point is that if "Mrs M.'s" boys spend more than 100 lire per day allowance, other chaps have to go short (at least that is the way we put it to "Mrs M").

By mid-January Italy was well in the grip of its most severe winter for many years, which meant both that more and more escapers made their way to Rome from exposed hiding-places in the country, and that the position at the front, in the south, was more firmly static than ever. I had to face the fact that for the time being the organization would have to cope with an increasing number of new arrivals without hope of a compensating outflow of departures, and Simpson and the priests spent most of their time finding new billets, although some of these, in Simpson's words, were "not very bright."

It had always been my practice to provide money, clothes, and whatever other facilities were possible for any escaper who wanted to make his way south to the lines, and I continued to do so when requests were made, though without optimism.

When the United States Chargé d'Affaires, Mr Harold Tittman, asked me for a route to the lines for some American escapers in the care of the organization, I had to reply:

> I regret I am unable to give a route down to the lines, as ex-prisoners who have recently been dispatched on our recommended route have all returned. They state: (a) that it is practically impossible to obtain food when some distance from the lines; (b) that snow on the mountain slopes makes going very slow; (c) that they have seen several British ex-prisoners-of-war, especially Indians, dead on the mountains, apparently having died of exposure and/or hunger. While I realize that it is the duty of all ex-prisoners-of-war to try and rejoin our forces at the earliest possible moment, I cannot help but feel it is exceedingly unwise to attempt to get through to the lines now.

The blocking of the escape line to the south added to the difficulty of finding sufficient accommodation in Rome for escapers, and there were many minor complications: as on the occasion when Pasqualino Perfetti, the pseudo-priest, who had been my first contact in Rome, brought in from the country two South African soldiers who happened to be ebony-black Negroes. There was, of course, no colour bar in the organization, and, indeed, it was not difficult to find Italian 'padrones' to look after the South Africans, but even the least racial-conscious observer had to admit that they looked conspicuous on the streets of Rome, so we had to order them to remain permanently under cover, in their billets.

There was also a steady stream of Arabs at the Santa Marta, all claiming to have fought for the Allies in North Africa, and all demanding (good Moslems that they were) the protection of the Vatican. John May used to go down to the gate and deal with them, but in almost all cases their loyalty was suspect, and we never took them into the care of the organization in the ordinary way. On the other hand, we could not afford to take chances, so John May gave them money, and instructions to return to the Porta Santa Marta if they needed more, and eventually we organized a system of fixed allowances, which the Arabs collected at the gate once a month.

Then there was the problem of the Indians, which was rather more difficult. I knew as well as anybody of the gallantry and loyalty of the units which had fought with us in Africa, but I also knew that the Germans had played on the political sensitivity of the Indians they captured, telling them that British Imperialism had been keeping them down for centuries, and urging them to join an Indian regiment to fight the British, and so—as the Germans put it—strike the first blow for the independence of their country.

Tragically, some Indians fell for this line, putting their sweat and skill at the disposal of the wrong side, and I always had the fear that the loyalty of others was weakened by the persuasive Nazi propaganda. Often with regret, I had to treat requests for help from Indians with a certain amount of caution, but my best defence lay in an ever-growing intelligence system, and information elicited during the interrogation of new arrivals from various camps gradually enabled us to build up a fairly comprehensive knowledge, fully recorded and indexed, of the activities of the more dangerous characters.

Thus, when one particular Indian came to us for help I was able within minutes to identify him as a renegade who had gone over wholly to the other side, and who therefore needed to be kept under surveillance until he could be handed over to the British authorities. One of the group leaders, Lieutenant Panwar, a King's Commission Indian, volunteered to "befriend" the turn-coat, take charge of him, and keep him out of trouble until the liberation, which, in fact, he achieved with complete success. Unfortunately, the renegade later escaped from his prison cell at Naples.

But we had friends, too, and one averted a disaster for Mrs Chevalier. It was only ten minutes before curfew one night, when Mrs Chevalier answered a ring at the door to find there a lame Italian youth, whom she knew vaguely by sight. He whispered urgently, "You are hiding some British prisoners. The Germans are coming to raid you after curfew to-night."

The youth told her he would take the escapers to his home if they would get ready at once.

Mrs Chevalier, torn between suspicion and anxiety, asked him to wait, and told her 'lodgers' of the message. They came, rightly, to the conclusion that it was better for them to take the chance of walking into a trap than to risk death for Mrs Chevalier and her family. They scrambled their belongings together, and got out of the flat with four minutes to spare before curfew, leaving Mrs Chevalier, her son, and six daughters to cram their mattresses into cupboards, and remove all other obvious traces of their occupation.

Almost exactly on the hour of curfew the S.S. pounded on the door with the vicious urgency characteristic of their terrorism: they never knocked on a door, but always kicked it with their jack-boots or clouted it with carbine-butts. Mrs Chevalier slipped back the latch, and the German commander strode in, taking in at a glance the middle-aged woman, the youth, and the six girls.

"Papers," he demanded, and flicked quickly through their identity cards.

"Who else is here?" he asked, but without much conviction. Standing before him were eight Italians, all with papers perfectly in order, and it was not conceivable that there could be any further occupants of such a tiny flat. He made only a cursory inspection of the apartment, failing to find any of Mrs Chevalier's vast surplus of mattresses and foodstuffs, and decided that the denunciation had been a false one. He apologized for the intrusion, and asked quite courteously if she had seen any strangers coming and going in the neighbourhood.

Mrs Chevalier had already come to the conclusion that the denunciation had come from the family next door, whom she knew to be of Fascist sympathies, so she replied innocently, "There have been some strangers coming to this building—but they all went next door."

The German commander thanked her, and ordered his men to the adjoining flat, and for the next half hour Mrs Chevalier derived singular satisfaction from the noise of crashing furniture and hysterical protests, which filtered through the wall. In that half-hour the S.S. men, who had spent only a few minutes with her, and caused little trouble, practically wrecked the adjoining apartment, wrenching open doors, stripping beds, up-turning drawers, emptying cupboards, and puncturing upholstery.

The five escapers who had been at the flat were housed in temporary billets, but when Lieutenant Simpson called on Mrs Chevalier the day after the raid he found her very concerned about them, though not in the least daunted by her own unnerving experience. "She is very worried about her boys," Simpson confided to me. "She wants them back, but I say no. She is willing to help us in any other way possible."

But within four days Mrs Chevalier had managed to get in touch with her beloved "boys" again, and had talked Simpson into allowing them to become reunited in the home of a friend of hers.

A day or so later Simpson was given a sharp reminder that he should be constantly on his guard. He was now back at the comfortable flat of Renzo and Adrienne Lucidi, where his new fellow-lodger was a Polish saboteur known as Rafaelo, and they were all in bed when the front door shook under the unmistakable hammering of the S.S.

In the moments before Renzo opened the door Rafaelo's little bag of explosives was hidden, the Pole was pushed into bed with Peppina, the housemaid, and told to pretend to be her lover, and Bill was told to look stupid, and to do his best with the rôle of the

Lucidis' half-witted nephew. It was a plot as fantastic as any ever directed by Renzo Lucidi in a film.

The jack-booted Germans accepted the Lucidis' explanation without question and showed no further interest in the English officer and the Polish saboteur, but, to every one's horror, they arrested Renzo's eighteen-year-old stepson, Gerard. As soon as curfew was lifted next morning, Simpson and Rafaelo changed their billets, while Renzo Lucidi went to the Via Tasso headquarters of the Gestapo to find out what had happened to his stepson. He found out nothing—and that evening the Germans returned to the flat, and arrested Renzo. They also asked about the unbalanced nephew, but Adrienne said he had gone out for the day, and she did not know where he was.

That was true enough: Simpson had come post haste to the Vatican to report to me, and had gone away with firm orders to post himself to another billet forthwith, leaving me to do what I could to assist Renzo Lucidi and his stepson. I knew that the boy, Gerard, Adrienne's son by her former marriage, was French by birth, so I immediately got in touch with my friend De Vial, at the French Legation.

He persuaded the Vichy French Minister to take up the matter with the German authorities, and within five days Renzo and Gerard were released, little the worse for wear, and apparently without having been subjected to extreme interrogation. From De Vial I gathered that the only reason for the Germans taking the boy had been that his name appeared in a list of students' addresses found in the notebook of a professor arrested on suspicion of subversion, and they had nothing on his stepfather beyond the accurate belief that he was a leader of socialist thought.

Lieutenant Simpson made his own inquiries into the cause of the raid, and in due course confirmed that it was only a political business, and nothing to do with us.

Now that I was taking none of the personal risk myself, I was increasingly conscious of the danger to which those doing the operational work hourly exposed themselves, and there were constant reminders that the risk was very real. On the day that we so nearly lost Lieutenant Simpson the organization did, in fact, lose another valuable helper, a gallant little Italian woman, whose arrest was a direct result of her work for escapers.

To the organization she was just "Midwife." To the people

of the scattered villages in a rural area a few miles north of Rome, she was Concetta Piazza, the district nurse, who dressed their bad legs, took them medicine when they were ill, and brought their babies into the world—a busy little body, who fulfilled all the duties of an English district nurse as well as many of those of the general practitioner. To twenty British ex-prisoners-of-war, hidden in odd corners of farms and villages, she was the cheerful courier who, regularly as clockwork, brought them money and supplies.

When Concetta Piazza was arrested she had just completed her long round of visits, and that was her one stroke of luck: she had none of the incriminating money or supplies left. She was taken off to Rome, and bundled into the notorious Regina Coeli gaol, where she was charged with giving aid to Allied escapers and evaders.

"Midwife" knew she had been denounced, which probably meant that the Germans had little real evidence against her, and no knowledge of the whereabouts of her ex-prisoners. She also knew that she was facing a capital charge, but she pinned her faith on her record as a nurse who had given medical attention to all in need, including Germans, and was convinced that if the highest authorities were aware that a nurse such as herself was being kept away from her vital work because of a mere 'unfounded' suspicion, she would be immediately released.

On prison toilet-paper she wrote a long letter to Field-Marshal von Kesselring, setting out all she had done in the course of her vocation, and emphasizing the danger of epidemic over part of the countryside close to Rome, in her absence. She knew, of course, that such an epistle would never have got beyond the stark walls of the Regina Coeli if she had tried to have it delivered through official channels. Indeed, she would probably have been punished for writing it, since any form of communication was forbidden. But "Midwife" also knew that in the Vatican were those who would help her even in the apparently hopeless task of laying a petition before the field-marshal himself. She therefore persuaded a prisoner being released to smuggle her letter out of gaol. It reached me, and her outline of her work seemed to provide as good a case as any for her release, for I knew that the hygiene-conscious Germans, aware of the general shortage of medical attention in the provinces, and also of the astonishingly primitive nature of rural sanitation, were in constant fear of the outbreak of some sort of epidemic.

It therefore remained only to retype the letter on paper more fitted for the eyes of a fastidious field-marshal, and arrange its delivery. This would have to be through one of the neutral Ministries, but I had to proceed with caution, for the Swiss Legation was already suspected of going beyond strict diplomatic limits for the British, and at the French Ministry De Val had shot his bolt for the time being by persuading the pro-German Minister to intercede for Adrienne Lucidi's son. On the other hand, there was still the Irish Legation, where Dr Kiernan reigned with such strict and unimpeachable neutrality that even the naturally suspicious Germans could scarcely have harboured any doubts about him. Blon Kiernan therefore arranged for the letter to be placed before her father, and in this way the most strictly neutral man in Rome came to pass a petition, typed at the headquarters of the British underground organization, to the field-marshal; furthermore, he marked it, "For the personal attention of Field-Marshal von Kesselring."

A day or two later, without a word of explanation, Concetta Piazza, the little nurse, was released.

This result was gratifying, for the loss of agents and helpers was becoming all too frequent. Often Italian helpers and Allied escapers alike were picked up simply because they happened to be in the wrong place when the Germans were rounding up men for forced labour—almost a daily occurrence. Occasionally the loss of an agent had an extra poignancy, such as when one messenger, a Jugoslav returning from delivering money to a group at Viterbo, was killed by machine-gun fire from a ground-strafing British fighter aircraft.

January was a black month, but as disaster followed upon disaster, there came a new beacon of hope—Anzio. After months of deadlock on the Cassino line, the Allies took a sudden leap up Italy by a seaborne invasion at Anzio, on the Tyrrhenian coast, not much more than twenty-five miles south of Rome, and established a firm bridgehead on January 21, although the B.B.C. news broadcasts did not mention it until the next day, and the German-controlled Rome Radio ignored it altogether.

Rumours reached me within an hour or two of the landings, and later I was able to see for myself, from the high roof of the

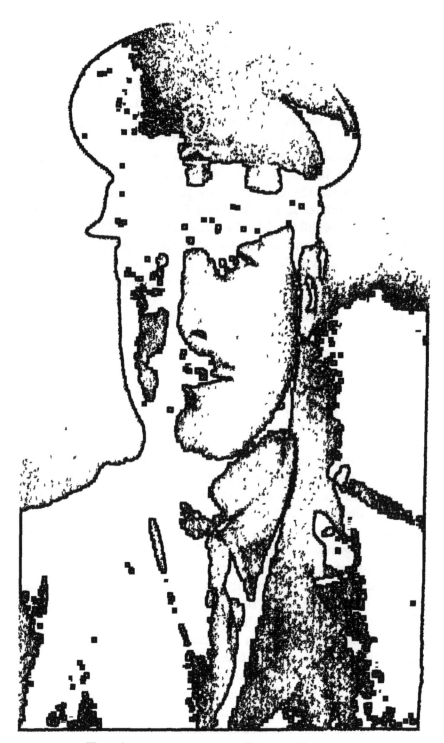

THE AUTHOR BEFORE HIS DESERT CAPTURE

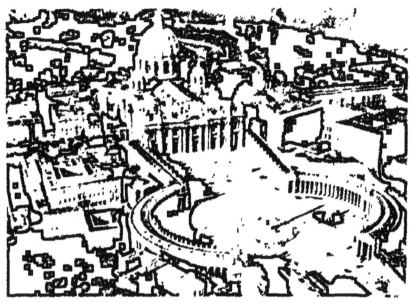

ST PETER'S SQUARE, ROME

It was here the author first met Monsignor O'Flaherty The large building on
the left is the Collegio Teutonicum

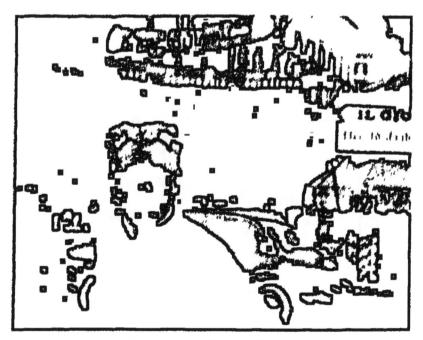

SNAPSHOT OF MONSIGNOR HUGH O'FLAHERTY IN ROME
(1958)

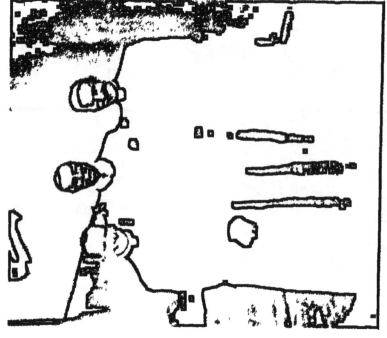

The Author, Father Owen Snedden (*right*), and Another Helper

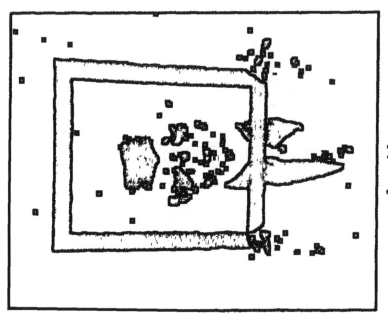

John May

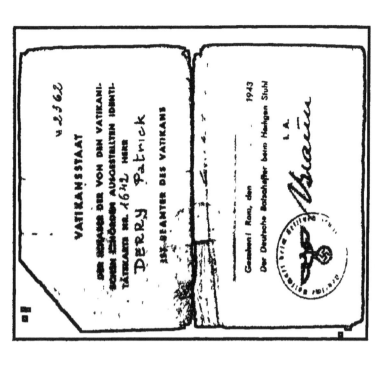

VATIKANSSTAAT

DER INHABER DER VON DEN VATIKANI-
SCHEN BEHÖRDEN AUSGESTELLTEN IDENTI-
TÄTSKARTE NR. 1642 HERR
DERRY Patrick

IST BEAMTER DES VATIKANS

Gesehen! Rom, den   1943
Der Deutsche Botschafter beim Heiligen Stuhl

i.A.

THE GERMAN PASS ACQUIRED BY THE AUTHOR,
AND SIGNED BY THE GERMAN MINISTER

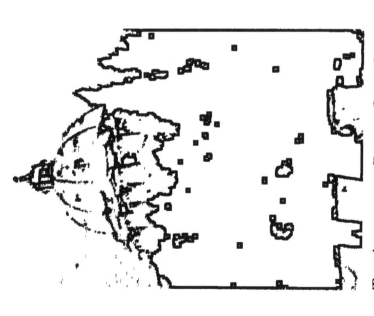

THE AUTHOR AND FATHER OWEN SNED-
DEN, NEAR ST PETER'S, ROME

An enlargement of a tiny snapshot smuggled
to England at Christmas 1943

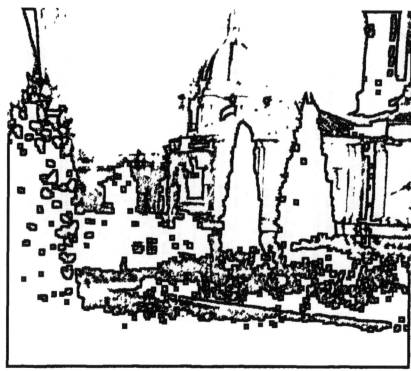

THE VATICAN GARDENS

The daily records and receipts of the Rome Organization were buried nightly in sealed tins.

LIEUTENANT JOHN FURMAN

He is seen here after his promotion to Captain following the liberation of Rome.

LIEUTENANT FURMAN'S NOTE FROM THE REGINA COELI PRISON

It measured approximately two and a half by four inches and bore some two hundred words, telling the story of his capture.

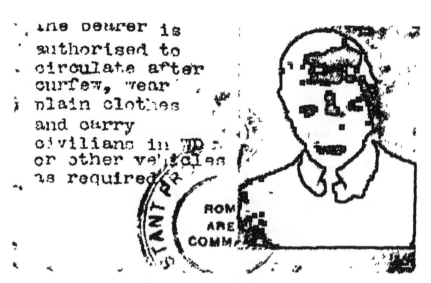

he bearer is
authorised to
circulate after
curfew, wear
plain clothes
and carry
civilians in jeep
or other vehicles
as required

ROM
ARE
COMM

THE AUTHOR'S BRITISH MILITARY POLICE PASS

THE MEDALLION PRESENTED TO THE AUTHOR BY
POPE PIUS XII TO COMMEMORATE HIS AUDIENCE

hospice building, the flashes of battle on the southern horizon. Overnight I was placed in a quandary, for the whole underground organization, which we had come to look upon as operating deep in enemy territory, was now only a score of miles from the front line. But everything depended on the reaction of the Germans. If they intended to defend Rome there would be little hope of maintaining the organization, quite apart from the fact that the neutrality of the Vatican would probably be the first casualty, but if they intended to withdraw to the north my task was clearly to maintain the organization intact, and keep the escapers free until the Allies swept into Rome. I was therefore faced with the alternative of ordering every man to make the best arrangements he could to link up with the Allies, or telling everybody to sit tight until further notice.

My own view was that the Allies would not attempt to storm Rome, for the capture of Rome, while good propaganda, was of negligible military importance compared with relieving the pressure on the Cassino line, and perhaps cutting off the German forces holding out there. But the decision was too important to be based on my own forecast of military tactics; what I wanted was knowledge of the German reaction, and the only way to get that was from the Germans themselves.

Blon Kiernan, the Irish Minister's daughter, was on good terms with the Bismarck family, and readily agreed to call for tea with Prince Bismarck, first secretary at the German Embassy to the Holy See. During tea they chatted casually, and by the time she returned to me, Blon was able to confirm that the Germans considered they would have to withdraw northward.

The main danger was that the escapers, learning of the proximity of the Allies, would act prematurely, and get recaptured at a time when they would be more likely to be shot out of hand than bundled off to distant prison camps. A few small groups south of Rome, who were virtually within sight of the battle, made their own way to the line, and were able to join the Allies without much difficulty during the first twenty-four hours, when the Germans were still off balance. Indeed, in that period I could easily have evacuated all the escapers in and south of Rome, myself included, but that would have meant abandoning the hundreds of others north of the city, at the time when it was most necessary for them to remain an organized unit. In any case,

I presumed that my freedom was being delayed for only a day or two.

To Lieutenant Simpson I rushed the order:

> Tell all that they are to remain in their billets after the occupation until they receive orders.

In the stress of the moment I had not said quite what I intended to say, but Simpson, with admirable discipline, circulated the order to other agents before he permitted himself to observe:

> I have noted your remarks about the boys staying in billets when the time comes, and have passed the order on. I wonder if they will, however.

> I did not mean this quite literally [I wrote back hastily]. But I do not want the boys dashing all over the place so that we get complaints, and then orders for us all to be concentrated in some camp. What I mean is that I want the boys to continue to live in their billets, as opposed to dashing off to live in brothels, etc.

Even Lieutenant Furman and the other prisoners in the Regina Coeli were aware that the war in Italy had taken a dramatic turn, for two days after the landings all their regular guards were withdrawn, and battered front-line troops, obviously resting from battle, were put in their place. I knew all this because I had at last heard from Furman. On a flimsy piece of paper, measuring only two and a half inches by four, he had written two hundred words outlining the story of his capture, warning that one of the priests was under suspicion, and listing the names of escapers he knew to be in the prison. The tiny epistle, folded over and over and placed in a capsule, had been smuggled out of the gaol, secreted on the body of an Italian, who went in periodically to shave the prisoners because the Germans thought it was necessary for hygiene, and because the men were not allowed their own razors.

Addressed "Dear Toni," and dated January 23, the letter read:

> We were taken by the S.S. at Via C. on the 8th Jan. They had already grabbed Tug and Pip and knew all about Via F. We were taken straight to the Regina C. where we still are. None of us has been interrogated, and we don't know what they intend to do with us. We are in different cells, and liaison is difficult, but I learned from Tug that Padre B. is known to them. They

got into Via C. with the assistance of Tug's cook, who brought them along. To-day all our guards have been changed, and rumours are rife. I hope the most optimistic ones are true. What is certain is that there is small chance of escape from here, but if they try to take us away—well, "chi la sa." Officers here are Wilson, Gardner, Macauley, Stewart, Selikman, Kane-Berman, Furman, O.R. Billet, Knox-Davies, Gibb, Churchill, Hands and Eaton (U.S.A.). In addition I have seen two coloured troops and a Pole. Also brought in with us were Herta and Bruno. Since I arrived I have seen and heard nothing of Macauley and Bruno, nor have I heard or seen Joe. If I don't get back please see my wife, and give her my love. Best luck,

JOHN

Two days later, at half-past eight in the morning, Furman wrote another letter, which reached me by the same method.

Dear Toni [he said], I have just had notice that all British prisoners are leaving here within the next two or three hours. It is the most damnable luck to have missed the bus by just over two weeks, but who knows—perhaps I shall see you in Rome yet. In any event, I know you will see my wife and Diana when you get back. Would you also ask Bill to remember me to all our friends here who have been so kind to me? And would you greet our Irish golfing friend for me, and also John, who made such an excellent dish of porridge not so many days ago. I still hope to see you all, but, as you know, the opportunity may just not arise, or it may end in a "Jock Short." In the event of the latter, I would like you to know that I had a balance of 4000 lire at Chieti, which should be worth about £50. But that is, of course, taking the gloomiest of views. I have already sent you the names of the people here—all men from Via F. and Via C. except Tug and Pip. I will sign off now, with the hope that you have an uneventful voyage back to England, and that the work you have done here is duly rewarded. My very best wishes,

JOHN

I could not imagine that anyone else in such circumstances would have betrayed so little self-pity, but there was still no doubt that in a month of many letters this was the saddest of all; it read far too much like a last will and testament for my liking.

"What might a 'Jock Short' be?" asked the monsignor, when I showed him the letter.

"It was the name of one of our chaps at Sulmona," I explained.

"He was shot down when he tried to make a bolt for it at the railway-station."

"I see," said the monsignor slowly. "And do you think John could be after doing the same sort of thing?"

"No . . . no, not quite. He's got too much initiative to commit suicide. But I'm sure of one thing, Monsignor : if there's the ghost of a chance of escape he will jump at it."

I was depressed by the news that our men in the Regina Coeli, within reach of liberation, were being sent north to the prison camps in Germany—at least, we prayed that was the correct interpretation of the transfer; the alternative was that they were being taken out to be shot. I was also depressed by the general situation around me. Furman's reference to missing the bus by a fortnight made it clear that he was still under the impression that the Allied occupation of Rome was imminent, but I was no longer so sanguine.

After the elation of the first day or two, it rapidly became apparent that Prince Bismarck had been too pessimistic about the outcome of the Anzio landings, and that I, consequently, had been too optimistic. The Germans, rather to their own surprise, had succeeded in containing the bridgehead, and they were now even talking confidently about "throwing the Allies back into the sea." I did not believe that this was likely, but I could have kicked myself for assuming a German withdrawal from Rome, because I now knew that I could have evacuated dozens of escapers safely from the city and its environs during the confusion of the first twenty-four hours.

So far from withdrawing from Rome, the Germans, in their new confidence about containing the Anzio bridgehead, were turning the Eternal City into a sort of front-line base. Divisions from all over northern Italy were converging upon it, and the whole place was alive with grey-uniformed troops. Each day brought added danger for Lieutenant Simpson and the other agents whenever they ventured on the streets, every night the curfew was more and more strictly enforced, and troop concentrations made it difficult and, in some cases, impossible for us to maintain the regular flow of supplies to groups in the country.

On the other hand, all this activity under our noses provided more opportunities than ever before for the information service which had been built up on the military side, and we were able to keep useful reports flowing out of Rome in a fairly steady stream. These included regular information about German reactions at top level, for Blon Kiernan was taking tea regularly with Prince Bismarck, and the knowledge was useful, because the Germans did not subsequently about-turn their reactions as violently as they had in the first two days of the battle.

From the growing information service, we drew the consolation of doing something active again for the war effort, but as January slipped away, and the red line on my calendar scored through a week, and then a fortnight of February, with no hint of an advance from either Anzio or Cassino, I realized that the Rome Organization would have to be kept intact for an indefinite period. Fortunately, there was no clairvoyant around, for I would have learned that although the Allied guns were barely a score of miles away, the Rome Organization was still only half-way through its chequered life.

8
Homing Pigeon and Caged Lion

BEAMING all over his benign face, almost bouncing with excitement, and obviously bubbling over with delight, Monsignor O'Flaherty burst into my room, thrust a scrap of paper towards me, and commanded, "Just read that, me boy!"

It was February 14, but I had scarcely expected that it would bring me a Valentine. Uncertainly, suspecting some sort of a prank, I unfolded the paper, and immediately recognized the small, neat writing.

> Back in Rome [it said]. Where the hell are you? Only consolation for my sore arse will be when I see your smiling face.
> JOHN

I could not believe it. Was John Furman really back in Rome?

"It's true all right, me boy," grinned the monsignor. "I've seen him with my own two eyes, and talked to him as I am talking to you now."

"But this is marvellous news! It seems like a miracle!"

"It is that," Monsignor O'Flaherty agreed. "But I think John rather helped it on its way."

"Nothing could surprise me less. How did he manage it this time?"

"Took a leaf out of your book, so far as I can gather—hacked a hole in a train, and jumped out. Then he and another chap named Johnstone rode bicycles here up and down mountains from the other end of Italy."

"That explains his cryptic comment," I laughed. "Monsignor, do you know, these last few days I've been thinking of myself calling on John's wife, and telling her that he got shot as a spy or something, because of a job I let him in for. Not the sort of thing one looks forward to, I can tell you. But I should have known better—I should have known they could never hold a chap like John for long. How is he—apart from the complaint he mentions?"

"Furious because he can't get straight in to see you," answered

the monsignor. "But seriously, I imagine all this unorthodox
travelling has not done his dysentery much good. He needs a bit
of building up, and a few nights in a comfortable bed."

Meanwhile Furman and the other man were having their first
good meal for weeks. I wished I could have gone with the monsignor to see them, and half hoped he might suggest some means
of smuggling me out of the legation, but I was a prisoner, not
just as a matter of expediency, but also as a matter of honour.
It was practical common sense that I should not allow the cloak
to slip from the secret of my existence while 2500 escapers and
evaders, scattered in and around Rome, depended for the maintenance of their freedom on the organization. There was also the
information service, which was of some value to the Allies, and
I had to remember that a moment of carelessness on my part
might lead to such extreme measures as the expulsion of the
British Minister, the closure of the legation, and the collapse of
the whole organization. It would not have been hard to talk the
monsignor into lending me his soutane again, but I knew that to
walk out through the gates would be to break faith with Sir
D'Arcy Osborne, if not with all those who depended on the continuation of the organization. With a jolt of conscience, I realized
that I was not now just a gunner underground : I was not merely
a 'ghost,' but something of a diplomatic secret.

Nevertheless, I was personally as well as professionally interested in methods of escape, and eager to hear from John Furman's own lips how he had completed his hat-trick of escaping
from German hands three times in six months. Bit by bit I pieced
the story together, although it was to be a long time before Furman himself could fill in all the gaps, and I think it was one of
the most daring and efficient escapes of the war. At the time, I
summed it up more directly as "bloody marvellous."

All the odds had been against Furman from the start,
for the Regina Coeli itself was virtually escape-proof, and
there was nothing equivocal about the German commander's
warning when the British prisoners were lined for transportation
northward. "Your guards have been warned to shoot to kill at the
first signs of an attempted escape." Small wonder that Furman,
in his hastily written second note, had visualized himself meeting
the same fate as Captain Jock Short.

The first ninety miles of the journey north were made by

motor-coach, under the constant surveillance of a singularly tough-looking group of guards, who kept their carbines at the ready. The only bright moment came when the coach broke down, and had to be towed by two oxen, commandeered by the Germans at pistol-point. At a transit camp Furman teamed up with Lieutenant J. S. Johnstone, R.E., a blond giant of a man who had been with us at Chieti, and together they hatched a hazardous plan for escape over the wire, but they were moved on, perhaps fortunately, before they had the opportunity to try it out.

Before entraining for Germany, together with nearly a thousand others, they were thoroughly searched, but Furman was even more successful than at the Regina Coeli, from which he had emerged with his money still secure in a loaf of bread. He not only retained a pair of scissors, stolen from the unsavoury black-marketeer at Regina Coeli, but gained an excellent cigarette-lighter. Seeing a box full of "forbidden items," like lighters and fountain-pens, confiscated from other prisoners, he used his fluent German to tell the officer in command that a lighter had been taken from him which was completely unserviceable but of very great sentimental value. Rather to his surprise, the German gave him permission to look for it, so Furman rummaged around in the box, and took the best lighter he could find, salving his conscience with the thought that the rightful owner would no doubt prefer him to a German, as the new owner.

The train in which the prisoners were to travel was not a sight to inspire confidence. Every two or three wagons had a turret from which armed guards could get an excellent view, and the wagons themselves were closed box-cars, with only small ventilators, which had been securely boarded up and wired. Even Furman recognized that breaking out of such a mobile dungeon with a pair of scissors was likely to be difficult, but as he craned around the door for a last breath of air before the wagon was sealed, he saw on the tracks a few yards away a rusty iron bar. His pleas of dysentery, vocally supported by his companions, were eventually heeded by the Germans, who allowed him to leave the wagon. Furman walked away from the train, threw his jacket carelessly over the iron bar, and settled down. There he sat, watched by a dozen armed Germans, and then, picking up the bar in his coat, scampered back to the train. By the time he reached the wagon a large part of the rusty iron bar was protruding from his coat, but the Germans did not notice it. His fellow prisoners, however, had cottoned on, and eagerly hauled him and his trophy aboard.

A break-out, to have a reasonable chance of success, had to be made while the train was in motion (because of the noise), and at night (because of the guards), but all through that night the train remained in the sidings, and next day Furman had to sit impatiently and impotently for hours as the train put more and more miles between him and Rome. As evening approached, the work began. Laborious carving made two deep cuts in the woodwork at the end of the wagon, and a single mighty blow with the iron bar left a neat hole two feet square.

Furman and Johnstone clambered out on to the buffers, fortunately concealed from the turrets in each direction, but the train was rattling along at nearly fifty miles an hour, and they could feel themselves slowly freezing as they waited for it to slow down sufficiently for them to jump. When at last it slackened speed they jumped in opposite directions—and the firing opened up at once.

Furman dashed into a back garden adjoining the tracks, and Johnstone hurtled past him a few seconds later, and plunged through a hedge. They lay panting, and listening to the continuing firing as other prisoners took their turn to jump farther down the line. But the train kept moving, and when at last all was quiet again they got up, and padded away in their stockinged feet. Their boots had been confiscated before they entrained, and when they were told they could have them back if they gave their parole not to escape their reply was a derisive laugh.

Furman, who was always ready to make the bold approach to Italians, and was invariably lucky in those he found, soon organized food and footwear, and eventually a change of dress for Johnstone, whose ragged prison-camp clothing was all the more conspicuous by its contrast to his companion's smart city suit. As a final master-stroke, Furman purchased two ancient bicycles, for through all his tribulations and searches he had contrived to retain 3000 lire of the Rome Organization money in his possession at the time of his arrest. They were only a few miles from the borders of Switzerland, where they could easily have spent the rest of the war in internment, but they never gave it a thought. From the moment that he was driven out of the gates of the Regina Coeli, Furman had never wavered in his determination

to return to Rome, and Johnstone had caught his infectious enthusiasm—although Rome was more than 200 miles away.

The next fortnight was a marathon of country lanes and mountain passes, of wide detours to avoid towns, guarded bridges and
road-blocks, of dragging climbs and exhilarating descents, at the
end of one of which Johnstone complained that his bicycle did not
seem to have responded quite as it should have done round the
innumerable hairpin bends. Furman inspected it, and found that
the front forks had parted company completely from the rest of
the ancient machine. They had help from many Italians, but none
more valuable than the information they gleaned from a farmer
they met near the outskirts of Rome, for it was he who told
them, first, that bicycles were not permitted to enter the city, and,
secondly, that trams from the near-by village of Monte Mario
were never checked at the road-blocks. The two officers gave their
bicycles to the village priest of Monte Mario, for the benefit of
his poorest parishioners, boarded the tram, and, with a combination of amusement and amazement, watched over the top of their
newspapers as the road-block guards checked every form of traffic
going into Rome except the tram in which they sat.

Within twenty minutes they were in the heart of the city, and
Furman led Johnstone to St Peter's Square, but he realized that
great caution was required : he had no way of knowing how far
the disaster of January 8 had spread, how many billets had fallen,
and how many more had been compromised, or even if the organization still existed at all. To go to any of the addresses he
knew might be to walk straight back into captivity, and to approach the Collegio Teutonicum without knowing if the monsignor and I had been arrested was unthinkable. With the calm
discretion that is so often the corollary of exceptional initiative,
Furman deposited Johnstone, a conspicuous giant who looked
more like a German deserter than a British escaper, in a quiet
corner of the square, where he was unlikely to come in contact
with the German sentries, who rarely moved from their appointed
stations, and went off on his own.

With the confidence that comes from familiar surroundings,
Furman made his way to a small shop facing the square, where
the proprietor had, he knew, rendered small services to us in the
past without becoming deeply involved in the organization. The
Italian agreed to get a message to Monsignor O'Flaherty that

a friend was waiting for him in the square, and it seemed only minutes later that the tall priest was striding towards him, hand outstretched, face beaming, and rich brogue bellowing, "In the name of God, John, it's good to see you back."

Furman took him to where the bewildered Johnstone was waiting, and the monsignor led them to the house of Fathers Claffey and Treacy, where he left them while he rushed off to inform me of the good news.

That afternoon the monsignor returned to them with one of his own suits for the down-at-heel Johnstone, the monsignor's great height having once again proved an advantage. He led the two officers back to the square, where Lieutenant Simpson and Renzo Lucidi were waiting for them, and, after a joyous reunion in sight of the Germans, they made their way to the flat of a loyal Italian helper, Pestalozzi, where there was another reunion—with Adrienne Lucidi. In the evening they all had a party, but Furman was anxious to get back into action, so Renzo Lucidi and Bill Simpson spent most of the next day putting him in the picture.

Furman was appalled at the effect on the organization, and was hard to convince that there was no prospect of our meeting. Since I was already accustomed to conducting most of my conversations with the aid of an elderly typewriter, I lost no time in writing to him.

I cannot possibly say how pleased I was to hear of your triumphant re-entry into Rome [I wrote]. When I got the news I just didn't believe it until "Golf" confirmed that he'd actually seen you; it was just too good to be true. Recently I had been imagining seeing your wife and daughter, wondering if they would hear from you before my arrival, and thinking of handing over the presents which I was holding for you. Now I hope we shall all go home together—what a time we shall have! I might add that, in my humble opinion, the initiative and determination you have shown in your three escapes is absolutely terrific.

Incidentally, John, the work done by Bill, Joe, and you during the last few months is beyond all praise.

Furman did not reply for four days.

I had been hoping [he wrote apologetically], a letter would not be necessary, optimistically thinking I might be able to see you within a day or two. I'm looking forward to a yarn with you, and the sooner the better—in fact, I have been looking forward to it ever since the "break." All the way down here, when I wasn't thinking of my sore bottom, I pictured your face when you heard I was back. The warmth of my reception on my return was such as almost to compensate for the trials and tribulations of the preceding month. But we should all be better off without these excitements.

By the time he got around to writing, Furman was already thoroughly back on the job, somewhat to my concern, for my idea had been that he should remain under cover for a time. Activity by the authorities was intense at the time, for the Germans were making continuous round-ups, to secure forced labour for the defence positions being constructed around Rome, and the Italian Fascists were making no less frequent raids aimed at the black market, which had already made nonsense of the Roman rationing system. The black market had the enthusiastic support of our organization, for we had a vested interest in any illicit trade that enabled us to obtain food and other supplies without the formality of ration documents. One weird effect of our black-market transactions, incidentally, was that tobacco supplies reached the very people for whom they were originally intended, via complex roundabout routes. The cigarettes were packeted in America for issue to Allied troops, but had been captured by the Germans, and issued to their soldiers. They, in turn, sold them to Italian black-marketeers, from whom they were bought by our agents, and eventually distributed among the escapers.

Furman drifted back into work by attaching himself to Simpson as an unofficial assistant, helping to escort escapers to new billets, delivering supplies, and checking on reports of enemy activity; I soon became resigned to the fact that he was fully operational again, whether I thought it safe or not, and I could not order him to stay underground while the load on Simpson was so heavy. I contented myself with warning him to be careful, and not to try to work at the speed which had been possible in the days when he last knew Rome.

One day Monsignor O'Flaherty said that if John did not see me soon I would find him breaking into the place.

"I'll see him to-morrow," I laughed. "At long range. Tell him to be in your room at three o'clock. I'll give him a wave from the window."

At the appointed time I looked out from the high legation flat, across a jumble of buildings and squares, to the distant Collegio Teutonicum, and at a third-floor window I could just make out a figure. I waved cheerfully, wondering if Furman could see more of me than I saw of him. In fact, he could—he was using binoculars. As I left the window, I wondered if the gesture had been worthwhile, for it had made me feel my isolation more keenly than ever.

Out in the city Simpson and Furman divided the duties equally, but agreed it was not wise for them to continue to share the same billet. Furman organized a home for himself with a middle-aged clerk, Romeo Giuliana, whose eighteen-year-old son became one of his principal helpers, with, ultimately, calamitous consequences.

It was through Furman that Mrs Chevalier's ever-ready apartment came back into use. One day he learned that an Italian, who had guided four escapers into Rome, had been arrested, and had started to talk. The man knew nothing about the organization, but he did know where the four escapers were billeted. Sure enough, the house was raided, but Furman, forewarned, had already moved the escapers. He had put them in "Mrs M.'s." I was not very happy about this, because it was only an unexpected tip-off from somebody outside the organization that had averted disaster there before, but, in fact, Furman had set the pattern for the use of Mrs Chevalier's flat in the immediate future. It was to be the temporary home of escapers whose billets had become unsafe.

It was also, by chance, to be pressed into service as a make-shift nursing-home. We had to arrange a good deal of medical attention for the escapers in the country areas during the hard winter, but the report that came in from a group at Subiaco, some miles from Rome, was more disturbing than usual. A Cameron Highlander, Private N. I. Anderson, had acute appendicitis, and needed an immediate operation. The supply of medicines and even qualified medical attention was no great problem, but we did not have a fully equipped operating theatre.

I therefore decided that Anderson would have to be brought to Rome, and deposited at the door of a suitable hospital, where he would lose his freedom but gain medical attention. "White-bows" (Brother Robert Pace), who had for some time acted as the link for this group, went to see him, but returned a few hours later with a surprising reply.

"He won't go," said Brother Robert. "All he says is, 'I've come this far, and if nothing can be done for me I'd rather die than give myself up to the Jerries.' "

I admired his spirit, but had no intention of letting him die. I did not know the answer, but was sure Monsignor O'Flaherty would.

He did. He got in touch with an old friend of his, Professor Albano, surgeon at the Regina Elona Lazzaretto, a big hospital, to which at this time the Germans were sending many of their seriously wounded troops from the Anzio battlefield, and the professor agreed to carry out an emergency operation that night on "the monsignor's friend" without giving any information to the authorities. However, an official check of the hospital was imminent, so the patient would have to be removed immediately after the operation. It was impossible for him to be taken to a ward, even for long enough to recover from the anæsthetic.

A second difficulty was that of getting Anderson to and from hospital. Ambulances were out of the question, taxis were non-existent in Rome, the distance was too great for a horse-drawn *carrozza*, and the few private cars were mostly in the hands of the Fascists, since elaborate permits were required for their use. That left only the small group of cars belonging to the few members of the Corps Diplomatique, who were still able to move freely, and one of these was in the possession of the Irish Ambassador, Dr Kiernan. The monsignor was on good terms with the strictly neutral Irishman, but he knew that there was nothing to be gained by a request that he should allow his car to be used for clandestine purposes. On the other hand, there was nothing to be lost by an appeal to Mrs Kiernan. . . .

When the Irish "C.D." car swept out of the city that evening it carried an Irishman who was no diplomat—the massively built Father John Buckley, known in our organization as "Spike." Father Buckley had qualified for the job because he was the biggest and most powerful of the monsignor's helpers, for that night he was to do the work of two stretcher-bearers. At Subiaco he carried the almost insensible Anderson bodily into the car, and at the hospital he carried him into the reception hall, and placed him gently on a trolley in the care of two nurses, who were in the professor's confidence.

The professor, who had already that evening carried out four operations on German soldiers, turned his attention at once to Anderson, and within an hour the Scot, sewn up and still unconscious, was wheeled out of the operating theatre, and gathered again into the vast arms of Father Buckley.

Monsignor O'Flaherty, working on the basis that Anderson's biggest need would be for a selfless motherly care, which could not be provided in many of our billets and was certainly not available at Subiaco, told Father Buckley to take the patient to Mrs Chevalier's flat, where they arrived to find Lieutenant Furman waiting in a state of some concern.

He had learned that the place might be under observation, so it was essential that anybody billeted there should be able to get away in a hurry if necessary. "This chap doesn't look as if he can move very fast," said Furman.

"That he can't," said Father Buckley. "But the point is that if the poor boy isn't put to bed soon he'll be a corpse."

It was Mrs Chevalier herself who settled the issue, commanding Father Buckley to take Anderson up without further delay. "It will be all right," she assured Furman, and by the time the massive priest had toiled up three flights of stairs with the grey-faced Scot in his arms, she had a bed all ready.

I received the reports on this enterprise with a mixture of relief and anxiety. I was relieved that the operation had been completed, because Anderson had been suffering from severe appendicitis and peritonitis, and might well have failed to survive another day, but I was concerned by the news that the surgeon still considered the patient's condition to be "very grave," and I was seriously worried about the possibility of another raid. "Mrs M." was already looking after five escapers who had been forced to move from other billets, and we had gone to great lengths to ensure that they all had an efficient evacuation drill worked out in detail and thoroughly rehearsed, but it was obvious that it would be a long time before Anderson could, in emergency, do anything to save himself or, even more important, the woman looking after him.

The raid we had all feared came just seven days after Anderson's operation, and he was still immobile, and by no means out of danger. Once again, however, Mrs Chevalier was forewarned, by a young Italian who worked in a minor capacity at the German headquarters. Possibly without knowing that she had anything to hide, but purely as a neighbourly act, he called on her shortly after five o'clock, and told her, "Your flat is to be raided at seven."

Mrs Chevalier informed the five fit escapers, who left unobtrusively at five-minute intervals, and sent one of her large family rushing off with a message to Monsignor O'Flaherty. When he received it there was only an hour to spare, but in that time he saw Mrs Kiernan, again 'requisitioned' her husband's car, rounded up Father Buckley, and dispatched him post-haste to Via Impera. Father Buckley gathered up Anderson, now conscious but in considerable pain, ran with him in his arms down the steep stairs to the car, and swept away, watched by a tearful Mrs Chevalier, who was sure Anderson could not survive such a journey.

By the time the security men arrived, punctually at seven o'clock, the apartment bore an outward innocence, but Mrs Chevalier was lucky, nevertheless, for once again it was the size of her own family that saved her. Faced by so many people in such a small flat, the police made only a cursory examination for signs of more.

I breathed again, expressed my congratulations and thanks to those responsible, and once again issued orders. "No more lodgers for 'Mrs M.'"

So far as Private Anderson was concerned, I would not have believed that any man's constitution could withstand being carted about like a sack of potatoes immediately after a major operation, and now I was pessimistic about his chances of surviving a second move in a week. He was sent "up the hill" to our safest billet, in the grounds of the Collegio Americano, which now held the largest of our groups in Rome, under the command of Lieutenant Colin Lesslie, of the Irish Guards. Lieutenant Lesslie spent half his time working out new schemes for rejoining the Allies, and just before Anderson's arrival he had returned 20,000 lire, which I had advanced to him for a plan involving sailing a boat to Sardinia, which he reluctantly abandoned after running into a host of insurmountable difficulties. Anderson presented Lesslie with a new problem, and he did everything possible to ensure that the sick man had comfort, quiet, security, and good food. After hovering between life and death for a fortnight, the dour Scot, whose own will to live had never weakened, began to gain rapidly in strength, and by the end of the month was well on the way to recovery. His eventual restoration to health was, in fact, complete, and I suppose it could be said that rarely has a man owed his life to such strangely assorted factors as a scholarly monsignor, with the incisive brain of a business tycoon; a giant priest, with the strength of a lion and the gentleness of a lamb; an Irish lady, whose humanity overwhelmed political propriety; a little Maltese widow, with a gallant heart as big as her own expansive family; and an Italian surgeon, who, with his enemies all around him, risked his life to save a life.

As February ran out the pace continued to increase. In four weeks we added 338 names to those on the roll of escapers and evaders in our care, bringing the total to 2591, in spite of recaptures, escapes into Switzerland, and, in a very few cases, successful returns to Allied-held territory.

The flow into Rome itself remained the biggest problem, and it was intensified by the arrival of men from the front at Anzio, who had been cut off from our forces without ever falling into enemy hands. We were also receiving an increasing number of American bomber crews, who came in groups of six or seven at a time, all largely unaware of the German grip on Rome, and generally expecting to find that the best hotel in the city had been taken over for their reception. From beginning to end of February the number of escapers actually in Rome rose from eighty-four to 116, and on several days it was very much higher, for new arrivals often outnumbered the day's dispatches to country groups.

The basic policy of the organization remained, as ever, to reduce the numbers of escapers in Rome, because keeping them in the city had two disadvantages: first, their maintenance cost much more than in the country, and secondly, there was the never ending difficulty of finding Italians prepared to take the risk of housing them for a return that barely covered costs, and this at a time when police activity was constantly increasing, and prices in the shops were rising steadily.

When the Allies landed at Anzio a good many Italians, thinking the end was near, decided to get back on the right side of the fence, and endeavoured to contact organizations such as ours with offers of assistance, but as the weeks dragged on, and the bridgehead forces came no nearer to Rome, that shallow source of supply dried up. Indeed, even some of the families who had helped us in the past began to get a little discouraged.

In a report to Sir D'Arcy Osborne ("Mount") I wrote:

> While we do all we can to discourage ex-prisoners from coming to Rome, still the number keeps increasing. It becomes more and more difficult to find billets for them—but I am afraid the number will still increase as time goes on.

From experience, I knew what the rising numbers must mean to Lieutenants Furman and Simpson, on whom the burden of billeting rested to a large extent.

> It's a hell of a job finding billets now [Furman wrote], and, of course, when you do find them they insist on having officers.

Furman's view was that if the Italians insisted on having commissioned guests, then officers they must have—even if it meant that the Rome Organization had to do some unorthodox promoting on its own. When one Italian agreed to take in two escapers provided they were officers Furman moved in two smart young men—both privates—and promptly gave them the very temporary (and unpaid) rank of lieutenant.

On another occasion Furman received a message from the Greeks, who now called their movement "Liberty or Death," that they had in their hands a British major who had been parachuted behind the lines as a saboteur, and now appeared to have about half the Gestapo on his heels. Furman had just made arrangements with a well-to-do business woman, Luciana Zoboldi, to take in an officer, so he called on her, and told her to be ready to receive the major. Then he went off to meet Mario, the Greek agent, and found him accompanied, not by one man, but by two, for the saboteur had teamed up with another escaper. Furman thought he would be able to overcome that difficulty with Luciana, but the next snag almost stopped him in his tracks. The saboteur, addressed by Furman as "sir," looked uncomfortable, and explained that he was not a major but a sergeant-major. The Greeks had got hold of the wrong idea, and he, not knowing that he was to be transferred into British hands, had decided not to disillusion them. His companion was a private. Furman came to the conclusion that the fewest complications would arise if the deception was maintained; he had promised Luciana a major, and a "major" she got, together with another "officer."

Furman might not have gone to such pains with this couple if he had known about them what I was able to tell him after he had reported their arrival. They had, in fact, already been through the organization once, while Simpson was working on his own, and had disappeared from Rome, owing their 'padrone' about six weeks' rent. As soon as I learned of their return, I put Furman in the picture, but in the meantime the pair, having stopped long enough to collect money separately from three sources in the organization within an hour, had departed from Rome again, ostensibly to head southward, in an attempt to re-join Allied forces.

We 'promoted' escapers only rarely, but we came across scores who, since their escapes, had 'commissioned' themselves, and many of them clung tenaciously to their assumed officer-status, even when we had been able to confront them with particulars of their true identity, as we frequently could, thanks to the extensive card-index system built up by Captain Byrnes. Indeed, there were few men who had been in prison camps in Italy about whom we did not have an outline history. Most of the self-commissioned 'officers' seemed to be South Africans, and I wrote to Furman and Simpson :

> During the past week I have received letters and applications for assistance from no less than ten officers, who, when checked up, proved to be sappers, privates, or lance-corporals (unpaid). All are S.A. I wonder why they do it? I suppose you know that Lieutenant Koster Kelly is really Private Kelly. . . .

The truth was that the organization was now so vast that the people passing through were bound to include a few doubtful characters, particularly since any one who knew the ropes could turn our services to personal financial advantage. I issued money to several sources, to be handed out against the name and number of escapers, in order to ensure that new arrivals in Rome should have prompt assistance, and some of the cuter ones quickly discovered that they could achieve a useful working capital by making the rounds. This was reprehensible, to say the least, yet there were occasions when I felt inclined to take a lenient view of such duplication of assistance, which of course always came to light when I checked the numbers of those given money.

There was, for instance, the case of the private who was taken in the Via Chelini raid, but left in the Regina Coeli when the others were transferred. He was later moved to a prison camp, from which he immediately made good his escape, arriving back in Rome on the same day as Furman. Knowing the ropes, he collected, in a couple of days, 2000 lire and a suit of clothes from our contacts at the Swiss Legation, 3000 lire from me, via John May, and 1440 lire from Lieutenant Simpson. It was a pretty cool round-up, but I was so delighted with the man's success in having escaped again that I decided against taking any action—beyond making sure that everybody concerned was warned not to make any further payment to this particular customer.

The main purpose of our meticulous records was not, in any case, to protect us against the wiles of over-enterprising escapers so much as to preserve the security of the organization, for they indicated those whose behaviour while in prison camp had been suspect, as well as those who had never been in prison camps at all. I knew that some of the forty Arabs on the books were of dubious loyalty, since many of their race had come to Italy voluntarily, to continue their profitable services to Italian or German officers. I also had reason to be cautious with the Indians coming into contact with the organization, for I knew that several of them had been, as mentioned previously, sufficiently swayed by "anti-Imperialist" propaganda to give active assistance to the Fascists. Men about whom we could not be absolutely certain— although they must, in many cases, have been fully trustworthy— were never billeted with Italian families, but sent to caves and other similar hides in the country. They were never visited by members of the organization, but had to call at pre-arranged points to collect a monthly subsistence allowance. Nonetheless, they occasionally approached the 'staff' for help, and Lieutenant Simpson's accounts once included 150 lire to enable an Indian, Atma S., to buy a hat. Taken prisoner while wearing a turban and beard, he had cut off his beard when he escaped, Simpson explained, and naturally he needed a hat.

I knew something about Atma, because he was one of those receiving a monthly allowance, and shortly afterwards I was able to give Simpson the more definite information that he was a rogue, and at one time had a job as batman to a well-known Fascist.

When Simpson reported later that he had received a request

to keep a rendezvous with Atma and some other Indians, whom he claimed to be guiding into Rome, I flashed back a warning at once. Simpson did not keep the appointment, and, though Atma remained on the monthly pay roll, there was no sudden influx of new Indian names to give credence to his story.

One new arrival had to be side-tracked from the normal channels for an entirely different reason—he bore a famous name. Towards the end of February I received a report that Paul Freyberg, a lieutenant in the Grenadier Guards, was in hiding in the Pope's summer villa at Castel Gandolfo, normally the only place ever visited outside Rome by a Pope during his reign, but at present a lonely outpost, virtually in the middle of the German line ringing the Allied bridgehead at Anzio.

Freyberg had been cut off while on patrol, and captured, and though he escaped with commendable promptitude, he was unable to find any way through the German forces massed round the brideghead. So he gave himself up at the palatial villa, which was clearly labelled as Vatican extra-territorial property. The priests there took him in, but with discomfiture, for he was the son of Major-General Bernard (later Field-Marshal Lord) Freyberg, V.C., C.B., C.M.G., D.S.O., commander of the New Zealand Corps.

Freyberg's name made him an embarrassment for the Rome Organization too, quite apart from the fact that it was impossible to make any direct approach to him because the Germans had established field workshops all round the villa, and how he got through without detection I could not imagine.

Monsignor O'Flaherty discussed the situation with me, and we agreed that this was the one case where, if possible, we ought to organize an official internment in the Vatican, for, on the one hand, Freyberg would be a tremendous prestige-prize to the Germans if they succeeded in recapturing him, while, on the other, his confinement in the Vatican should not be too protracted, since the Allied advance would soon liberate Rome.

"But how do we move him along the main road from the battlefront?" I mused. "Then there's the problem of getting him through those German workshops."

"Leave it to me," said the monsignor, after a moment's thought. "I'll see if anything can be arranged, me boy."

I cannot remember how often the incredible cleric had said

exactly this to me in varied circumstances, but I did know, from repeated experience, that when he said it the impossible task was as good as accomplished. The monsignor arranged with the priests at Castel Gandolfo to stow Freyberg into the boot of the official Vatican car, after its next routine call with supplies for the staff at the villa, and in due course the car, a familiar enough sight to the Germans, swept unhindered through the workshop area with a crumpled grenadier slowly suffocating in the back. The car covered the eighteen miles to Rome in half an hour, swept through the gates of the Vatican, and stopped close to the barracks, where Freyberg emerged gratefully, to become the first escaper to be officially interned since the guards had been given their orders to expel forcibly any unauthorized person attempting to enter the Vatican City.

He was also the first new arrival I had been able to welcome personally for some weeks, and one of the earliest things I learned about him was that he was on the verge of coming of age. The ubiquitous major-domo, John May, received this news with unconcealed delight. Always ready to organize a party, but rarely presented with the excuse for one, John May jerked all his black-market strings violently, and my small room became the setting for the only official party the Rome Organization ever organized. John May and I were joined by several of the British internees, who regularly called at the legation to relax in the club-room, which had once been the generous Mr Hugh Montgomery's study, and to the guest of honour it must all have seemed slightly unreal. A day or two earlier he had been in the midst of a violent battle, and now, twenty miles deeper in enemy territory, he was involved with other British officers in a riotous celebration of his twenty-first birthday, with everybody shouting joyfully in English, and singing English songs, as though there was not a single German within a couple of hundred miles.

Luckily for me, the party came just when Lieutenant Simpson had succeeded in smuggling in a small supply of spirits. I was almost overwhelmed when the first bottle unexpectedly arrived, and wrote: "Gratissimo multi for the medicine—it is just what the doctor ordered." The phrase stuck, and from then on the cash which I sent Simpson often included, with 'the firm's money,' some of my own, for what came to be known to us both as "the medicine account."

Not without some interest did I read in a publication called *The Tablet* that "the presence of the ex-prisoners, all naval and military men, had considerably enlivened diplomatic life in the city." The article continued:

> The circumstances in which they succeeded, not without diffi-culty, in making their way into the jealously guarded precincts of the neutral sovereign state of the Vatican will some day be worth reading. They are lodged in what used to be the infirmary of the Pontifical Gendarmerie Barracks. . . . The ex-prisoners are well fed at the barracks, though they find the endless *pasta* a trifle monotonous. They also suffer somewhat from the cold, as the winter has been exceptionally severe in Rome, and the barracks, like the rest of the Vatican, with the single exception of the diplo-mats' quarters, has remained unheated.

The Tablet was slightly wide of the mark, when it spoke of the forced inactivity of the cut-off diplomats, for our own legation was a hive of industry, and several of the others, like the Polish and the Jugoslav, seemed to be very active.

Even I was by no means limited to one room, although I rarely ventured farther out of doors than the *piazza*, since the gendarme on duty would have recognized at once that I was not one of the thirteen official internees. However, I saw De Vial and De Blesson of the French Embassy practically every day, called on the Jugo-slav Chargé d'Affaires, Tzukitch, three times a week, visited the American Minister, Mr Harold Tittman, periodically, and was constantly in and out of the Polish Legation, which was on the floor below our own. Between us we had a pretty thriving social life, and I attended many happy bridge parties with my French, Jugoslav, and Polish friends.

At the Polish Legation, no matter how often I called, there was always a wonderful welcome, and it was there that I met Casimira Dabrowska, who had been a well-known portrait-painter in her own country. She was distressed because she was trapped in the Vatican, with practically no contact with the outside world, and so was unable to do much to help the organization's work. One day I was showing her the tiny photograph of my wife, Nancy, which I had managed to retain, through all my changes of fortune, in the screw-on back of my wrist-watch: the only one of my original possessions that had remained with me through-out.

"So nice," said Casimira, "but, oh, so small. You must lend it to me. If I cannot do anything for your work I will do something for you : I will make a big copy of it."

The result, produced a day or two later, was a magnificent drawing which I shall always treasure, for from the tiny snap-shot, she had built up a glowing, lifelike portrait of astounding integrity, guessing, with remarkable accuracy, the shoulder line, which the photograph did not reveal, and equipping Nancy with a dress which suited her perfectly.

One way and another, my contact with representatives of Allied nations was satisfactory, but there were times when I wished that it was equally close with the British forces. By various means, I was able to send a good deal of information out of Rome, but it was a one-way traffic, and the lack of news from the opposite direction occasionally led to complications undreamed of by Allied Force Headquarters.

At one stage we were concentrating escapers in an area which was ideal—a valley nestling in a curve of hills, miles away from the city and trunk-roads, admirably suited for air supply-drops, well equipped with farms, where escapers could be billeted, yet with hills providing hiding-places in emergency. Above all, it was singularly free from German military occupation. Its principal link with the outside world was a railway viaduct running across the valley.

To the planners of Allied special operations, the viaduct was an inviting target, and one night they parachuted down a couple of 'cloak and dagger' men, who made a thoroughly effective job of blowing it up. The immediate result was that furious German troops and S.S. units swarmed into the peaceful valley, and, assuming the sabotage to be the work of subversive Italians, went through every farm and every house with a toothcomb. In search-ing for explosives and indications of Italian activity, they inevit-ably unearthed a good number of Allied ex-prisoners, who, with their hosts, were promptly arrested. Fortunately, many of the escapers had intelligently rushed to the hills immediately the viaduct disintegrated, and most of the men we had sent to the valley maintained their freedom. On the other hand, we lost one of the best concentration centres we had ever found, but it would have been asking too much to expect the 'cloak and dagger' boys to let us know what they were going to blow up next.

Nearer home I was more concerned at the lack of direct contact with my principal assistants. The letter-ferrying system was working well, all things considered, and hammering away at my typewriter, I found it fairly easy to convey instructions and advice, but it often took a long time by written question and answer to collect all the details I needed.

The quiet, methodical Lieutenant Simpson seemed to be capable of sitting down in the monsignor's crowded, always noisy, room, and writing a detailed, flowing report, undistracted by the babel of criss-cross conversation, but the more mercurial Lieutenant Furman had no love at all for the system. Plaintively he ended one brief report:

> I can't think of anything else to say, but there are probably a thousand and one things. Writing letters in "Golf's" room, in company with twenty other people, all talking, is not the lightest of tasks.

However, those who knew the circumstances accepted that it was impossible for us to meet.

I never needed the advice of my lieutenants more than at the beginning of March, when the growing number of men in our care was beginning to swamp the organization, and I was really worried as I left my room one day, to consult the British Minister about a situation that was developing into a financial crisis.

I closed my door pensively, and turned to walk down the long, straight corridor to the Minister's office. Then I stopped dead, astonished at what I saw. Standing at the end of the corridor, looking for all the world like a small lost dog, was the unmistakable figure of Lieutenant John Furman.

9

Ides of March

TORN between delight at seeing Lieutenant Furman again and the fear that his sudden appearance meant the pace had become too hot for him, and he had been forced to seek sanctuary in the Vatican, I could not get him quickly enough into the security of my own room. There, as we broached 'the medicine bottle,' he rapidly dispelled my fears.

"Just a social visit," he grinned. "I've been trying to get in to see you ever since I arrived back in Rome, you know."

"But how the devil did you manage it?" I asked.

The fairy-godmother had been the Princess Nini Pallavicini, an old ally of mine from my days at the Collegio Teutonicum. One of the leaders of the group of Roman noble families who had consistently refused to co-operate with the Fascists, she had dramatically escaped through a rear window of her palace apartment as a raiding Fascist party entered through the front door, and had made for the Collegio Teutonicum, where Monsignor O'Flaherty gave her refuge, and where she eventually became one of his most loyal helpers. She had a great deal to do with the activities which enabled us to obtain Italian identity documents.

She had mentioned in casual conversation to Furman that on one of the innumerable Italian saints' days she was going to attend service in the chapel, which formed part of the Vatican building where the British Legation was housed. He promptly asked to be included. Princess Nini agreed that there was a reasonable chance of getting him into the Vatican, as all seven or eight others in her party were already well known by sight to the Pontifical Guards, and were unlikely to be stopped for questioning.

Furman, a small inconspicuous figure, walked in the middle of the group as they entered the Vatican, and was relieved to observe that the only reaction from the guards was a glance followed by a salute. They walked unmolested through the quiet squares, and into the tall hospice building, where they all turned towards the ground-floor chapel except Furman, who bounded up the main stairs to the fourth floor. The monsignor had told him that the British offices were on the top floor, but had not pointed out that Furman would find himself in a long, deserted corridor, with unlabelled doors leading off on either side. Panting and puzzled, Furman was wondering which door would present the least risk of disaster when, by chance, I emerged from my room.

"When I got up here, and found myself all alone, it seemed a bit of an anticlimax," he said, "but your entrance was right on cue."

We were joined in my room by John May, Captain Byrnes, and the first secretary, Mr Montgomery, who suggested that before too much 'medicine' had been dispensed, it might be advisable to acquaint "Mount" of the unexpected visitor. Lieutenant Furman, who had expected at best to have a few words with me in some secluded corner, was not too happy about this, and expressed concern that his uninvited and wholly unconstitutional appearance in the legation might be an embarrassment, but I knew the Minister well enough to guess that it would take more than this to ruffle his equanimity.

When I presented Lieutenant Furman in as matter-of-fact a manner as possible Sir D'Arcy Osborne did not reveal surprise by so much as the lift of an eyebrow. He greeted Furman with calm and warm courtesy, and I was once again lost in admiration of the ability of this polished diplomat to create, in any surroundings, the gracious atmosphere of an English country-house party. Furman, so fresh from the streets where terror marched in jack-boots, felt he had drifted into another world, and answered Sir D'Arcy's questions about prevailing conditions in the city in a slightly dazed manner. He left the legation that evening with the Minister's congratulations on his work still ringing in his ears, and with a new realization that his efforts and Simpson's, so far from being a demi-official and largely unknown enterprise, were fully appreciated in high places, and had the complete support of the British Government. Furman returned to the outside world with his little group of church-goers, leaving me to ponder on that strange, indefinable quality, which made three men who were as different as Sir D'Arcy Osborne, Monsignor O'Flaherty, and Lieutenant Furman, each, in his own way, a great leader of men.

Furman declared that the visit had been like a potent tonic, and said he had every intention of repeating the experiment, and although I warned him that he must not employ the same trick a second time, his ingenuity enabled him to get in once more.

He presented himself boldly at the Porta Santa Marta guardroom with a large parcel prominently labelled *To be delivered personally to Sir D'Arcy Osborne, K.C.M.G.*, and demanded, in voluble Italian, to be allowed to accomplish his mission. The guard, not surprisingly, told him to leave his parcel at the guardroom, but Furman protested that he must hand it over himself or not at all.

After further argument, the exasperated guard telephoned the British Legation for some official to come down to the gate. John May took the message, went to the guardroom, and, giving no hint of recognition of the visitor, inspected the parcel carefully, and then told the guard that he was sure it would be all right for the bearer to deliver it personally. Uncertainly, the guard admitted Furman, and John May took him to the legation, where he led him, not to Sir D'Arcy, but to me.

I was, of course, delighted to see Furman, and we had another gay little party, at which the guests this time included the latest internee, Lieutenant Paul Freyberg. But while admiring Furman's initiative, I felt that the risk was not justified. Without any suggestion of reproach, I tried to convey to him my growing concern at the chances constantly taken by Monsignor O'Flaherty, who had already incurred the displeasure of the Germans, and was in danger every time he stepped beyond the confines of his college.

The latest of the monsignor's escapades involved our senior escaper, General Gambier-Parry, who, since his early eulogies of the advantages of his secret room, had found its disadvantages increasingly irksome. His messages to the monsignor clearly revealed growing impatience at his enforced inactivity, and the monsignor decided that the general should be taken on an outing. He chose to take him to—of all things—an official celebration of the Pope's birthday—a reception at which our enemies would outnumber our friends. Brother Robert collected the general from the secret room, and took him by tram to St Peter's Square, where they were met by the monsignor and some of his varied acquaintances. The monsignor swept them along, introducing the general on the way as an Irish doctor friend, in tones loud enough to be heard by anybody they passed. At the party the "Irish doctor" was happily introduced right and left by the monsignor to high-

ranking diplomats and other guests, and even collected a few
invitations to call at various legations. His charming personality
made a considerable impression on the distinguished gathering,
and I have no doubt that he found the party a great joy after the
social restrictions of his life in a doorless room.

But I heard about all this with mounting alarm, and it was not
for the general that I was concerned. Although he had waived his
unquestionable right to take over my command, he was still a
general, and I could scarcely order him to remain in his billet,
particularly since he was aware that many junior officers working
for the organization were moving about Rome fairly openly. The
safety of Monsignor O'Flaherty, however, was a different matter.
The organization he had founded remained heavily dependent
upon him and the priests who helped him, and we could not make
light of the fact that if he should be arrested his fate would not be
enviable.

At the first opportunity I took the monsignor to task, telling
him quite frankly that I considered he had taken an unwarrant-
able risk.

"Ah, the poor fellow needed a breath of air," he replied simply.
"He's been cooped up for weeks. Not good for him, you know."

"Now look, Monsignor," I said earnestly, "you know damn
well I can't give him orders. He's a general, and if he chooses to
go out and get himself recaptured there isn't much I can do about
it. But I have every reason for wanting you to stay in circulation,
and, heaven knows, you've attracted quite enough attention already. I do beg you to be as cautious as you possibly can, at least
until the German interest in you has died down a bit."

"Never fear, me boy," said the monsignor, treating me to one
of his vast, room-filling grins. "Ah, a pity it is I haven't brought
me clubs. We could have done a bit of putting practice. Nothing
like golf for knocking all the troubles of this poor world out of
your mind."

That was as far as we got. I sometimes suspected that Monsignor O'Flaherty's overriding interest in golf was a sort of secret
weapon which enabled him to change the subject at will. Nevertheless, he did agree, eventually, that it was desirable to find
something less alarming than visits to Vatican receptions as exercise for General Gambier-Parry, and by mid-March the general
was moved to a new billet, where he had some freedom, although

less luxury or security. He became a 'patient' at the hospital run
by the Little Sisters of Mary, known as the "Blue Sisters," at San
Stefano Rotondo, where he was able to exercise in the grounds
without endangering himself or the organization, and there, in
fact, he remained safely until Rome was liberated.

The visits of General Gambier-Parry and Lieutenant Furman
to the Vatican were only two incidents in a period of audacious
enterprise, in which the gallant Greeks, as ever, were prominent.
I was intrigued when Angelo Averoff and Theodore Meletiou
("Mario"), leaders of the newly constituted Liberty or Death
movement, reported to me that they had managed not only to
hire a car, which was unheard of at that time, but also to obtain
all the complicated permits and coupons necessary to run it. These
they had borrowed from a leading Fascist, who, like many of his
kind, had an eye on the prospect of an early occupation of Rome by
the Allies, and was anxious to put himself back on the right side
of the fence, provided it did not involve him in any personal risk.

Equipped with car and documents, Averoff and Meletiou decided to make an extended tour of northern Italy, to contact as
many Greek escapers as possible, and, as usual, they offered their
services to me. The offer was most timely, because I was ex-
periencing considerable difficulty in delivering supplies in the
north. In one district I was wholly reliant on a woman with a
donkey for distributions to more than eighty allied escapers.

When the car set off the Greeks carried with them 100,000
lire of Rome Organization money, and a large stock of clothing,
including dozens of pairs of boots, crammed in the back. I secretly
doubted if they could be successful, even with their library of
documents, in getting such a bulky cargo through the innumerable road-blocks, and I should have been even less hopeful had
I known that their personal equipment included the most dangerous of all 'verboten' possessions : a miniature camera.

The gallant Greeks were confident—and, in the event, un-
believably successful. When they returned three weeks later they
had motored for more than two thousand miles, reaching as far
north as Milan, and had contacted dozens of groups of escapers,
distributing clothing and money, and collecting information. They
brought back with them up-to-date lists of escapers, with names
and addresses of their next of kin, reports on the disposition of
German forces all over northern Italy, and—to crown everything

—an interesting series of photographs of German preparations for a final defence line, only a few miles on the Italian side of the French border.

I did not risk sending the photographs back to our lines, for they revealed nothing of immediate value, but had them packed in a tin, and buried in the Vatican gardens, pending the arrival of Allied intelligence units. The new lists of escapers, and particularly of next of kin, were of more immediate interest, as I always considered that one of the important tasks of the organization was the prompt dispatch of news of escapers who, so far as their families were concerned, were simply missing, and we had developed a number of secret ways of achieving the flow of this welcome information out of Rome.

Much of the other information collected by the Greeks was filtered back to Allied headquarters, but what I should have most liked to send at that juncture was a heartfelt plea to get on with the advance, for the delay was making it increasingly difficult for us to maintain an adequate supply of billets.

There was also another factor, over which we had no control, which was making the finding of billets daily more difficult for Furman and Simpson. Inflation was galloping through Rome. The rationing system had broken down almost completely, and prices were soaring. The German Military Government had withdrawn their earlier ban on the importation of food into the city, and, in fact, were now trying to foster it, but this had resulted in only a small increase in supplies alongside a substantial expansion of the black market in food-stuffs at sky-high prices.

> To find billets is becoming more and more difficult, principally because the food question is becoming more and more serious [wrote Simpson]. The position now is very different from even two months ago : in that time there has been an average increase in the price of all commodities of from 80 to 100 per cent.

Close on the heels of this depressing report came another.

> Here are particulars of three others, whom we are due to collect on Wednesday—God knows where we are going to put them.

The billeting officers were pressing for more money, but what they could not know was that the total cost of the organization was now running at about two million lire a month, or more than a thousand pounds a week, and there was no margin at all. Sir D'Arcy Osborne had already worked miracles in securing fabulous quantities of lire notes, but I was plagued by the fear that the supply might suddenly dry up.

About this time I found myself in a dilemma from another quarter. On the one hand, Furman and Simpson were pleading for an increase in the billeting allowance of 120 lire a day, and on the other, the British Minister was passing on complaints from other legations that our billeting allowance was too high. I discussed the Rome problem from all angles with the Minister, but the 'official view' I had to relay back was not encouraging for Furman and Simpson:

> 120 lire a day is higher than the subsistence paid by other Allied nations (Poles, French, Russians, Jugoslavs, etc.), and, in fact, we have been criticized by the others for paying out at the 120-lire rate—they say it has cut them out of the billet market. Of the money paid out, the odd 120 people in Rome cost much more per head per day than the remaining 2500 : in fact, 120 in Rome cost us about half a million in February while the remaining 2500 cost us about one-and-a-quarter million (and, by the way, officially, cigarettes are not regarded as necessary for living). I fear, John and Bill, that all this will be answered by one rude word, but I just can't help it.

By anticipating that my hard-pressed lieutenants would respond with a terse epithet, I misjudged them, for Simpson's reply was thoughtful, tolerant, and sympathetic.

> We think they are all very reasonable points [he wrote]. I certainly sympathize with you in your position—you get all the knocks from both sides.

Simpson had, however, no intention of accepting defeat without stating his case, and he continued :

> Rome is, as you already know, an entirely different proposition from the country; we all know that, having experienced both, and having lived quite well in the country without any money at all. The Romani, on the other hand, are money-conscious. . . .

All this argument did result in one small victory, and we were able to arrange payment on a flat rate of 4000 lire a month, representing an extra ten to fourteen lire a day.

It was perhaps unfortunate for the billeting officers that just at this time the British Minister was receiving reports that some of our officers had been seen dining in luxurious hotels. Many had managed to make their own arrangements with well-to-do Italians for cashing cheques or providing lire against an IOU payable after the arrival of the Allied forces, and so long as they used this money for the purchase of extra comforts, or even to finance parties in the safety of their billets, I was not concerned, but some were indiscreet.

Although they did not go out of the way to draw attention to themselves, the whisper began to pass round, "Rome is starving, yet escaped British officers are dining in the best hotels." On both points it was an exaggeration, but in its more dangerous form the whisper became, "Why should I risk my life to help ex-prisoners when British officers can be seen in the best restaurants?" Italians spoke to their parish priests; the priests passed it on to the bishops; the bishops reported it to the Vatican; and from the Vatican Secretariat of State the British Minister would receive an austere inquiry whether he was aware that British officers had been seen dining in the same restaurant as Germans.

I asked Simpson and Furman to ensure that escapers with money of their own spent it discreetly, making it clear that I was excepting them from the general complaint. They were now working and living separately, and kept in touch with each other by meeting for a meal or a drink, which was more pleasant and less dangerous than calling at each other's billets. I had no doubt of their ability to deal with trouble. Unlike the men in their charge, they were accustomed to moving openly about Rome; they spoke the language, and knew how to behave as Italians; they had friendly contacts in the places they visited who could be trusted to warn them of impending danger, and, above all, they were both capable of carrying off difficult situations with astonishing sang-froid.

On one occasion Simpson was waiting for Furman in an otherwise empty bar when a group of German officers strode in, accompanied by a flat-nosed giant, who was immediately recognizable as the idol of Germany—the heavyweight boxing champion, Max Schmeling. Simpson knew that if he attempted to walk out the Germans would interpret his action as a protest by an unfriendly Italian, and would immediately haul him back, but if he remained where he was, silent and alone, they would probably become suspicious anyway. He therefore did the only other thing he could think of : he invited them all to join him in a drink. The Germans accepted, and in due course returned the compliment, and before long they were all gathered round the piano, singing popular songs together. Simpson became quite the life and soul of the party, but when the Germans invited him to join them for dinner he decided that it had gone far enough, so, with diffidence and charm, excused himself, and departed.

It was not only the spending of officers that gave me cause for concern. As the days dragged on, and the relief of Rome, which had seemed near in January, remained as far off as ever, the men in the billets became frustrated and bored, and some got drunk with money borrowed against IOU's, or, in a few bad cases, with money which should have been given to their Italian 'padrones.' They seemed to be incapable of realizing that they lacked the native capacity for *vino*, and I began to receive disturbing reports of men wandering drunkenly back from wine-shops to their billets—disturbing, because there was no surer way of attracting attention to the homes of our Italian helpers. The thoughtless few were never more than a tiny proportion of the men in Rome, but they were a dangerous minority, since the arrest of a single drunken escaper could easily lead to the execution of an Italian and the imprisonment of his family.

I clamped down firmly on this crack in discipline, and every case reported was investigated at once. Sometimes the circumstances revealed were not very serious, but even in these cases I issued stern warnings. To one private I wrote :

I have heard of the affair of a few nights ago, when you were in an intoxicated condition. I really wonder if you can realize what is being done for you by various people (for example, the people in whose house you live, and the padre friends). Do you understand that as the result of an affair like that of the other evening, these people might have lost their lives? And if anything like that happened you, and you alone, would have been responsible; a thing that would be on your conscience all your life. Any future conduct contrary to good order and discipline will have serious consequences afterwards. In the circumstances under which you are living at the moment an affair of this kind is made all the more serious because the safety of your comrades is endangered as well as your own.

To an Indian soldier I wrote :

It has come to my notice that you are taking unnecessary risks, which not only may lead to your recapture, but may also lead to the recapture of your comrades. Apart from this there is the danger of reprisals on the local people and their friends, who are assisting you and your comrades. In view of this you are to remain in hiding, and go out only when absolutely necessary. I realize that you have probably been confined now for a very long period, but I am sure you would not wish to endanger others.

These were relatively mild cases, but in really serious instances, as well as preparing (and burying) reports for disciplinary action in the future, I did not hesitate to expel offenders from Rome. To one trooper I wrote :

I have received a full report on your atrocious behaviour during the last week. I have made out a full report which will be sent to the proper authorities. You are to get out of Rome at once. Immediately after the liberation of Rome by the Allies, you will have to answer charges.

It was a difficult time all round, and one billet in particular seemed to be occupying a good deal of Lieutenant Furman's attention. It was a flat run by a woman named Teresa, who was, I think, the only one of our 'padrones' who ever attempted to make her living by looking after escaped prisoners-of-war.

I had first come into contact with her when I was doing the outside work now done by others. She was an acquaintance of Mrs Chevalier, and agreed to take a couple of officers in her furnished rooms. When the firm for which she worked was evacuated to another part of Italy she gave up her job and her rooms, but approached John Furman with an offer to take the lease of a flat, providing the organization would give an undertaking to billet a couple of escapers with her. Furman agreed with the idea, but was captured in the January raids before he had made any firm agreement with her about payment, which was a pity, because during my time she had put in such enormous expense accounts that I had to move her lodgers elsewhere.

When Furman returned to duty he was promptly presented by Teresa with large expense accounts, and, referring them to me, he pointed out that the position was very tricky because it was clear that Teresa had spent her own money on building up stock.

Furman had a long session with Teresa, but even his nimble accountant's brain could not break down her claims, and he reported back sadly, "We argued about it, but there is little that can be done."

"Well, try to keep her down to the minimum," I replied. "Billets are far too hard to find now—but tell her to keep the bills down, anyway."

Realization of the existence of people like Teresa, willing to make a full-time job of looking after escapers, led us to establish, for the first time since the fall of the Via Firenze and Via Chelini flats, an 'elastic billet,' capable of holding large numbers temporarily in emergency. It occurred to Furman that if we could obtain a large apartment cheaply, and install our own 'padrone' in it, many of our present troubles would be overcome. I approved, and, through Princess Nini's lawyer, Furman obtained a suitable flat at a nominal rent. The lease was signed in the name of a woman known as Sara, who was installed there to take charge of it. She was, it need hardly be added, a friend of Teresa.

The two original clearing-houses were now, of course, distinctly out of bounds, and we kept well away from them until there came what seemed to be a message from the dead. The telephone rang at the home of our friends, Renzo and Adrienne Lucidi, and Renzo, answering cautiously, as always, said simply, "Hello?" "Renzo," said a once familiar voice at the other end. "This is Joe Pollak."

"Where are you?" asked Renzo excitedly.

"In Rome," replied Pollak. "At the Via Chelini flat."

"Good God!" said Renzo. He had reason to be horrified because he knew that the flat was now in the occupation of Dr Ubaldo Cipolla, who had helped Monsignor O'Flaherty to obtain it in the first place, and had allowed it to be registered in his name, but subsequently, we discovered, had worked as a secret agent for the Germans.

Renzo Lucidi had another reason to be astonished. For a long time after Pollak's arrest we had been unable to get any news of him at all, and when at last we did it was to the effect that he had been shot as a spy.

In the eight weeks since we last saw him the little Cypriot, whom I had once suspected of treachery, had gone through some incredible adventures, and they had taken their toll savagely upon him. When he was returned to Sulmona with the Italian girl, Iride, after his arrest on January 6, Pollak was shocked to find that all the principal Italian helpers of escapers in Sulmona were in custody, for the Australian medical orderly, who had posed as an R.A.M.C. captain, had made a thorough job of his denunciations. This man, picked up drunk and subsequently plied with more drink, cigarettes, and other creature comforts, had led his German captors systematically from billet to billet. Every 'cell' known to the Australian fell, and many of our escapers, as well as more than a dozen Italian families, were arrested, with his wine-fuddled co-operation.

Pollak, heavily implicated in a statement by Iride as the man who had distributed money to the billets, claimed he had been carrying out instructions by a British officer whose name he did not know, but he ran up against an unexpected difficulty in that he was unable to establish his own identity as a prisoner-of-war. The Germans, realizing that he was not English, accused him of being a Jew (which, to the Nazis, was a capital offence), and beat him up several times, leaving him without blankets or heating in a cold cell, where, not surprisingly, he contracted pneumonia.

Then Pollak was charged with being a traitor and a spy, and the firing-squad seemed inevitable, but on the way to the court he passed a group of British prisoners-of-war, who were being marched to the gaol. Among them he recognized an officer he had known at Chieti camp, and, in the nick of time, succeeded in establishing his prisoner-of-war identity. He was merely sentenced to be returned to a prison camp.

At the same court three of our Italian helpers from Sulmona were sentenced to death, several others were deported to Germany, where their expectation of life would be little more favourable, and all the rest were sent to prison. Fortunately, the three men who had received the ultimate sentence all managed to escape before the Germans could carry it out.

Joe Pollak was among several who escaped when, at the very moment they were being loaded on to a train bound for Germany, the R.A.F. chose to bomb the station, and with a companion he turned his footsteps at once to Rome.

Using his excellent Italian, Pollak organized a lift in the back of a lorry, and all went well until they reached the road-block outside Rome. Pollak slipped over the side as the lorry halted, and crawled underneath, but his companion was promptly discovered by the guards, who did not take long to come to the conclusion that he was British. Two armed soldiers were put aboard as escorts, and the hapless driver was told to set off for the nearest German barracks. Pollak was clinging to the underside of the lorry, and could not let go without immediately attracting the attention of the road-block guards, so he hung on painfully until it slowed almost to a halt at the sharp turn into the barracks, and then gratefully released his frozen grip. Picking himself up, he walked on into Rome.

Believing that the calamity in which he was involved on January 6 had been confined to Sulmona, and knowing nothing of the Rome disaster of January 8, he was completely unaware of the changes that had occurred. It was therefore natural for him to make his way to the Via Chelini flat, and give the familiar secret ring on the doorbell, expecting to be welcomed by Bruno Büchner, or Herta. He was alarmed when he found that the apartment contained nobody he knew, and was occupied by the plump Dr Cipolla and his Russian-born wife, but there was no turning back, so he told them frankly who he was.

Surprised, but not put out, they invited him in. Pollak was in luck because his sudden appearance was the answer to Dr Cipolla's prayer, for the doctor saw in Joe a means of getting back on to good terms with the British Organization. We had gone to great pains so satisfy ourselves that he had revealed nothing of the little he knew about us to the Gestapo, and had been in no way responsible for the raiding of the Via Chelini flat. Cipolla, in fact, sought to be a double-agent, working for friends on both sides, so that he was safe while the Germans remained in Rome, yet with something to plead in his favour when they were evicted.

He treated Pollak with generosity and consideration, telling him repeatedly that he was anxious to do anything he could to help British escapers—an anxiety doubtless strengthened by the rumble of Anzio gunfire, which occasionally rattled the windows of his home. However, it was with some misgiving that Renzo Lucidi agreed to Joe's request to take a new suit to the apartment of frightening memories, and when he left he carefully side-tracked Cipolla's friendly inquiries about their destination.

Pollak's somewhat rash descent upon the Via Chelini flat had given the Rome Organization at least one useful piece of information—we knew exactly where Dr Cipolla stood. From what I knew of the character of the man, I was sure that whatever help he gave to the Germans in other directions, he would not risk certain retribution by revealing any information about the organization, so I kept in touch with him, and made use of him in many small ways. The situation intrigued me no end: it was the only time I ever had a known German agent on my staff.

Pollak was moved to one of our safest billets under the care of Lieutenant Simpson, and I authorized payment to him at the 'staff rate' of 200 lire a day, made up his back pay, including the sum of his own money, which he had lost when he was arrested, and ordered that he should lie low for at least a fortnight.

I wanted Pollak to be kept out of the way until I had made quite certain that there would be no double-crossing by Dr Cipolla, but there was, in fact, a much stronger reason, which I did not know at the time, for Pollak to rest: his pneumonia had turned to tuberculosis.

When Simpson and Furman realized that his condition was serious they suggested that he should be smuggled into the Vatican, but I knew that this course would ultimately amount to handing Pollak over to the Germans. "Getting him into the Vat. would not help in the least," I explained, "because when people are sick here they are sent out into Rome nursing-homes. If he really has T.B. I would strongly recommend Switzerland. The chaps there are having a hell of a fine time. It would mean the end of the war before he could get home, but he would stand a good chance of getting cured."

The two lieutenants agreed that this course—and it was one which we could organize with little difficulty—was the best, but Pollak settled the issue by proving to be as stubborn as Private Anderson had been. He flatly refused to accept medical attention if it meant his removal from the war.

"No, thanks," he said. "If I am only fit to work one day a week I shall do more good here than I would in Switzerland. Anyway, it can't be for long now."

With both front lines completely static, I was not so certain, but I would not consider ordering Pollak to leave Rome against his own inclination. Besides, I could understand his determination to remain on active service at all costs. After being beaten up several times and left to freeze by the Germans, he had a personal score to settle. On the other hand, it was clear that he was quite unable to take over responsibility for a complete group of billets, so I instructed Furman and Simpson to use him as an assistant whenever he was fit, and to see that he was well looked after whenever he was ill. Pollak was content with this arrangement, and willingly dragged his weakened body about the streets of Rome, but there were many occasions when he was confined to his bed for long periods.

Most of the escapers had no knowledge of the existence of the organization, and sometimes the admirable caution exercised by new arrivals was so extreme that we were quite unable to establish contact with them. On one occasion Lieutenant Simpson spent days searching in vain for a group of Americans, who had sent out a call for assistance by such devious and circumspect channels that he never could trace it back.

Another time Renzo Lucidi wasted a valuable day searching for an American-born Jugoslav whom I was already watching fairly closely because I had a suspicion that he had appropriated for his own use money collected ostensibly for a group hiding some distance outside Rome. I had no idea that Renzo Lucidi was looking for this dubious character until Lieutenant Simpson wrote :

> I enclose a photograph of this American, who is supposed to be suffering from appendicitis. "Rinso" traced him as far as a hotel in Rome, and he had apparently left a few days before. Do you know anything about him?

> Yes, I know all about him and his location [I replied at once]. We can do nothing for him at present as the U.S. Legation will not accept him until he is checked by the Swiss. He has had clothes from us—and, I rather think, cash that was intended for the country.

> I was only interested in his appendix [replied Simpson laconically].

If some escapers were difficult to find, others were a good deal too conspicuous for our liking. The diminutive Lieutenant Furman, who could always pass in an Italian crowd, even with his red hair and moustache, had a particular aversion to guiding big, blond, obviously British types through the busy streets. He was never more shattered than when he answered a message from Monsignor O'Flaherty to pick up a couple of new arrivals, and found himself face to face, in St Peter's Square, with two vast six-footers—a guardsman named Bensley and a highlander named McBride. Both would have been conspicuous enough in conventional clothes, and in the ragged and tattered remains of their prison-camp dress they could hardly fail to attract attention.

Shuddering, Furman led them to the tram stop, and then, deciding that he could not face a ride in such spectacular company, changed his mind and hailed a *carrozza*. As they jolted off in the cab, Furman, feeling that every eye in Rome was turning towards them, wondered if he had done the right thing, and his heart sank as he observed two mounted policemen trotting up behind them. Wordlessly, he motioned to his companions to remain silent, and, for a heart-thumping age, watched warily as the policemen drew gradually closer. They were almost up to the *carozza* when suddenly they wheeled smartly into a side-street and were gone, entirely disinterested in the two tattered giants and their dapper little companion. At the billet he had arranged for them Furman found another shock awaiting him, for the door was locked, and there was nobody at home. He had to leave Bensley and McBride standing conspicuously outside, in full view of inquisitive passers-by, while he went off in search of the 'padrone,' and it was with astonishment that on his return with the Italian he found them still there, stoic and unmolested.

"Taking Bensley and McBride through Rome," an exhausted Furman reported to me later, "is like carrying a Union Jack in each hand."

Lieutenant Simpson also was having his moments. Leaving Monsignor O'Flaherty's office one day, he found himself walking through the colonnades towards a bearded, uniformed Fascist, whom he recognized at once as the man who had been the despised adjutant at the Chieti prison camp. The Fascist was walking slowly with a pretty woman, and Simpson stepped in front of them, stuck out his hand, and announced in Italian, "Remember me? I was one of your guests at Chieti."

Dumbfounded, the Fascist ignored the proffered hand, stared at the British officer—a smart, confident figure, very unlike the ragged subaltern he remembered—and then exploded. "We are enemies, you know. What makes you think I shall not have you arrested immediately?"

"You are an officer and a gentleman," Simpson replied blandly. "You could never bring yourself to take advantage of a social meeting like this."

He had judged his man's conceit shrewdly. The Fascist, acutely conscious of the eyes of his pretty companion upon him, controlled his anger with a visible effort, and jutted out his bearded chin.

"Don't be too sure of yourself. If I were you," he said, playing his rôle of officer and gentleman carefully, "I should exercise a little caution in future."

"No doubt you are right," replied Simpson, turning away. "I should pick my acquaintances with greater care."

This incident was not reported to me at the time, for Lieutenant Simpson knew well enough what would have been my reaction to such an unnecessary risk, taken by the only one of my military assistants who had so far managed to avoid recapture.

On the whole, however, it seemed that with Furman and Pollak back in Rome, we had entered into a fairly satisfactory period. There were no raids on billets, there was a steady stream of supplies to escapers, and we successfully developed one or two 'sidelines.'

Among these was the establishment of contact with Allied prisoners-of-war in hospitals in and around Rome. Their numbers had been increasing since the Anzio landings, and they were under direct German guard, so there was little we could do to help them escape, even had they been physically capable of making the attempt, but we were able to smuggle cigarettes and other small luxuries in to them. Thanks mainly to Brother Robert Pace, whose own Order ran one of the hospitals used as casualty clearing stations, we were fully informed of the arrival and condition of all wounded Allied prisoners-of-war, and were able, not only to distribute comforts, but to send news of their safety to their next of kin.

We also contrived, chiefly through the expenditure of more than 6000 lire in bribes, to establish contact with most of the recaptured escapers held in the Regina Coeli, the Forte Boccea, and other prisons in Rome, and we managed to get parcels of food, clothing, and money—which we knew, from Furman's experience, could be put to good use—through to most of them. "Sorry we didn't think of it while you were inside," I told Furman.

Things were going so smoothly that even if I had studied the calendar more closely I should not have thought that after nearly two thousand years it was still necessary to "beware the Ides of March." But on March 15, 1944, there were three grim portents of trouble.

There was nothing ominous about the first : the mass bombing of the mountain monastery of Monte Cassino. The town of Cassino had been the anchor of the stubborn German defence line in the south throughout the long winter, and above it, massive, unapproachable, and impregnable, perched the great monastery, overlooking the whole of the Allied lines west of the mountains. To what extent it had been fortified by the Germans was uncertain, but it was a unique observation-post, and its effect on the morale of the troops was depressive. Every concentration and every move they attempted was in the conscious knowledge that the great stone vulture hanging in the sky above them had its beady eyes fixed firmly on what they were doing. It was therefore no surprise to any member of the Allied forces when, on the return of bombers' weather, every available aircraft unloaded high explosive on to Cassino and its forbidding monastery, and the men in the line must have felt a curious relief as the stone-clad mountain-top disappeared in the smoke of more than a thousand tons of bombs.

But the raid was a psychological disaster from the point of view of the Rome Organization. All our Italian helpers were good Catholics, who had always thought of Allied bombing as being directed against specific military objectives, although they appreciated that damage might be done to other property in the process, and they could not understand how a Catholic monastery, still occupied by its monks, could be a military objective. Our priests were placed in a particularly delicate position, and it took all the tact and persuasion of which Lieutenants Furman and Simpson were capable to assuage the doubts of loyal Italian helpers, who had never before questioned the morality of any action taken by the Allies.

The second omen on March 15 was the unexpected death of a

member of the administrative staff who was in good health, and in no danger from the Germans. Sub-Lieutenant R. C. Elliott, a young naval officer, who was one of the first four Britishers interned at the Vatican, where he celebrated his twenty-first birthday, had been working as principal assistant to Captain Byrnes, on our records.

But he was a survivor of one of the most terrible experiences that can befall a man in war, and night after night, in the relative security of the Vatican, he relived in vivid nightmares his desperate struggle to escape from a submarine plunging to its doom after being torpedoed in the Mediterranean. In the small hours of March 15, rushing from his bed in a nightmare panic, he crashed through the window, and fell three storeys to his death on the flagstones below. He was the only internee to die within the city throughout the war, and the Vatican authorities arranged an impressive funeral. I could not help thinking, as I sadly watched the cortège pass, that if tragedy could strike so suddenly at those of us in safety, then the lives of those who walked with danger in Rome hung, indeed, on a slender thread.

The third portent of that ominous day was more clearly a threat to the organization. I received a warning that an Italian named Grossi, who had helped us in a small way on one or two occasions, had been seen working with the Fascists. Although his denunciation had not so far seemed to be connected with us, I was fearful that he might know some of the Italian families providing billets. I was especially afraid that he might, through her own lack of caution, get on to Mrs Chevalier, whose tiny flat had once again been pressed back into service. I immediately informed Lieutenants Furman and Simpson of Grossi's liaison with the Fascists, but was relieved to learn that they already knew about it, and had taken precautions.

To Simpson, who was responsible for Mrs Chevalier, I wrote :

"Mrs M." is a wonderful woman—but no idea of security. It is essential that Grossi does not know that we know of his activities. My suggestion is that "Mrs M.'s" is used as little as possible for permanent places; also, if possible, she should not be told the exact position of permanent places.

"Mrs M.," etc., are fully aware of this gentleman's recent activities, and are on guard [Simpson replied]. "Mrs M." has had five people staying with her for about ten days now, and because of new arrivals I have not been able to reduce the number so far.

Denunciation by somebody on the fringe of the organization was the threat I feared most, and I had all Grossi's movements observed as closely as possible. In our sort of work, to be forewarned was half the victory, but I did not want Grossi to suspect that we were watching him, because I thought it possible that he, like Dr Cipolla, was playing some sort of double game, and I did not intend to risk putting him wholly against us.

But I never foresaw that the causes of a coming crisis for the Rome Organization were a bogus priest and a bomb in a rubbish cart.

10

Denunciation

BY mid-March the Rome Organization was big business. The total number of escapers and evaders on our books had risen in less than three weeks by 800 to 3423, and the number in Rome itself had gone up by sixty to 180.

Our operations on the black market were so immense, it is not improbable that we were a primary factor in the farcical breakdown of the Roman official rationing system. Apart from our constant search for food, we were always on the lookout for clothing, since the supply of surplus garments given by Italian helpers had by now dried up almost completely. Our expenditure on the black-market clothing rose from 107,000 lire in January to 157,000 lire in February and to 187,000 lire in March.

'Customers' now included 400 Russian escapers, to whom help was being channelled through a Russian priest, Father Dorotheo Bezchctnoff, appointed by Monsignor O'Flaherty, and assisted by two Russian women who had formerly served in the Red Cross. During March this group was joined by a lieutenant-colonel, who sent a charmingly worded message of thanks to the organization for all the help that his countrymen had received.

As the total numbers swelled, so the financial burden increased, but it was eased to some extent by the departure of two or three hundred who, as the winter reached its peak, found their mountain hides in the north of the country no longer tenable, and made their way over the border into Switzerland. Others joined the armed bands of Italian guerillas, gradually being formed behind the German lines, who were adequately supplied with money, clothing, and food of their own. At least one group outside Rome made itself financially independent by negotiating a large loan from local industrialists.

With the organization generally going along so smoothly, it was irksome as well as distressing whenever any escaper was re-captured, although less alarming than the arrest of an Italian helper or 'padrone,' whose life in German hands was not likely to be worth much, but I was especially annoyed when one particular officer was taken.

Captain Milner was the last of our Roman residents I would have expected to be captured, because he had never given us cause for a moment's concern. Because of his very English appearance and almost complete lack of understanding of Italian, he had been warned at the outset that it would be dangerous for him and those who helped him if he ventured out, despite the fact that his billet was most uncongenial.

He never complained, but eventually it became clear that he was unhappy, and when a vacancy occurred we arranged to move him. This time his luck was in, for we had found him the luxury flat of a glamorous Italian film actress, Flora Volpini. Two or three days later, bounding with joy and new confidence, he set off on his first lone outing to his former billet, to pay off a debt of a few thousand lire. But he never arrived, and he never returned to his new home. Swiss contacts discovered that he was languishing in the Regina Coeli, where he had been taken after walking slap into a routine police check. There was nothing we could do for him beyond smuggling the usual comforts into the prison, but it seemed a pity for his splendid billet to be wasted, so Lieutenant Simpson packed his bag, and moved in.

The capture of the captain was unfortunate, but the next blow landed on our most vulnerable point: the priests. On March 16 Brother Robert Pace went to a village on the outskirts of Rome to collect a couple of escapers who were to be taken straight to a billet. "Whitebows," as usual, accomplished his mission with success, but as he introduced them to their hosts, Andrea Casadi and Vittorio Fantini, the two 'escapers,' instead of extending their hands in greeting, pulled out ugly revolvers. They were Gestapo agents.

Brother Robert and the two Italians knew that they were trapped. They were marched at pistol point through the streets of Rome to the headquarters of the Gestapo, in Via Tasso—a place more dreaded than even the worst of Rome's notorious prisons, as it was the undisputed centre of the fine art of torture. They were separated, and eight days later the two Italians were shot. Brother Robert knew only too well what this meant, for the survivor, from whom the Gestapo aimed to extract information, could expect only inhuman torture right up to, but never beyond, the point of death.

He thought little of his chance of survival, but stuck doggedly to his story that he had received a request from a village priest to guide two people to an address in Rome, and had naturally, and without question, agreed to render this small service to a brother in the Church. He also pointed out that he was well known to his captors' military superiors in Rome, and this registered on Teutons well trained in subservience to senior rank. As a result, "Whitebows" was allowed to send a message to the superior at his Mother house—a school now being used as a casualty clearing station.

At the hospital Brother Robert had provided little gifts and comforts for the wounded Germans with the same unselfish generosity that he had shown towards Allied prisoners. The German army therefore thought highly of him, and indicated that they would like to see him back as soon as possible. Doubtfully, the Gestapo allowed him to return to his Mother house for the time being, but warned him that he was likely at any rate to be recalled for further "questioning." We all realized that the Gestapo, frustrated for the moment, would continue their investigations, so it was agreed that the time had come for Brother Robert to 'disappear.' Thus, although a life was saved, the organization lost yet another of its most valuable helpers.

But it was the bomb in the rubbish cart that really made things difficult. The various Communist underground organizations in Rome had shown gallantry and initiative on many occasions, but we never saw quite eye to eye. They constantly derided the idea of giving help to escaped prisoners-of-war, and insisted that the proper function of all enemies of the German Reich was sabotage. The destruction by our own men of the railway viaduct had provided one painful example of the disadvantages of blowing things up, but another even more spectacular lesson was to come.

The Communists kept a close eye on everything done by the Germans, and their plans were frequently assisted by the Teutonic characteristic of uniformity and routine. In Rome, as elsewhere, the Germans insisted on doing everything in exactly the same way at the same time day after day, and it did not take the Communists long to discover that at two o'clock every afternoon a large squad of German soldiers marched down the Via Rasella on their way to the bath-house.

When the grey column tramped along the street on March 22 it passed an unattended rubbish cart, which at a glance looked innocent if unsavoury, but which, in fact, contained a bomb carefully constructed and placed there by the Communists. The Germans, as usual, were absolutely punctual, and so was the timing mechanism devised by the saboteurs. At the instant that the column came abreast of the rubbish cart, the giant time-bomb went off with a shattering roar.

The cart vaporized, window-glass clattered to the ground from end to end of the smoke-filled street, and, like flotsam on the edge of a sudden wave, bodies and bits of bodies were spread in a bloody, groaning semicircle. The explosion had caught the Germans absolutely in the centre of the passing column, and the result was indescribable chaos. Thirty-two of the Germans were killed outright or died soon afterwards, and most of the survivors had some form of injury.

I had known nothing in advance of this devastating operation, though aware—few in Rome could fail to be—that the various Communist groups made a practice of letting off small explosions regularly throughout the city. The first news within an hour of the big bang in Via Rasella was somewhat garbled, but, even allowing for exaggeration, I could see that this time our Communist associates had achieved more than usual.

It was, of course, a most effective piece of sabotage, for even an Allied bomber, while perhaps doing more widespread damage, could scarcely have expected to write off a larger number of German troops in a single blow. But I had the suspicion that this was the sort of blow that would turn into a boomerang, for although the Germans were frequently confused by the destruction of property, they always retaliated sharply when German life was destroyed, usually on the principle of half a dozen eyes for an eye, and I was anxious. My official responsibility was for the Allied escapers and evaders directly under my command, but I felt even more strongly my moral responsibility for the lives of the Italians who were looking after them; a recaptured escaper still had a reasonable chance of survival, despite his civilian clothing, but an Italian arrested on any pretext at the present time was virtually doomed.

I decided to reduce evidence for Germans making round-ups and minimize the risk of re-arrests by emptying all billets as far as possible. Our messengers were sent scurrying about Rome, and before the blood had been swabbed from the Via Rasella, dozens of ex-prisoners had already moved out of their billets into inadequate temporary hiding-places, in parks and public gardens. The men for whom I was responsible were uncomfortable and in considerable risk of recapture, but the homes of their 'padrones' were innocent again.

If anything I underestimated the lengths to which the Germans would go. Their immediate reaction was as I had expected: they brought the curfew hour forward to half-past five in the evening, and enforced it rigidly, shooting first, and asking questions afterwards. I had surmised that the next step would be an intensified series of raids and round-ups, followed by the beating-ups and shootings, which had become the hallmark of Kultur, and I was surprised when no reports flooded in of families roughly shaken awake in the middle of the night, and carted off to the dungeons. Instead, the Germans revealed another form of retribution, and it was a horrible object lesson in ice-cold inhumanity.

Indiscriminately, from the prisons of the city, they took ten prisoners for every soldier killed in the bombing—a motley miscellany of political prisoners and prostitutes, outspoken journalists and unthinking juveniles, pilferers and petty offenders, many of whom had faced no trial, and some of whom knew not with what they were charged. Their hands tied behind their backs, the 320 prisoners were taken through the streets of Rome to the Ardeatine Caves, at Domitilla. There they were bundled in batches into the forbidding cavern entrances, and mown down by machine-gun fire. The terrible slaughter lasted through several hours of the grim night: hours during which those who were to die stood impotently, and watched their comrades fall.

When the hot barrels of the machine-guns were silent at last the Germans placed land-mines in the rock, and blew in the entrance to the caves, presumably to save the trouble of burial, but possibly to prevent Italians from recovering the bodies, and perhaps getting help to any who might have escaped death. That some did survive the savage machine-gunning was proved later, when post-mortem examinations revealed dust inhaled into the lungs. They had been entombed alive.

Piecing reports together with growing horror, I was acutely conscious that more than forty of our escapers and Italian helpers had been in the prisons when the Germans selected (if such a word can be used without irony) their hostages, and I put all available contacts to work on the task of ascertaining who had been the victims of the barbaric butchery. When the position clarified we knew that five of our Italian helpers had perished, including the gallant radio-operator, Umberto Losena, who had given such tremendous help to me during my first few weeks in Rome, and who had been in the Regina Coeli ever since his arrest.

German security forces in the city were substantially strengthened, and as many as 2000 extra S.S. and security men were brought into Rome. Enemies swarmed everywhere, seemingly armed to the teeth, and never alone, doubling the danger of the work of all our agents, and making any violation of the curfew, however small, completely impossible.

The worst development of all was the return to prominence of the most vicious elements of the Italian Fascist movement, who were formed into a special security gang, with full German support, and powers overriding those of the police and the Republican Guard (which the military governors knew very well would, in the main, go over at the first opportunity to the Allied cause). This Fascist neo-Gestapo, answerable to no judicial authority, and consisting largely of brutal, sadistic morons, rapidly established itself as the most terrifying body in Rome. It set up its headquarters in a block of flats, and within a week all the other tenants, unable to stand the screams of the victims of its 'interrogations,' quit the building.

I realized that the sudden increase in the tempo of enemy activity was not aimed at the capture of Allied escapers, but at the destruction of the Italian and other subversive movements, which were a growing threat to German rule, but we had so much in common with their organizations, and, indeed, overlapped at so many points, that a search for one was only too likely to unearth the secrets of the other.

The number of visits made by our agents to the billets and to the Vatican was therefore reduced to the minimum, and orders went out to all 'cells' for detailed evacuation drill, under which the escapers were, in the event of any large-scale scare, to try to make their way to the age-old catacombs of Rome. We gave them directions for entering and—equally important—not getting lost in the fabulous complex of subterranean tunnels, in which, I knew, a whole army could be hidden if necessary; the catacombs had served the early Christians well enough against the heathen Romans centuries before, and now offered similar protection to the Allied men against an enemy no less pagan.

Conditions for our work became more and more difficult as the Germans and Fascists started rounding up all males between the ages of fifteen and seventy for forced labour, ostensibly to prepare earthwork defences north of Rome, but more probably, I thought, to reduce the number of potential enemies in the city, and to move any who might be subversive agents as far away as possible from the front line. The priests were still relatively safe from seizure, but few others could walk safely on the streets unless in possession of formidable documents, and during the long hours of curfew searches and round-ups by the S.S. and the Fascists became more and more frequent.

Unexpectedly, just as the Via Rasella bombshell had been a boomerang against the Roman underground, even more un-expectedly the Ardeatine massacre proved a boomerang for the Germans. The Fascist neo-Gestapo, who went about their bestial business with sadistic satisfaction, were by no means typical of their race: for the most part the cold, calculated cruelty of the Germans, which the Fascists aped, was something wholly foreign to the passionate, volatile, yet essentially warm-hearted Italian nature. As a people, the Italians never cared much for the Germans; during the occupation of Rome they learned to dislike them actively, and after the Ardeatine massacre their dislike turned to a glowing, loathing hatred. Many Italians who had found it ex-pedient to collaborate, now turned their backs on the Germans, and many more who had barely tolerated them now sought means of working against them. Outside the Fascist gang there were few Italians left who looked upon the expected Allied entry into Rome as merely the substitution of one occupying force by another. It was a hoped-for, prayed-for day, which would be a day of libera-tion.

In this atmosphere the Rome Organization found itself many new and valuable helpers—men and women who cared nothing about the small sums of money we distributed or the black-market supplies that we could organize, but wanted only to do something active against the hated Germans.

Despite the value of this extra help, however, the most valuable assistance that came my way was a strictly commercial proposition, and possibly the best bit of business the Rome Organization ever did.

"Know the Questura?" asked John May one day, his eyes creased by an expansive grin.

"Of course—though I've no wish to make close acquaintance with it," I replied. "You mean the headquarters of the S.S. and the Fascist Carabinieri?"

"How would you like to get hold of their routine orders when they come out?" he asked. "I think I've found a way of laying hands on those orders."

"Now, John," I expostulated, "I'd be the first to agree that you're a bloody marvel, but you are now talking through your elegant hat."

John May explained. "I'm in touch with a chap—name of Giuseppe—who says he's got a pal working in some sort of clerical capacity in the Questura. Betwen them they're prepared to float an extra copy of the gen from the routine orders in our direction. They will, of course, expect rather more than thanks."

"How much?"

"A thousand lire a time."

We discussed the idea, but the only thing holding me back was that I was too old to believe in fairies any more. My most optimistic plans had never contemplated a sight of the Questura's routine orders, but John May and I hammered out details of a roundabout route for reports to reach us with the minimum risk to our informant and ourselves. I had little hope of getting anything at all, let alone something useful, but when a report appeared a couple of days later my surprise at receiving a return for my money soon gave way to astonishment and delight at its contents: for this was indeed a full and detailed transcript of the S.S. and Fascist orders most affecting us in the Rome Organization. In addition to information about the general activities of the security forces, the report also listed the areas in Rome on which the authorities, with their customary insistence on committing all plans to paper, intended to make 'surprise raids' within the next two or three nights.

"This is terrific," I enthused to John May. "If your boys are going to produce this sort of thing they're underpaid."

I told him that if his little friends had wanted to take us for a ride they wouldn't have filled their first report with stuff that could manifestly be proved to be true or false within a few hours. Anyway, I cleared the billets in the danger areas, knowing that we should soon find out where the Questura gang had been paying their social calls.

Everything worked out as the report had forecast, and it was clear that the organization had never made a better financial investment. We now had an inside contact with the very people who were searching for, and rounding up, escaped prisoners. It did not, of course, give us anything like complete protection, for the Gestapo were likely to turn up anywhere at any time, and the Questura orders only covered routine raids. They did not refer to checks resulting from a denunciation or information. But it was a tremendous stride forward in security, and the reports regularly received thereafter frequently enabled us to prevent recaptures and arrests by evacuating escapers from danger areas.

These evacuations called for some fast thinking, since the routine orders and detailed raids scheduled for the same evening were not published until midday. Then it took time to cover the devious route from the Questura to the British Legation, and the vital information did not reach me until quite late in the afternoon. Orders for raids usually related to a fairly broad area, and I had to rush through our card-indexes and maps to find out if any of our 'cells' were in danger, for with the increasing number of new billets, and the sheer number in occupation in the city, there was too much detail to be committed to memory. If billets were found to be in danger areas there still remained the physical task of warning the occupants and arranging evacuations. This was complicated by the security precaution that any one messenger should know of no more than a handful of 'cells.' Consequently, we sometimes found that to get warnings to four or five billets quite close to each other, we had to trace and dispatch as many messengers.

Sometimes the messengers directly concerned could not be contacted in time, but we never sent a neighbouring messenger to take warnings to 'cells' which were not in his own group. Only

four people knew the location of all the billets: Monsignor
O'Flaherty, Lieutenant Simpson, Captain Byrnes, and myself.
Even Lieutenant Furman, who had taken over half Simpson's
list since his return to Rome, did not know many of the 'cells'
which had been established while he was away. Of the four of us,
Byrnes and I were confined within the walls of the Vatican, and
the monsignor could not venture beyond its immediate surroundings without risk of instant arrest. So, for the second time, the
quiet, methodical Simpson found himself the key outside-man
of the organization. Whenever the contact-man for a threatened
billet could not be traced at short notice it was Lieutenant Simpson who had to take the warning, and one of the minor mysteries
of the war—or even minor miracles—was how, when Rome
swarmed as never before with German soldiers and security forces,
Simpson managed to travel incessantly about the city without ever
being stopped and questioned.

Everything had to be done at the double, for it was now virtually impossible to deliver messages or move escapers once the early
curfew clamped at half past five, and public transport services
had largely broken down. Even where in existence, they were subject to constant scrutiny by the Germans, so some of our priests
were now regularly covering eight or nine miles on foot in a day,
during their routine calls on billets.

Nevertheless, whatever the difficulties of making practical use
of Giuseppe's reports, it was a tremendous advantage to be able
to circulate warnings at all, and in time we had the whole complicated business of translation, pinpointing affected billets,
selecting messengers and briefing them, boiled down to a high-
speed drill.

Apart from details of official orders, Giuseppe began to include
background information, and I realized from repeated references
to "anonymous" denouncements, that a good many of the arrests
which had been put down to bad luck in routine checks
might, in fact, have been due to denunciation. For example, he
reported:

As a result of several denunciations, the Via Merulana is being
closely watched these days, since British and American ex-
prisoners are reported to be hidden there. Houses will shortly be
searched.

On another occasion he wrote:

A denouncement has arrived declaring that a coffee-house keeper has an English ex-prisoner under an assumed Italian name, who he pretends is his helper. A search by the Republican Fascists is imminent.

And later:

Another denouncement reports that a baker in the San Giovanni district is hiding some British and Badoglian soldiers in a walled-up garret.

It was from Giuseppe that I confirmed a suspicion that the Germans were now sending out agents dressed as priests, who got in touch with British escapers, and offered help, undertaking to conduct them to secure hiding-places—a promise which, looked at in one light, they often fulfilled all too thoroughly.

Giuseppe also reported that every access to the San Roberto Bellarmino Church, which was about a mile north of the ancient city wall, on the far side of the Rome Zoo, was being watched, as the Germans suspected that the priests were giving money and hospitality to escaped prisoners-of-war. This was particularly disconcerting, for the prospects were certainly poorer if the Gestapo net was beginning to tighten round Monsignor O'Flaherty's priests; I urged him to warn all his helpers to be on their guard, and, since he disliked others taking risks that he cheerfully took himself, the warning was passed on.

Giuseppe's reports caused me great concern, because the details given in denunciation were so accurate, but when they revealed at last the source of the betrayal it was only confirmation of what I already knew.

Pale and tight-lipped, the Free French leader, De Vial, had told me, "That bastard, Perfetti, has gone over to the Boche."

It was not really surprising. I had never liked the greasy Pasqualino Perfetti, who wore priest's clothing though he was not a priest, and who had been my first contact in Rome, so I had allowed him to slip gradually out of the organization, although he had continued, for a remuneration, to find billets for the French. Nevertheless, the news was alarming, for Perfetti had been an important link in the monsignor's original organization, and he knew the location of too many of our present billets, as well as those occupied by French escapers.

"We knew Perfetti had been arrested," De Vial continued, "but we were not too worried. We thought it was all routine. Then we heard that he was about again, limping heavily, and obviously badly battered about the head and face. And, mon Dieu, he was not alone. He was with the Gestapo. Sometimes in a car, sometimes on foot, he was guiding them from place to place. We lost a dozen billets before we could do anything, and a lot of our men have been taken in by that Fascist gang, and badly beaten up."

"How do you know?"

"One of them got away—Captain Martin. He climbed down a drainpipe from four floors up, and ran through Rome with his face and clothes covered with blood. From him, we learned about Perfetti."

Thus it was confirmation rather than information when Giuseppe's next report told me:

I have been informed that one Pasqualino Perfetti had been collaborating with the Fascists and German police. He helps them in their searches for ex-prisoners. Before, Pasqualino Perfetti has helped or feigned to assist ex-prisoners-of-war. It has been confirmed that he has given much information.

By this time I had rushed urgent warnings to the billeting officers, and a sort of general post had begun among the underground Allies in Rome, but despite our speed, the bogus priest's wholesale denunciation moved faster, and half a dozen escapers and their 'padrones' were arrested. Giuseppe's reports began to lag behind developements, filling in details of known disasters, rather than providing warnings, but they were still valuable. For example:

The German police have arrested the lawyer, Eramo, who had very generously helped ex-prisoners and Badoglian soldiers [he wrote]. He is imprisoned in the prison of the Via Tasso. It appears that he was betrayed by Don Pasqualino Perfetti, who had been in contact with Eramo over the financing of the above-mentioned soldiers. Arrested himself some time ago, Perfetti has given the addresses of all those in hiding, accompanying the German police in their searches. Without a doubt, Perfetti now works for the Germans.

Perfetti's perfidy had gone beyond the bounds of an understandable breakdown under torture. From Captain Martin and other sources, the French learned that Perfetti not merely guided the Germans from house to house, but at each gave the secret signal on the bell, and held the door open while the Germans burst in, so that there was no hope of escape for the ex-prisoners.

I was hoping that we had been able to clear most of the billets known to Perfetti from earlier days, but the scope of his denunciations became evident when Lieutenant Furman, after a frantic couple of days, reported on March 26:

> Du Toit: I enclose this man's identity card. Du Toit was Pasqualino's escaper; he was picked up with Ireland, who had only been at the billet a few days. Matthews must be considered taken; he went away from his billet and hasn't returned. Flynn and Wynn have been taken. Macdougal, I hear, has been taken; one of Pasqualino's, I believe.

Perfetti's treachery caused us grievous losses. By the end of March twenty-one escapers had been recaptured, and more than a dozen Italian helpers arrested. We tightened up on security in every possible direction, and to reduce the amount of incriminating paper floating around Rome, I ordered that no further receipts should be collected from people to whom money was given. Sir D'Arcy Osborne gave authority for the reports written by Lieutenants Simpson and Furman, in the comparative safety of Monsignor O'Flaherty's office, to be accepted as sufficient acknowledgment for the vast amount of British Government cash now passing through our hands.

Yet, even at a time of high drama, it was impossible to forget the trivial problems of my work, as "the pay bloke"—to use the term given me by Simpson. While reporting on the arrest of Du Toit and Ireland, Lieutenant Furman also pointed out:

> The elderly lady who looked after them wants to make some claim in respect of Du Toit. I don't think she really expects to get all she has put down, but I might mention that Du Toit was wearing a watch of her husband's, and also she bought an accordion for 5000 lire, which Du Toit said he would pay personally.

I had financial troubles enough, without trying to extract payment for a wrist-watch and an accordion from the British Government, but I had already foreseen this sort of development, and was devoting most of my spare moments to planning the establishment of some sort of commission, which, after the Allied entry into Rome, would be able to sift and settle the claims of all Italians who had suffered loss through their help to the organization. So I told Furman:

I suggest you give her a couple of thousand lire, and tell her that we have got all her details for the commission, which will investigate and deal with all claims. But, anyway, I should think she would be able to get a good price for the accordion. . . .

As March turned to April, it seemed that the crisis had passed. The cold blue of the sky took on a gentler, golden mantle, setting aglow the great ruined temples, sending melted snow coursing under the seventeen Tiber bridges, and clothing the boughs and branches beyond my windows with bud and blossom. Nowhere in the world could have been more beautiful than Rome in the spring of that year, and as I looked out from the safety of my comfortable prison, I felt a new hope. Better weather would surely hasten the liberation, and now that the leak which had brought such tragic results had been stopped, I hoped to preserve the freedom of those anticipating reunion with their comrades.

I started to breathe easily again—but out in the beautiful city Lieutenant John Furman was aghast. He had been discussing Perfetti's perfidy with his young assistant, Gino Giuliani, the son of his 'padrone,' and quite casually, as though it were of no importance, the youth mentioned that he knew the betrayer. Furman elicited that Perfetti also knew Gino was helping us, and that at least one of the billets which Gino had provided for Furman's escapers had been passed on to him by Perfetti.

Lieutenant Furman acted promptly, evacuating the billet which was known to be in danger, and moving his own quarters to his reserve billet, in the home of a widowed countess. He advised his 'padrone,' Romeo Giuliani, to take his family away, but the little clerk would not hear of moving, although Gino agreed to go and stay with his young friend, Memo, who also had occasionally helped in the finding of billets.

When nothing happened in three or four days Furman decided

that the danger had passed, and returned to the Giulianis' home on April 5. The Fascists struck during the night of April 7, but, by pure chance, Furman was not there. He was attending a birthday party, and because of the curfew the convention had developed that such parties should last all night. The spare bed on which Gino slept whenever Furman was in the house had been dismantled and packed away, and there was no obvious sign of the tenancy of an escaped prisoner-of-war, but the Fascists were equipped with a detailed denunciation by Perfetti, and took away both Gino and his father, Romeo. After maintaining his ignorance of anything to do with British escapers all through a night-long interrogation, Romeo was released, but his son was held.

The organization knew nothing of this new blow until Furman returned to his billet next day, to find it occupied only by tearful, haggard women, for Romeo had gone back to the Fascist headquarters on his own, to find out what had happened to his son. Furman urged the remainder of the family to vacate their home at once, but again they refused to move.

He rushed off to meet Joe Pollak, who was enjoying a brief spell of relatively sound health, and together they drew up a list of all the billets known to Gino, and worked out a plan for the warning of all the families involved. Several were on the telephone, and they decided to contact these before setting off to call on the others, but in no single case could they get a reply. Hearts sinking, they realized that they were already too late. Gino had talked.

Abandoning their plan of separating to visit all the billets, they decided to go together to one for a check. The idea behind this dangerous but utterly unselfish plan was that if one of them walked into a trap the other would be able to get away, and report to headquarters. They made their way by tram to a billet occupied by Privates Groundsell and Allen, where, while Pollak waited below, Furman went upstairs, and gave the secret ring on the doorbell. The face of the girl who answered the door was enough to tell him that here, also, he was too late. She told him that the Fascists had burst in without warning the previous night, and had taken away the two escapers and her father. She and her mother had watched the Fascists kick the three men down the long stairway.

Furman and Pollak became increasingly depressed as their investigations continued, for of all the escapers known to Gino, they could find only two still safe, and these they moved at once to another billet. Furman, now without a home of his own, remembered with a sudden shock that although he had not given the address of his emergency billet to Gino, he had told him the telephone number. He rushed to the house to warn the countess and her two daughters that they must leave Rome at once, at least for a few days.

Lieutenant Simpson, meanwhile, unaware of the latest disaster, had gone to the basement flat, which had been used for the past few weeks as the principal clearing-house, and to which Monsignor O'Flaherty sent all new arrivals. He found that the Fascists had already called and dragged the 'padrone' away, but the five British escapers using the billet were still there. In the few moments before he opened the door, in answer to the harsh and unmistakable Fascist summons, the Italian (Paolino) had the presence of mind to bundle the five into a cellar, and push his bed over the trap-door entrance. The Fascists searched the flat without finding any trace of escapers or the hastily concealed trap-door, but they took Paolino. Since they were armed with detailed denunciations, they no longer needed material evidence. Simpson immediately moved the five escapers to other billets, and once again we were left without a clearing-house.

I had sent out warnings throughout the organization as soon as Perfetti started out on his long trail of treachery, but the Gino development caught me off balance: I did not know what he knew about the organization, although I had a suspicion that we should have to write off a good proportion of the billets for which Furman was responsible. Furman's first written report on April 11, after a hectic period in which there was time only for brief verbal messages, confirmed my foreboding.

The situation is now a little clearer [he wrote], but I'm afraid the clearer it gets, the blacker. Nearly all my lads have been taken, so it is quite clear that Gino spilled the beans. All were taken on Saturday between 1 A.M. and 5 A.M.

Groundsell and Allen: taken together with the 'padrone,' Cardinali. I went to the house yesterday, and saw the daughters, and left them 2000 lire.

McBride and Bensley: I haven't been to the house, but have phoned constantly, with never a reply, so it is fairly conclusive. It would seem that Renato Peoletti and his mother have both been taken.

De Lisle and Gardner: I haven't been there, but the Cardinalis' (whose friends they are) told me the worst. I don't know which members of the family have been taken. Incidentally, there were also two Jews in hiding there, so I suppose they have been taken.

Doug. Bennett: He must have been taken, as, again, I get no reply on the phone. That also means Signora Ingoramo and her maid.

Memo: He also was taken on Saturday night, but I learn has now been released; he thinks, however, that he is being tailed. I shall try to make contact with him if it can be done safely.

Countess Morosini: I stayed a few nights in this lady's house, and Gino knew the phone number. Accordingly, I advised her to move, together with her two daughters, and in view of their expenses thus entailed, I left 2000 lire with them. If you think this is not justifiable I'll pay it myself, but it is on our account that they're having to move.

Hudd and Conlon, who were known to Gino, fortunately are safe, and I've shifted them. It is quite right that as soon as some one is taken it is necessary to assume that everything he knows is also known to the enemy. . . .

This depressing list was by no means complete, and in his next report Furman told me that an underground agent named Zachan, with whom he had an appointment at the business premises of an Italian 'padrone,' had been arrested while in possession of a pistol.

Neither Z. nor his 'padrone' was there [wrote Furman, reporting on his appointment], but the 'padrone's' wife was, and this is the story I had from her :

At about 1 A.M. four Guardia Republicans came to the house, and gave the proper signal. They took away the 'padrone' and Z., who was armed.

The 'padrone's' wife has had an interview with her husband at the Regina Coeli. He had a black eye, and was bruised about the head and face. He told her that Gino had been badly beaten up, and that his head was swollen like a pumpkin; also that Perfetti had been badly beaten up about the body. Gino, he said, was now also at the Regina Coeli, and no longer at Via Principe (the Fascist neo-Gestapo headquarters). He confirmed that they seem to know everything about everything, and said they are particularly anxious to locate me : apparently all the 'padrones,' who have been taken have been asked where the English lieutenant who used to visit them is to be found.

Memo, Gino's friend, who also worked for me, has been released without apparently being beaten up; he visited this lady at her house, and told her that wherever he went he had two Fascists with him. It appears that they threatened him with death unless he led them to other prisoners—and, it would seem, particularly to me. However, he knows no other prisoners, so far as as I am aware, and I don't believe that he would give me away even if he saw me in the street. But I don't propose to take any chances. If I see him about I shall promptly put on a gallop in the opposite direction.

I gave the lady 2000 lire, for which she was very grateful. I think it is the least we can do.

Hudd and Conlon, the only two of his escapers that Furman had been able to save, were not at liberty for long : they and their new 'padrone' were arrested within a few days.

"What do you put it down to?" I asked. "One of the Pasqualino gang?"

But Furman replied that he thought it a common case of denunciation.

Three more escapers were taken in quick succession, and this time they were all uncomfortably close to Mrs Chevalier's crowded flat.

I really am worried about her place [I warned Furman and Simpson]. That son of hers is such a damned chatterbox : he tells them practically everything at the Swiss, and we know there are at least two people there who get paid on results, by the Huns. Both of you are to keep away as much as possible from her flat.

Unfortunately, Lieutenant Simpson was destined never to receive this message. At this time he was playing with the idea of taking advantage of the improved weather by making an attempt to rejoin our forces. He had asked for permission to join in a scheme with others to get away by boat from the west coast.

I had to reply, somewhat discouragingly, that none of the many 'boats trips' had succeeded from the west coast.

The last [I wrote], cost the French nine men and 80,000 lire (the men being in gaol). However, I am naturally interested in any show for getting the chaps back, so although I should be sorry to lose you, of course you may go in the event of the proposition sounding reasonable, and we shall provide the cash for you.

But I warned him that Germans posing as French patriots had been infiltrated into many escapes by boat, and reports from the north showed that many so-called boating-parties were merely a Fascist ruse to collect as many prisoners-of-war as possible. However, there had been several successful evacuations on the Adriatic side.

These warnings, too, were never to reach Bill Simpson, for before the ink of my signature had dried, the calm, methodical lieutenant, who had worked on undismayed through eighteen weeks of turmoil, suddenly vanished.

11

Thrust and Parry

JOLTED by a series of straight lefts, a boxer can be forgiven if he raises his guard against another, and then finds himself caught by an unexpected right uppercut.

The Rome Organization was on the defensive, and concentrating on fending off more blows, following the Perfetti and Gino revelations. I felt that in the haze of sudden raids Lieutenant Furman had become a marked man, since his habits and description must have been well known to the Fascists. So I decided that for the time being he would have to be taken out of action, and set about making arrangements for him to be hidden in a seminary, which, to all intents and purposes, would be as safe as the Vatican itself. But long before the plans were complete, other events decreed that Furman must remain on active service.

I was also worried that the Perfetti poison would spread in other directions, for although the Fascists had not yet laid hands on any of the priests, Perfetti knew enough for complaints to be passed through to the ecclesiastical authorities. Sure enough, two of our most stalwart assistants, the Maltese Father Borg ("Grobb") and the Irish Father Madden ("Edmund"), were shortly afterwards confined by their superiors to their religious houses. With Monsignor O'Flaherty virtually restricted to the Vatican, Brother Robert Pace ("Whitebows") out of the game, and Joe Pollak limited to occasional assistance because of his health, our outside staff was drastically reduced, just at a time when more movements than ever were taking place. The burden on the few who remained was thus increased enormously, and Lieutenant Simpson was carrying his full share.

Then on April 18, the only billeting officer to have evaded recapture during the winter disappeared. It was a body blow. Simpson had been of such vital importance to the organization that, in Furman's absence, I had ordered him never to sleep in the same billet on successive nights. It is true that after Furman's reappearance Simpson made his 'permanent' home in the perfumed apartment of the film actress, Flora Volpini, but he had continued to move around a good deal, for he knew the position of every 'cell,' and was never at a loss for a bed.

On April 18 he was spending the night with an American friend, Lieutenant E. Dukate, who was billeted with two Italian black-market operators. In the middle of the night the flat was raided by S.S. men, which was fairly unusual at a time when most of the attacks against us were launched by the hated Fascist neo-Gestapo, but it was not black-marketeers they were after—they wanted Simpson and Dukate only.

> Things go from bad to worse [reported Lieutenant Furman]. Now Bill is in the bag. I shall try to get Bill's prisoners looked after, with the aid of "Rinso," but I want a complete list of them.

Simpson, the biggest fish the enemy had yet hooked out of the Rome Organization, simply disappeared. We had excellent contacts in so many places that normally we were quickly able to ascertain the whereabouts of recaptured escapers, but in this case we drew a long succession of blanks. Through our underground information lines we sent inquiries to the civil police and the Questura; at a less clandestine level the Swiss asked questions on our behalf, and the actress, Flora Volpini, herself made a direct approach to the Italian governor of the Regina Coeli, who was known to her. From all directions came the same response—no one had heard of Lieutenant Simpson. We knew that as he had not been taken by the Fascist gang, he would not be in the torture centre in Via Principe Amedeo, but the alternative was scarcely less encouraging, for if he was in the Via Tasso headquarters of the Gestapo he would be lucky to emerge alive.

While investigations continued, the ordinary work of the organization had to go on, and Lieutenant Furman himself decided to remain in action, and postpone what he called "coming inside."

I was not happy about his being out and about in Rome, though I understood and accepted his decision. But I tried to dissuade him from following Simpson's earlier system of sleeping in different billets every night, chiefly because I did not want him to venture on to the streets at all unless absolutely necessary, and also because I wanted to know where he could be found if he had to be moved 'inside' at short notice.

For the moment I will stay put, doing only necessary work, and otherwise lying low [replied Furman]. When you think the time is ripe for me to go inside you will be able to let me know, but I am still not sure that the time is ripe—with "Grobb" and "Edmund" out of action, in addition to Bill and "Whitebows," do you think I can be spared?

The question was rhetorical, for Furman had already decided the answer for himself : he could not be spared. He dyed his hair jet black, changed the position of his parting, and shaved off his moustache.

These alterations in appearance, which turned him into a typical Italian, were speeded after an alarming encounter. He reported to me :

To-day I went back to my old billet, and to my horror met Memo there—the friend of Gino, who was released after a couple of days' captivity. He was as alarmed to see me as I was to see him. He told me he was released on condition that he would look for me, and he had two guards with him for a couple of days, but they seem to have disappeared now. He thinks that Gino will be released within the next couple of days, also on condition that he helps look for me (Gino has already had most of his teeth knocked out or broken). He tells me that they have my description down to the very last detail of my clothing—which, incidentally, I have now changed—and also know a number of places which I frequent, and are watching them. He says, too, that the Fascists have told him I am a spy, and they will shoot me when they catch me. I have taken off my moustache, and am going to dye my hair, so don't be surprised when next you see me.

Furman was now staying at the flat which he had arranged to be taken over by an Italian woman, Luciana Zoboli, and he had another scare when she asked him if she could bring in two young Italians who needed refuge. One was a doctor who had helped Allied escapers in the country north of Rome, serving as our contact with a group of twenty, but the other man was wearing the uniform of an officer in the Republican Guard. Luciana hastened to explain : the visitor had been an officer in the regular Italian army, and had been forced into joining the Republican guard, but once he had moved his family, against whom he had feared reprisals, to a place of safety, he deserted, and went into hiding.

The faith that Furman had shown in our Italian friend, Renzo Lucidi, when he assured me that between them they would look after Lieutenant Simpson's billets, was not misplaced. Lucidi, who had helped the organization from the start, and had been Simpson's principal assistant, now dropped all his business commitments, and devoted his full time to our work. He and Furman together managed to deal with Simpson's long list of billets, and whenever I had occasion to flash a warning to Furman that it was specially dangerous for him to be seen about the streets, Renzo's gallant French-born wife, Adrienne, went out, and delivered the money and supplies to escapers.

My warnings were, unfortunately, becoming ever more frequent, for the hatred of Germans which had fermented among the population of Rome (overt and underground equally), was now erupting in a rash of minor explosions, assassinations, and other unfriendly acts all over the city. Every bomb and every bullet resulted in a sudden surge of activity by the inflated security forces, and the harbouring of prisoners became so hazardous that a few Italian families broke under the strain, and begged us to remove the men in their care. We did so, of course, though it meant a shuffle of escapers at a time when everybody would have been better lying low, and when billet-space was exceedingly hard to find.

I suppose the narrowest escape of this period was that of an Italian named Giovanni, who had taken into his home the five men who had been evacuated from Mrs Chevalier's flat. All five were at home when the Fascists hammered at Giovanni's door. There was no alternative exit, but he bundled them through the French window, on to the tiny balcony outside the living-room, and drew the curtains across.

He then admitted the impatient Fascists, who fanned out through the flat, searched, and found nothing incriminating—probably no new experience for them at a time when everybody was denouncing everybody else—but just as they were leaving, their sergeant pointed to the curtained French window, and demanded," What's through there?"

"Only a balcony," said the sweating Giovanni, and offered him a drink.

The Fascist thanked him, and said he would like one very much —after he had made a routine check of the balcony. Giovanni, all hope gone, waited for the inevitable as the sergeant strode to the window, swept back the curtains, and stepped out on the balcony. Utter stillness followed.

"Well, where's the drink you promised?" asked the sergeant, striding briskly back into the room. In a daze Giovanni handed him the whole bottle.

After the Fascists had gone, Giovanni crossed himself, wiped away the sweat dripping from his chin, ventured on to the empty balcony, and peered down at the bare flagstones below. Then he heard a whisper, and from the balcony above a ladder slipped down; one by one, five Allied escapers made a hair-raising descent high above the streets of Rome, and their Italian 'padrone' realized that he owed his life and their freedom to his habit of keeping his household ladder on the balcony.

About this time there returned to Rome, after a brief and abortive attempt to reach the Allied lines at Anzio, an escaper who had experienced one of the closest shaves of all—Flight-Lieutenant E. Garrard-Cole. He had been in Rome for some months, and had helped Renzo Lucidi delivering food, although he did not then know of the existence of the organization. Our security system was such that officers occasionally helped in this way under the impression that they were assisting in a small *ad hoc* arrangement to aid British escapers, operated by their 'padrone' and a few Italian friends.

Garrard-Cole, a big man, who had provided, like a number of others, rather a problem for our wardrobe department, was riding on a tram, when he noticed to his discomfiture that he had attracted the attention of two uniformed Germans. Deciding not to press his luck, he got off, but they disembarked too, and followed him, keeping about twenty yards behind, and stopping whenever he stopped. He set off more briskly, but the Germans overtook him, one on each side, and demanded to see his identity card. He produced the false documents with which he had been supplied, and the Germans gave him some orders of which he clearly understood only two words, "Via Tasso." He had no alternative but to walk with them, but equally he had no intention of accompanying them all the way to the Gestapo headquarters.

Noting that they were armed only with pistols fastened in black holsters at their waists, and that neither looked particularly bright, the tall flight-lieutenant suddenly stuck out his long leg. The German on his right stumbled, and as he fell forward, Garrard-Cole helped him on the way with a mighty blow on the back of the neck, and hared off down the street. A bullet from the other German's pistol whistled past his ear as he plunged round the corner.

He dived into a familiar block of flats, hid behind the door as the angry Germans clattered past, and then ran up the stairs to the home of Renzo Lucidi. Shortly afterwards Germans swarmed into the area, but Renzo had foreseen this, and Garrard-Cole was safely, if uncomfortably, squashed into the small covering on the roof, which housed the mechanism of the lift, thoughtfully put out of action by Renzo. Given a change of raincoat and hat, Garrard-Cole eventually emerged from the building, and made his way past two or three groups of Germans searching for him. He was hand in hand with the Lucidis' small son, Maurice, who chattered continuously in Italian to his "father" all the way to safety.

It was an example of something we had always believed: that if Germans were told to look for a tall man in a light raincoat and a dark hat, they would never think of stopping a tall man in a dark raincoat and a light hat. I mused that if the enemy could be confused by a small change of clothing, then the alterations in Lieutenant Furman's appearance should destroy the scent utterly.

April brought a shower of blows on the Rome Organization, and one of the heaviest was not an arrest but nevertheless meant the end of the tremendous help we had received from Captain Trippi of the Swiss Legation. From the start, he had directed to us all the new arrivals who turned up in Rome knowing nothing of the organization, but aware that Switzerland was Britain's protecting power. Captain Trippi had also distributed food and clothing to escapers who called at his legation, had issued Red Cross parcels to ex-prisoners billeted in Rome, and, above all, had been largely responsible for the distribution of supplies to messengers on behalf of groups in the country areas.

Therefore I was shocked to learn from Sir D'Arcy Osborne that the Swiss had indicated that they could no longer provide assistance to ex-prisoners-of-war or anybody else liable for arrest. This unwelcome decision resulted from a "friendly talk" between the Swiss Minister and the German Ambassador.

The latter had explained that the German military authorities were aware that the Swiss were aiding escaped British prisoners-of-war. If it continued they might be forced to arrest the member of the Swiss Legation most implicated. In the face of this warning, and of the threat of arrest of a member of the legation staff, the Swiss Minister had decided that these activities must cease.

The German Ambassador, who was very friendly throughout the talk, observed that, after all, it was unnecessary for the Swiss to do this job, since it was notorious that the British Legation to the Holy See financed British prisoners-of-war in Rome on so generous a scale that British officers were often to be seen lunching luxuriously at expensive restaurants!

The luxurious lunches, as the Minister and I both knew, were possible only for those officers who had made some arrangement with Italians for cashing their own money, but whether or not that cynical German barb struck home, the principal result was still the same: the Swiss Legation was now out of bounds.

This meant that escapers in Rome could no longer collect Red Cross parcels, and orders were circulated to all billets immediately, but the Germans acted even more promptly. Three escapers were arrested at the entrance to the Swiss Legation before they received the warning that the place which they had come to look upon almost as their village-store was now under German observation.

The loss of Captain Trippi's assistance meant that much of the supply line to the country groups now had to be directed through Lieutenant Furman, who was already carrying out an immense task. Noting his first reports on money sent to the country, I grinned to myself. This was new territory for Furman, and he was unaware that in our organization the "wide boys" were in the country rather than the city.

> John [I wrote], the country boys are up to all the tricks. Some are: giving false names and numbers; saying there are four men in one place when there are two; Italians collecting the money, and handing over only limited amounts to the ex-prisoners, and doing absolutely anything to get extra money—often the chaps never give a penny to their 'padrones,' and just spend the money on drink. Therefore, as a general policy, we usually give for twos and threes about 1000 lire per head to begin with, and for larger groups (say twenty chaps) about 10,000 lire, until we have got a

line on the fellows. When we have checked up contacts and got receipts, and the details of the men appear to be O.K., we send about 2000 lire per man per month. The snag is that the contacts are up to all the games, and collect from as many places as possible before going back to the country. Quite natural, but we pay out on names only.

It was necessary, also, to beware of stool-pigeons. In the country the Germans were up to all sorts of tricks—they even employed women to trace the source of cash, and used men dressed as "poor worn-out ex-prisoners-of-war!" They had all the answers, including army pay-books, numbers of camps, and so on. So I wrote, "Do be careful—and move about as little as possible."

The problems of escapers who turned most of their subsistence allowance into drink was always present. In Rome it led to rash behaviour at a time when Italian lives were already too cheap; in the country, where the risk to security was small, it usually meant that Italian helpers were kept short of recompense, since the allowance could not meet both subsistence and a generous supply of *vino*.

Although I had to take stern action in severe cases, I tried to remember that the men in hiding were leading lives of drab monotony, unenlivened by the interest, which active helpers had, of a worthwhile job to be done, so I sought to make the men realize their responsibility to the Italians, rather than merely to reprimand them.

To one group of five men who had been partaking fairly freely I wrote:

The one thing that an escaped prisoner-of-war must avoid is drawing attention to himself, and his freedom depends on thinking and acting quickly. It is now several months since the Italian armistice, and it seems probable that the Allied occupation will soon take place. Yet the number of ex-prisoners-of-war recaptured recently has been greater than at any other period. More than ever now, our enemies are making strenuous efforts to recapture as many ex-prisoners as they can, and more than ever now, the only reasonable course is to lie low. Remember the risk is not only personal, but will involve the people who have risked everything in order to try and keep you from being recaptured. I realize that you are not living under the happiest circumstances, but you must apply a little self-discipline : you risk recapture—others risk much more. If, after reading this note and after careful thought, you feel incapable of carrying on the unnatural existence of living indoors the whole time, then in fairness to others the only decent thing is to push off again into the country. We will help you as far as we can with money—but, whatever you do, think first before you chuck away at the last moment all you've gone through since you escaped.

Although life was both safer and cheaper in the country, I knew, even in the security of my office in the Vatican, that the escapers in the rural areas were leading a precarious existence. I had good reason to realize this, for in April I received many disturbing reports from the country of recaptures, and some of shootings.

There was little the organization could do for escapers who, caught in civilian clothes at a time when the Germans were not much concerned about the Geneva Convention, were promptly sentenced to death, but we did at least manage, in one or two cases, to get a last letter home from the doomed man. These letters, written with paper and pencil supplied by a village priest, who, if his action had been discovered, would undoubtedly have faced the firing-squad with the ex-prisoners, were often stark in their simplicity.

One written on April 15 by a Glasgow boy read :

DEAR MOTHER AND FATHER AND FAMILY,

This is the last letter I will be able to write as I get shot today. Dear family, I have laid down my life for my country and everything that was dear to me. I hope this war will soon be over, so that you will all have peace for ever. Your ever loving soldier-son and brother,

WILLIE

A brief accompanying note just said :

Just a few words to tell you that your son, Willie, was shot because he was caught and arrested in civilian clothes. I assure you that he received the comfort of our religion, and died in peace.

THE REVEREND FATHER IL CAPPELLANO,
P. ANTONIO INTRECCIALAGLI

The priest's note might have seemed stilted, and even a little austere, but he had risked his own life to enable a doomed man to give his family all he had left to give—a word of farewell.

I read such notes with an ache, yet while they were saddening, they were inspiring too. They strengthened my determination that the 3739 men now in the care of the Rome Organization should be kept out of German hands until they could be liberated to fight once more against the cold inhumanity of the most bestial enemy that ever faced the forces of Christianity and civilization.

It was, however, becoming difficult to fulfil that determination. In a month eight escapers had been shot, and forty others returned to prison camps, and more than twenty Italian helpers had been arrested. Most of the recaptures had been due to denunciations, but no fewer than sixteen escapers had been picked up in the streets during routine checks, three of whom would have evaded arrest if they had not been drinking.

Putting Lieutenant Colin Lesslie in the picture—for although his large group "up the hill" remained mercifully free from Fascist attention, they sometimes felt they were out of touch with what was going on—I wrote :

> We have had a very black time recently; eight chaps have been shot in the country (some forty kilometres north of Rome), Bill S. and over forty other chaps retaken; the Swiss have had to close down so far as ex-prisoners are concerned; and three of "Golf's" friends have had to go into strict hiding. Most of the denunciations have been due to a semi-padre; fortunately, he did not know anything about your position—although we are of the opinion that they will not raid any places like yours. Added to these black times, a lot of our boys have been going about contrary to orders, and some have been getting drunk. I think the waiting is getting them down (but it is slowly getting us all down). However, I am still full of optimism, personally, in spite of all. There is definite evidence that the Huns have pulled out a hell of a lot of their heavy stuff. I only hope that the recent activity points to them pulling out too.

For all my expressed optimism, I knew that the odds against us were mounting. Enemy thrusts were coming more quickly than the organization could parry them, and all the time the number of escapers on our books was increasing sharply, while the number of helpers was falling drastically.

April added 300 names to the total strength of our underground army, but for the first time the number in Rome fell by thirty to 150. There were two reasons for this : firstly, many

of our "Romans" had been recaptured; secondly, I had decided
that there must be no new billetings in the city. This decision had
been forced by arithmetical common sense. Rome contained only
about a twentieth of our escapers, but absorbed a quarter of
our expenditure, and in the last four black weeks it had accounted
for three-quarters of our losses through recapture. Living in Rome
was thus both expensive and risky.

On April 23 I therefore issued a long general order through a
distribution list that would have made an administrative assistant
at the War Office boggle: "To Golf, Eyerish, John, Fanny,
Horace, Mr Bishop, Sandro, Spike, Emma, Dutchpa, Sailor,
Rinso."

After outlining the developments of the last few weeks, I told
them all:

Current propaganda in Rome is that the Allies will not arrive
before the Autumn. This is strong propaganda when coupled
with the food shortage and with the static condition of the bridgehead and Cassino fronts. The Fascists and S.S. have been, during
the last four weeks, and still are, far more active in the rounding
up of Allied ex-prisoners than at any time since the Italian
armistice. These facts point to the following conclusions:

1. Fascist gangs, working in collaboration with the Gestapo,
are out to make a name for themselves by rounding up all ex-
prisoners in Rome.

2. The work of finding billets, paying 'padrones,' contacting
and supplying men, is more difficult than ever before.

3. The longer men remain cooped up indoors, the more
desperate becomes their attitude of mind, and, stimulated by a
drink or two, the more likely they are to take ill-advised action.

In view of the foregoing I regret to have to issue the following
instructions: No more ex-prisoners are to be billeted in Rome;
any arriving in the city will be given financial help, and advised
to return to the country. Ex-prisoners must on no account leave
their billets unless they receive warning of an imminent raid. The
practice of going from one billet to another to visit friends must
cease forthwith. If forced to make a run for it ex-prisoners must
leave Rome, and hide out in the country. Dashing to another
billet only compromises additional people. A lump sum of 6000
lire per man for the month of May will be given to you. This is
for maintenance for May, and should allow for some ready cash
in an emergency. In some cases the lump sum may be paid

to the ex-prisoner; in other cases it will require to be paid in instalments, as some of the boys would convert the cash into assets of a more 'liquid' character.

As if we had not troubles enough, we suddenly lost the use of the centre which had been our operational headquarters from the very beginning of the organization. This followed further complaints from the Germans, which caused the Vatican authorities, without warning, to close all outside approaches to the Collegio Teutonicum. Monsignor O'Flaherty's busy room, for so long the hub of the organization, was now out of bounds, and Lieutenant Furman and the other outside agents were completely cut off from their headquarters.

For a little while there was no contact at all, until a tenuous line of communication was established by the resourceful monsignor, who arranged to meet agents actually inside the great basilica of St Peter's, to which he and they alike continued to have access. This expedient, however, was fraught with danger, for there were always people inside the church, and the tall monsignor was a familiar figure, whose meetings with others in such a public place must have been observed. Such meetings also meant considerable risk for the agent, and the passing of letters or supplies of money was virtually impossible. I felt it could be only a matter of time before this arrangement led to further arrests, including the one I feared most of all—that of Monsignor O'Flaherty.

It was the astonishing John May who finally managed to restore a link between headquarters and outside agents. He contrived, by means which he never fully disclosed, to persuade the Swiss Guards to permit a few people, including Lieutenant Furman, to visit their guardroom beside the gate. The Swiss agreed that when these privileged visitors called they would contact the British Legation on the internal telephone system. John May could then go down to the guardroom—the limit of movement permitted to him—and converse in relative privacy.

This arrangement meant that money could be handed out once again, and that I could send messages to Furman, who, after reading them, burnt them before leaving the guardroom. He, in turn, was able to write reports to me while in the guardroom waiting for John May. It meant, also, that Furman had to memorize all the instructions I sent him before leaving, and that he had to commit to memory everything that he wanted to report to me before arriving.

A damned nuisance, this present arrangement—not being able to get inside [he wrote in his first report, which covered half a dozen Vatican forms, used by applicants for appointments with priests and officials]. However, I hope it will soon sort itself out, one way or another. I'm dashing off this note while I am waiting for John to come. I am told I have half an hour to wait. . . .

Despite his annoyance with the new system, Furman was in a good mood, for the southern battle-front, after a long winter of immobility, was livening up again, and rumours had drifted up to Rome to dispel much of the apathy that had developed during April. Furman noted the changed atmosphere, and ended his report:

I have a feeling something is in the air. I can sense a curious excitement abroad, as though big things are about to happen—everybody knows except me! Anyway, I think they'll be here by the end of May. What are the odds?

Furman sent me more than just his greetings: despite all the difficulties with which he was now faced, his message was accompanied by a bottle of genuine Scotch whisky.

It is absolutely wonderful [I replied]. I enclose 2000 lire for the bottle already sent: buy a drink with the balance for self and "Rinso."

Back came a prompt reply from the irrespressible Furman:

The bottle was a present to cheer you up in your loneliness! However, I will keep the 2000 lire—and buy some more if I can find it. Cheerio!

Security had now been tightened to such an extent that many of the escapers billeted in Rome had no clear idea where their money was coming from, and occasionally even our own leading agents collided with each other in the deliberate fog of our security arrangements.

Reporting the discovery of a South African corporal in Rome, Furman told me:

I met this lad to-day. He hasn't yet had money for May, but
he expects 2000 lire to-morrow. The money apparently comes
from here, but is handled by several people before he gets it. Can
you check up on this?

I knew the real contact to be "Mr Bishop," an Italian named
Giuseppe Gonzi, who distributed through other Italians, but there
seemed to be no useful purpose in passing on this information.
There was only one way to preserve maximum security and
simultaneously satisfy my billeting officer's curiosity—I transferred the corporal to Lieutenant Furman's list.

In a later report Furman wrote :

To-day "Rinso" told me he had paid 4000 lire to an American
called Sergakis, who had received only 2000 from an Italian named
Messina.

On this occasion strict security had cost us a tenner, for Sergakis had received full allowance for the month, and I had a
receipt signed by the man himself.

Information about doubtful or difficult characters reached me
fairly frequently, and in the isolation of the Vatican I had to take
it all at face value, and circulate warnings accordingly, at the risk
of being excessively cautious.

On one occasion I wrote to Furman :

Sergeant B. has already received a full allowance for May, and
has now moved his billet against orders, and has said he will tell
S.S. everything if interfered with. Leave alone. I shall deal with
him afterwards.

The truth was, of course, that this was one of those cases,
happily rare, of a bumptious character who took a cocksure line
with priests and Italian messengers that he would not have dared
to take with officers. In this case Furman had the advantage over
me of first-hand knowledge, and wrote back about the blustery
sergeant :

Know all about him. He's a bit of a rogue, but the S.S. business is all balderdash.

Personal knowledge once led Furman to billet two South
African officers in Rome despite the general order that all new
arrivals were to be sent straight back to the country—and this
time I had the advantage of knowing something of these two.

They are all right [wrote Furman, reporting their arrival]. I vetted them personally, and we have mutual friends. I wonder if they could go 'up the hill' or to some other quiet but safe place?

I replied:

Both these gentlemen wrote to "Mount," who passed their letters to me: they appear to believe that the inside of the Vat. is like a large residential area, and "Mount" only has to invite them in. But they appear to have had a bad time, and obviously think we should do all we can for them. The hill is out of the question at the moment; can they be put in the apartment? Anyway, let them stay in Rome if they wish to.

Sometimes every one was in the dark. One lone British captain made his way to Rome, got himself taken in by an Italian family, and lived happily in the middle of the city for several months before either he or the organization became aware of each other's existence.

On another occasion Lieutenant Furman wrote to ask:

What English officer is living at Porta Pia? We have had a tip-off that some one there is to be raided, but I know of nobody living there.

We checked thoroughly through all the files, but they revealed nothing. However, I circulated warnings to all contacts in the Porta Pia area, in the hope they would reach the billet of the officer.

The circulating of warnings was of vital importance, but they did not always succeed in their purpose. The failure of two men to receive one message lost us the home of Mrs Chevalier, and put the gallant, selfless widow and her copious family out of the escape game.

We knew well enough that her house was being watched, for the alert Mrs Chevalier herself had been quick to take notice of the two thin men in plain clothes, accompanied by an Italian woman, who spent most of their day in the café on the other side of the street. When the two men strolled across, and casually questioned the porter of the block about her, the porter lost no time in warning Mrs Chevalier, who, through her curtains, could see them settling themselves comfortably again in the café—within arm's reach of the telephone.

There were, of course, no escapers billeted with Mrs Chevalier at the time, but she had been 'Mother' to so many living in other billets that she inevitably had frequent social calls from her grateful ex-lodgers. I would have been the last to presume that my "stay indoors" orders had succeeded in ending this somewhat thoughtless practice, but fortunately, Mrs Chevalier, who had rarely shown enough concern for her own safety, now realized that a single visit might be her death warrant. She managed to get a message to Lieutenant Furman that her house was under close observation, and without wasting time he immediately flashed warnings to everybody he thought might be tempted to call at the hospitable flat. He ordered escapers that under no circumstances at all were they to go near the place.

But two, Martin and Everett, an American, never received the warning, and next morning they strolled casually into the block of flats, unaware that hostile Gestapo eyes were firmly riveted on their disappearing backs. This was the very sort of situation I had sought to prevent by the general order to stay indoors, which they were flagrantly disobeying. With leisurely unconcern, they made their way up the five flights of stairs, but as soon as they saw Mrs Chevalier when she opened the door, they knew something was wrong.

"Go, go!" said Mrs Chevalier urgently. "The Germans are waiting outside!"

Martin and Everett realized that they might be heading straight into the arms of the Gestapo, but they turned without hesitation and ran down the stairs. Quite properly, their thoughts were fixed on putting as much distance as possible between Mrs Chevalier and themselves before they were caught. Slowing to a walk at the foot of the stairs, they strolled out of the main entrance into the street, and, forewarned, immediately noticed a thin man in a raincoat emerge from the café opposite. They quickened their pace, and so did the Gestapo agent, but at the first opportunity, before he had crossed the road, they swung into a narrow courtyard, and immediately broke into an all-out gallop.

Back at the flat, Mrs Chevalier had already put her last-ditch evacuation plan into operation. One at a time, at brief intervals, and without baggage of any sort, her daughters and son were leaving, turning in different directions as they emerged from the front door. Mrs Chevalier was the last to go, and had little hope that

she would be allowed to get far, but the simple ruse was successful. It did not occur to the remaining agent in the café that among
people constantly drifting out of the block of flats was an entire
family abandoning its home. Presumably, his orders had been to
watch for British ex-prisoners, and the possibility that the bait
might trickle out of the trap had never occurred to him.

By different routes, Mrs Chevalier and her family made their
way to the home of a friend some distance away, and one by one,
some after deliberately long walks, her family arrived, to meet a
growing chorus of welcome. Eventually, the whole family moved
to a farm comfortably on the outskirts, where they remained until
the Germans left Rome. We were able to send assistance to them,
though it could never represent more than a fraction of what the
Allies owed to Mrs Henrietta Chevalier.

The safety of this family was the only consoling feature of what
otherwise was a very sorry incident indeed. Reporting on what
had happened, Lieutenant Furman wrote:

A big flap ensued, and the family's evacuation may be a good
thing in one way, because there was always the danger that if
the place was raided they would have given the whole show away.
"Mrs M." told me she was hard up, and I gave her 3000 lire.

I sighed as I read. If only people would obey their orders,
including unpopular and even apparently unreasonable ones,
fewer good lives would be endangered. But I contented myself
with commenting to Furman on the evacuation of the Cheva-
liers. "A very wise precaution."

As for Martin and Everett, I had some thoughts ready for them,
but they had disappeared. Lieutenant Furman pursued energetic
inquiries, but could find no trace of them at all, and after three
days we had to presume that they were lost. Then, through Italian
contacts, Furman accidentally discovered that both had eluded
their German pursuer, and were safe and sound in a billet the
existence of which had been completely unknown to us.

Meanwhile inquiries were continuing in the attempt to find
out what had happened to Bill Simpson. Our efforts were
strenuous but unavailing, for, had we but known it, Simpson himself had completely covered his tracks. And the Gestapo had yet
another blow for us—they caught one of the priests, and dragged
him away to their dreaded headquarters at Via Tasso.

12

Open City

"DON'T lie!" shouted the Gestapo commandant, landing another vicious blow with the back of his hand across the face of the half-conscious, half-clothed priest. "We know who you are," he went on, "you are an English officer. You can't fool us, disguising yourself as a priest."

One of the things I dreaded most had happened—the Gestapo had pounced on a priest for 'questioning' in their own sadistic manner.

Father Anselmo Musters, the Netherlands-born priest who was coded as "Dutchpa," realized that the Gestapo must have got on to something, for he knew very well that I was the officer who had masqueraded as a priest. He himself, moreover, had been working continuously with Monsignor O'Flaherty from the earliest days, and he was horribly aware that he had knowledge enough to secure the downfall of the whole organization if the Germans could get it out of him. Silently, in the cacophony of shouted questions and savage blows, he prayed for strength to withstand.

On the previous day, in the bright May sunshine that turned Rome into a city of sparkling light, he had been striding through the streets, active on the organization's business. He had just left the billet of a South African sergeant, and was on his way to two others, when he realized that a grim-looking man in plain clothes was keeping an even distance behind him. He stopped for a moment, and the plain-clothes man stopped too, looking unconvincingly into a shop window. Thoughtfully Father Musters strode on, but he changed his course, and turned towards the cathedral-like church of Santa Maria Maggiore. Before he could set foot on the vast flight of steps which, running more than the width of the church's columned façade, marked the limit of Vatican extra-territorial property, the plain-clothes man overtook him, and ordered him to halt.

"Identity documents," he demanded, in a strong, guttural accent, which left no doubt about his nationality.

"I will show them to you on the steps of the church," said Father Musters, striding on, and resting his hopes on the moderate protection of extra-territorial sanctity.

The Gestapo man jumped in front of him, to bar his way, but Father Musters strode round him, and started up the side steps. Pulling a pistol from inside his coat, the German ran up after him, and commanded him to stop, but with only a glance at the ugly muzzle waving in his face, Father Musters pushed the man unceremoniously aside, and gained the top of the steps.

Then he felt a vicious blow on the back of his head, and as he crumpled in a daze, he fell forward almost into the church— and unmistakably on to Vatican property. A Palatine guard, who from within the door had seen the priest struck from behind with the butt of the pistol, rushed forward to drag the half-conscious priest into the church. The German, pocketing his pistol, turned angrily on his heel, ran down the steps, and disappeared across the *piazza*.

Helped by the guard into a small vestry, Father Musters got in touch with the Vatican authorities, who told him to remain where he was until the following morning, when he would be collected by an escort, and taken back to his Mother house. "You will be quite safe where you are for the time being," he was told by his superiors.

They were wrong. Less than half an hour later a large squad of uniformed S.S. men, all fully armed, completely surrounded the great church, and one group, led by an S.S. captain, marched up the steps, and into the church. Pushing aside the protesting Palatine guard, the jack-booted Germans, sub-machine-guns at the ready, clattered noisily through the still aisles to the room where Father Musters sat.

"On your feet," commanded the German captain. "You will come with us."

"This is extra-territorial property," replied the Dutch priest evenly. "You have no right to burst in here. I have been ordered by my superiors to stay here."

For answer, the captain turned, took a sub-machine-gun from one of his men, and swung it with all his force on to the priest's head. For the second time in half an hour, Father Musters crumpled to the ground, and he was barely conscious as two S.S. men grabbed him by the feet, and dragged him through the church, out of the door, and down to the *piazza*, his head bumping on each successive step as they descended.

He still had not fully recovered when he was bundled into the Gestapo headquarters at Via Tasso, but was sufficiently conscious to realize that his arrival had generated an atmosphere of triumph among the Germans. Gradually he became aware that they were under the impression that they had captured an English colonel in disguise.

His clothes were torn from him and searched minutely, every garment being stripped of its lining and opened up at the seams. Even his shoes were taken completely to pieces. The Germans found nothing that could incriminate him, but this did not deter them, and they screamed and bellowed constantly at him, "Confess—you're an English spy."

With his arms handcuffed behind his back, and his feet heavily manacled, the priest was interrogated daily for a fortnight by two S.S. officers, who questioned him endlessly about an organization which, they said, the authorities knew existed, to assist Allied ex-prisoners-of-war. They even showed him a diagram, disconcertingly accurate, which they had made of the organization, and threatened him with death if he did not tell them where he fitted into it. Steadfastly, through all forms of physical and mental maltreatment, he maintained he knew nothing about it.

Because of the circumstances of the priest's arrest, and the fact that he had contacted the Vatican, I was soon informed that he had fallen into enemy hands. While the ecclesiastical authorities went to work to secure his release, I immediately put our normal security arrangements into operation. Working on the assumption that every one of the billets known to the captured priest must be considered compromised, I sent warnings to all the 'padrones,' and had all the prisoners evacuated to other accommodation well before the curfew descended on Rome.

In the event it proved unnecessary, since not one of the addresses known to Father Musters was ever raided, for although constantly under threat of death, and brutally and repeatedly beaten up, the gallant priest stood up to his inquisitors for three dreadful weeks without revealing a single word about the organization. On the twenty-first day even the past-masters of interrogation admitted themselves defeated, and threw Father Musters into a dark cell. There he remained in absolute isolation for a fortnight, and then was put on a train for Germany.

Had he reached Germany, his fate would have been sealed, but Father Musters, though battered, bloody, and bruised, was by no means broken in spirit, and when the train halted at Florence he eluded his guards, made a dash, and got clean away. He headed at once for Rome, but by the time he arrived it was June, and he found a very different city from the one he had left.

On May 18 Cassino, the stumbling-block and pivot of the whole stubborn, static line in the south of Italy, fell at last. Polish forces marched into the hilltop monastery, and the Allies began to sweep northward through Italy. A new spirit began to surge through Rome, and I found myself confronted with a wealth of offers of help. Everybody who had the slightest suspicion of the existence of the organization now wanted to join it.

With the Allied occupation of Rome imminent, Italians whose co-operation had not been conspicuous in the past, were falling over themselves in the scramble to offer their services to anybody with the slightest claim to be an enemy of Germany. Every one who had denounced anyone during the long night of German occupation sought frantically to render some small service to the other side, and even the few renegade Allied nationals, who had earlier thrown in their lot with the Axis, sent out pitiful feelers, in the hope of putting themselves back on the right side of the fence.

I was delighted, for although I realized that most of these came from sources that we would earlier have avoided at all costs, there was no reason why we should not now make some use of them. Of course, I never contemplated using any of these Vicar of Bray characters for billeting or supply work, but there were two services which they could render without risk to our organization. They could take over a large part of the illegal and onerous task of buying up on the black market the prodigous supplies we needed, and they could act as one-way information sources, collecting odd scraps of knowledge about enemy activity, which we collated and passed to the advancing British forces.

Clearly the end was now at last almost in sight, but there remained plenty of time for a fatal slip before the cup of liberation reached our lips, so rather than slackening the security rein, I

tightened it still further. There was always the possibility that
the Germans would raid the Vatican as their hold on Rome
weakened, and my feeling of personal responsibility for 3500
escapers, of whom 136 were in Rome, grew with every passing
day, for with more and more of our enemies dropping back into
the city and its environs, the risk of recapture rose steadily.

For an escaper to be taken now, with liberation so close, was a
tragedy, yet there were constant reminders of the danger, and
Lieutenant Furman, although now travelling about the city much
less than before, seemed to be permanently poised on the very
brink of recapture. On one occasion he was out delivering Ameri-
can-issue tobacco, bought on the black market but still in its
original colourful wrappings, when the tram on which he was
travelling screeched to a sudden stop. The Italian Fascists had
set up an unusually impressive road-block, he was uncomfortably
aware of the incriminating evidence in his pockets. Two or three
American packets of tobacco would invite dangerous questions,
if only on the grounds of black-marketeering, but his small notebook was a much bigger risk, for although in a code of his own,
it contained the addresses of many of his billets. Yet he could not
throw it away, or even part of it, without being seen. With his
hand in his pocket, he tore out the pages, and screwed them into
a tight little ball. He did not dare to throw it on to the floor, but
as the passengers crowded together to leave the tram, he found
himself pressed against a stout Italian matron with a heaving
bosom and a crowded shopping-basket, so he dropped the incriminating pellet into the basket among the vegetables.

The organization's secrets would next, in all probability, be
found in some suburban kitchen, but Furman was not worried,
since the scribbled pages were completely meaningless in themselves, and none of the notes or addresses or other personal hiero-
glyphs were capable of interpretation by any one but himself.

He was still, of course, left with the gaudy American packets
of tobacco, but these were less dangerous. By now the men in
the tram were being marshalled out on the street, so working
again by touch, Furman tore open the packets, emptied the
tobacco into his pocket, and unobtrusively dropped the labels behind him. He had tactfully taken his place at the end of the queue,
and by the time he reached the checking-table there was nothing
incriminating about him except a pocket full of loose tobacco.

Unlike the disgruntled tram passengers who had gone before
him, Furman did not protest and gesticulate at the table, but,
with a silent, haughty smile, handed over his impressive collection
of identity documents. His Vatican card and his pass signed by
the German Minister were papers of a much higher level than
those the Fascists usually unearthed, and Furman could see the
Fascist officers looking curiously towards him as they conferred
over them in the background. Without speaking a word, he maintained his aloof, slightly patronizing attitude, as though he fully
understood that the common soldiery had to carry out its menial
duty. His papers were returned, and he accepted them with no
more than a patient smile. He nodded to the officer who seemed
to be in charge, turned and walked slowly away, swaggering
slightly—and not until he was safely round a corner of the street
did he give in to his urge to get away as fast as his legs would
carry him.

I presented my documents, and got away without having to
speak a word [Furman reported gleefully to me]. Herewith one
bottle of brandy, 800 lire. I still have 1200 of yours.

What an escape [I replied]. Please don't bother about any more
booze, John—it is far too much trouble. You and "Rinso" have a
drink with the balance, to celebrate your latest escape!

But Furman was still in trouble. When he returned on the
evening of his narrow escape to his billet, in Via Dalmazia, he
was warned to leave at once because a visit from the police was
imminent, not because of the organization, but following a
burglary at the business address of his 'padrone,' Luciana. Furman, fortunately, had an alternative billet within ten minutes'
walk, at the flat of Luciana's brother, Tonini, to which he had
an invitation to go any time he was in difficulties.

A week later he had to change his billet again, and this time he
made his journey through the streets in company with Bruno,
the Republican Guard deserter, who was still wearing his officer's
uniform, with revolver at the waist. Furman also was armed,
with a tiny ornamental pistol made for a lady's handbag, but
effective enough at close range. Moreover, his pockets were stuffed
with Rome Organization money and documents.

With this compromising evidence, they were stopped in Via

Clitunno by two men who demanded to see their identity documents, and at the same time produced their own, showing them to be plain-clothes Fascist police. Furman and the deserter handed over their identity cards, and as the Fascists studied them, Furman, one hand in his pocket, gently slid back the safety-catch on his miniature pistol, and his companion unobtrusively undid the button on his revolver holster.

Both had the same thought, that it was now too near the end of the road to be taken without a fight. But the documents satisfied the Fascists, and they waved the English officer and the Italian deserter on their way without further interrogation. Once again Furman got away without speaking a word—at any rate, only one, "Grazie."

So once again I have to congratulate you on a narrow escape [I wrote]. Please pay "Rinso" in full—and give a little to "Mrs Rinso" for her excellent work.

Adrienne's "excellent work" at this stage included an ingenious attempt to rescue Lieutenant Bill Simpson, who was, we were now sure, in the Regina Coeli. The blonde Frenchwoman suggested that she should go to the double-agent, Dr Cipolla, and ask him to approach his German contacts with the proposal that they should release two of the British officers held at the prison, ensuring that they knew their freedom was due to Cipolla's efforts. He was to tell the Germans that he would then be able to get in with the British, and so continue as a valuable agent for the Germans after they had been forced to leave Rome. The two prisoners whose release he was to effect were Lieutenant Simpson and Captain John Armstrong, who had never been in touch with the organization, but whom we knew to have been in the Regina Coeli for the last nine months.

The scheme was complicated but neat, and it put Dr Cipolla into as curious a rôle as any underground agent ever filled. He was already working simultaneously for the Germans and the British, but now, on behalf of the British, he was to pretend to be a German agent pretending to be a British agent, so as to send information to the Germans.

Cipolla welcomed Adrienne's scheme, for it gave him the opportunity to do something for the Allies, who would soon be in

Rome, and at the same time enhance his standing with the Germans. No double-agent could wish for more.

He went straight to the German commandant, explained the plan—which, of course, he put forward as his own—and asked if he could take out two British prisoners of his choice. The commandant, realizing the inevitability of an imminent withdrawal from Rome, and the desirability of leaving a well-placed agent in the city, quickly agreed, and handed to Cipolla a list of all the British prisoners in the Regina Coeli.

Cipolla, scanning through it, saw with alarm that it did not contain the names of the two men he had undertaken to collect. He could not inquire about them without giving the whole show away, and he could scarcely disown the scheme or suggest coming back another day, so he chose a couple of names on the list at random. That was how, much to their surprise, two English civilians, who had been interned since Italy's entry into the war, came to be prematurely released.

The ruse could not be used again, and Lieutenant Furman and the Lucidis could not imagine where it had gone wrong. But back at headquarters I had located the fly in the ointment. Blon Kiernan had told me that the German military authorities had made inquiries at the Irish Legation about an Irishman named William O'Flynn, who was supposed to be employed at the Vatican—and had received the inevitable reply that no one of that name was known to the legation.

This was bad news indeed, for O'Flynn was the name that had been used on Simpson's false documents, and the German inquiry meant that he was still sticking to a story which the Irish reply had now proved to be false. The position was thus extremely delicate. Simpson was not protected as a combatant prisoner-of-war, and no diplomatic intercession could be made for him without confirming that he was a British officer with an assumed identity, which would give the Germans every excuse for shooting him as a spy.

We were still seeking for a solution when we heard from Simpson himself, in a letter smuggled out of the prison, and delivered to us a fortnight later. He wrote :

Three weeks here to-day, and still waiting for something to happen. Not even interrogated so far. After one week they asked my name and occupation and nationality—William O'Flynn, Vatican, Irish, as always. I protested, and asked if they had inquired or would advise somebody that I was here. They say they can't do anything, and I'll have to wait the pleasure of the S.S. Don't worry—there will be no complications. I shall be very grateful if you will give the bearer 10,000 lire for me. If the pay-bloke wishes he can debit it to me, but let him understand that I shall only use part of it myself. Further, if I am still here when it arrives it shall be given to others—that's fixed. Kindest regards and auguri to all acquaintances; and many thanks to your good self for all your assistance.

BILL

I was acutely conscious that all the assistance we could give to Simpson at the moment did not amount to much. I sent the 10,000 lire at once, though without much hope that it would ever reach its destination, and I also sent something more important— a warning to Simpson that his claim to Irish nationality had already been broken down by the Germans.

In fact, the message did not get through, for he was now in the one wing of the prison, a semi-basement, guarded solely by Germans. We had managed to establish a fairly successful service of information and supplies to prisoners in the Fascist parts of the prison, but even the substantial bribes paid by the Rome Organization could not pierce the German wing. The Italian black-market go-between could find no way through to Simpson.

We now had no way of knowing whether Simpson was dead or vociferously claiming prisoner-of-war status. The only thing that was evident was that his future was not bright. Yet when things seemed blackest, and I was beginning to despair, Monsignor O'Flaherty had a surprising visitor.

The caller was a Roman nobleman, with whom I had been in contact earlier under rather different circumstances. I had helped to smuggle his sister into the Vatican, away from the clutches of the Fascists, who were searching for her. It was one of our more audacious enterprises, and was the only occasion when a woman managed to take part in the Vatican formality of changing the guard. Wearing the uniform of a Swiss guard, which had been 'borrowed' for her by John May, the lady slipped through the gate, and unobtrusively joined on the end of a troop while the guard was being changed at midnight. I was waiting with the monsignor and John May, hidden in the deep shadows round a corner which we knew the marching column would pass. Standing with our backs flat against the wall, seeing but unseen, we watched the Swiss Guards tramp by only a yard away, and as the end of the column passed us, Monsignor O'Flaherty reached out a black-sleeved arm, grabbed the imposter's shoulder, and tugged her quickly into the shadows beside us.

It was over in a second, and the Swiss Guards marched on without noticing anything amiss: the lady pulled off the uniform, and put on a raincoat which we had brought for her, and then accompanied John May and me to the British Legation, where, unknown to the Minister, she remained in hiding until we had been able to make arrangements for her to stay at the legation of one of the South American Republics.

This time the nobleman was calling as an emissary from none other than the man we hated above all in Rome, Piedro Koch, the chief of the barbaric Fascist neo-Gestapo, who were in charge of all the recaptured members of our organization in the Regina Coeli. Koch had seen the red light, and, realizing that if he remained in Rome after the liberation he was more likely to be physically torn apart than quietly shot, he was making arrangements to go north when the Germans withdrew.

"I think he has no illusions," said the emissary. "He wants to make a bargain with you. He says that if the monsignor will arrange to place his wife and mother in hiding in a religious house when he goes, he, in exchange, will ensure that the monsignor's friends are left in the Regina Coeli instead of being transported to Germany."

The monsignor, however, was far from confident that he could trust the Fascist to keep his side of the bargain, and, with his usual wise foresight, he decided to make sure.

"Tell Koch I agree to his suggestion on one condition," he told the emissary. "As evidence of his good faith, he must first deliver safely to me the two British officers who are in the Regina Coeli—Lieutenant Simpson and Captain Armstrong. If he does that I shall make the arrangements he desires for his wife and mother."

When Monsignor O'Flaherty told me what had been going on I became more optimistic, and wrote to Furman, "Have great hopes of getting Bill out to-morrow."

Koch accepted the condition imposed by the monsignor, and agreed to extricate the two officers forthwith.

Shortly afterwards, sitting in his cell, Bill Simpson heard a request for "Lieutenant Simpson" on the prison's loudspeaker system, but because my message had not reached him he was still unaware that his pose as an Irishman had been broken down. He thought it was a trap, and said nothing. Nor was Captain Armstrong forthcoming, and the emissary reported failure.

This placed Monsignor O'Flaherty in a dilemma. Realizing that Simpson must be maintaining his pose, he knew that it would be necessary to reveal the assumed name of O'Flynn to Koch, if the Fascist's desire to help his family was to be turned to Simpson's advantage, and there were obvious dangers in such a course. But the alternative was worse. The Germans already knew that Simpson was not who he said he was, and if he could not be released from prison before the withdrawal his future was black, for he would either be investigated and executed, or shot out of hand before the evacuation. The monsignor made his decision, and told the emissary to inform Koch that Lieutenant Simpson might be found under the name of O'Flynn, but what name Captain Armstrong was using, he had no idea.

This time I was not so optimistic, and I replied to an inquiry by Furman :

> Our efforts for Bill seem to be failing. However, we have not given up hope yet, and are still trying.

While Monsignor O'Flaherty concentrated on life-saving, a task at which he was singularly adept, I found many other matters demanding attention as the Allied advance rolled on towards Rome, particularly the collection and despatch of information on German troop movements. Beyond the city the sound of battle was already audible, but Furman and the other escapers could only guess what would happen next. They could see German columns being withdrawn from the battle line, and much heavy equipment moving steadily northward, but for all any of us knew, the Germans were still prepared to stand and turn the Eternal City into a second Stalingrad, defending it street by street, until nothing but ashes remained.

Cut off from most first-hand information, I was nevertheless in a better position than most of us to make a prediction about the immediate future of Rome, for Blon Kiernan, after another social call on Prince Bismarck, had passed on the information that the Germans intended to declare it an open city. This was splendid news, for although we had prepared to protect ex-prisoners during street fighting by sending them down to the catacombs, it would have been difficult, if not impossible, to keep going through a prolonged period of siege. But if the Germans withdrew without putting up a fight our escapers could remain in their billets without much danger.

Since I was still a prisoner in the Vatican, I was considerably surprised to find myself the first Briton in Rome to establish direct contact with the spearhead of the Allied advance. On June 2 an armoured attack thrust past the Pope's great summer villa at Castel Gandolfo, where Paul Freyberg had begun his strange journey to internment, and a British liaison officer came across the short-wave radio equipment used to maintain contact with Rome.

Shortly afterwards an excited John May came to me, and said, "I've just had a message from the Vatican radio-station. They are in contact with a British officer at Castel Gandolfo who wants to know if he can speak to somebody British."

"I'll deal with it," I replied gladly. "Where is it?"

"There's an operator already on the way here with a portable set. All part of the service," said John May blandly.

The Italian operator set up his equipment near my window, called up the villa, and handed the microphone over to me.

"Who are you?" crackled a voice.

"Major Derry, First Field Regiment."

"Where the hell are you?" asked the liaison officer.

"In the Vatican," I answered.

"Where did you say?" asked the unbelieving voice.

"In the Vatican. Can I help you?"

"Yes—have you any idea what is going on in Rome?"

At that moment I had a very good idea indeed. From the high window where I stood, there was a clear view of German vehicles and lines of infantrymen, in single file with their weapons at the trail, crawling comfortably northward along the Via Aurelia, which flanked the Vatican City's high wall. "The Jerries appear to be withdrawing from the city very nicely," I said.

"Is it orderly? Or are they going to do any street fighting?"

Feeling like a broadcast commentator at a state occasion, I swept my gaze along the grey line moving slowly below, and replied, "They seem to be pulling back in an orderly manner. There are no signs of preparation for street fighting. Are you now in contact with the enemy?"

"No," replied the liaison officer. "They broke off contact last night. Do you know the position regarding the river bridges in Rome? Shall we have difficulty in getting across?"

"So far as we know, they have not been mined, but if you like I can find out for certain, and get a message back to you," I answered.

We sent out agents to check on all the bridges nearest to the Vatican, and the report I was able to give the liaison officer an hour later was encouraging, for the bridges were intact, and the Allies would have a clear passage through Rome.

Among the units passing northward below my window had been a battery of anti-tank guns, a vital factor in defence, and all the indications were that the Germans would not stand and fight until they reached the defence line which we knew they had constructed forty miles north of Rome.

I could not refrain from asking the question in every one's mind, "When will you arrive?"

"Maybe to-morrow or the next day," he replied. "I can't be sure. We are still pretty far ahead of our main forces."

I replaced the telephone, with a glowing feeling that the end was near, but we had all thought the same when the Allies landed at Anzio, twenty miles away, and that was now eighteen weeks ago. Castel Gandolfo was eighteen miles from Rome, and the main Allied forces were apparently still far short of it. But it was a most exhilarating 'phone call.' It brought hope.

In the city itself the Germans and their Fascist henchmen were as firmly in command as ever, and there was still time for the whole organization to be rounded up, so no slackening was allowed on our part. As late as June 3 Lieutenant Furman was asking about a private who had turned up as a 'major':

Have you got any dope on this chap? His background is so odd that we should look pretty silly if he turned out at this stage to be a wrong 'un.

I replied with a warning :

Have no dope on this man—but treat him with the utmost caution.

There was more danger than ever before that the Germans would try to infiltrate a spy into the escape line. In the past such an attempt would have been aimed at uncovering the organization, but now, with allied occupation near, it would have the more sinister purpose of planting an agent behind our own lines. I hoped the Germans would have been lulled into a false sense of achievement by the Cipolla incident, but I did not intend to take chances. I was particularly conscious of the danger of being left with a spy in our midst, because I had just helped to play the same trick on the Germans, and among the Fascist refugees trekking northward were four Italian radio-operators who had been working in close co-operation with the organization.

The biggest worry, however, was always the fate of our members and helpers in the prisons of Rome. There were twenty-four recaptured escapers in the Regina Coeli, three in the Gestapo prison at the Via Tasso, and six in the small Forte Boccea, as well as fifty of our helpers in the Italian sections of the Regina Coeli. I was immensely relieved when reports began to reach the monsignor of the reappearance of some of the Italians in their own homes. The Germans were still in command, but the Italian guards at the prisons were beginning to desert their posts, leaving the cells unlocked as they departed.

As the reports of the reunion of Italian families increased, Monsignor O'Flaherty and I found our initial delight becoming more and more subdued, for none of the ex-prisoners-of-war were among those released. The German-controlled parts of the gaols were still under supervision as close as ever.

Furman shared this concern, and with a nagging worry about the fate of Lieutenant Simpson and the others amid the excitement of obviously approaching liberation, he and Renzo Lucidi found it difficult to concentrate on making up their accounts. Even as they sat in the Lucidis' comfortable flat in Via Scialoia, Furman knew that the end, though near, had not yet come. Visiting billets that morning, he had found the streets more than ever full of Germans and Fascists, and he had noted with regret that the retreat of the grey columns along the road showed no signs of being a rout.

He and his host were discussing this when the doorbell of the
flat rang. It brought Furman and his companion to their feet
with a sudden shock, for it was the secret signal known to Pasqualino Perfetti and passed on to the enemy, but discarded by
the organization. Reliving the terror of that moment in January,
when Büchner, the Jugoslav, now dead, opened the door of the
Via Chelini flat and unwittingly admitted disaster, Furman
listened tensely as Peppina, the maid, crossed the hall. He and
Renzo heard her open the door, and in the same instant they
heard her screams.

A moment later they were racing to the doorway too, for the
scream was not of terror but of joy. Smiling in the doorway stood
Lieutenant Simpson.

Furman and Lucidi dragged him in, detached the tearful Peppina from his shoulder, and pumped both hands at once. In a
flood of relief they admitted to each other for the first time their
fear that Simpson had been nearer than any of them to the firing-
squad.

Beaming at the warmth of his reception, Simpson was
astonished when at last he learned of the complications caused
by his adherence to his false Irish identity, or what Furman called
his "change of *cognome*."

Until Furman and Lucidi made it clear to him, he had no idea
how lucky he had been to be left behind when the Germans suddenly withdrew their guards, and handed over to Fascist thugs
who promptly deserted. Rome was clearly going to be unhealthy
for any known Fascist. Members of the Italian underground who
had been imprisoned took over, but knowing that the Germans
remained fully in control of the city, they wisely arranged an organized and disciplined release scheme.

The first to leave were those who had homes near by, but high
priority was given to Allied ex-prisoners-of-war. Simpson was
among these, but the reason he took so long to return to the fold
was completely characteristic of the man. He was released from
the prison with others, and he placed them all in safe billets before finding a bed for the night for himself. Under the noses of
the Germans flocking the streets, he had emerged from prison,
and gone straight back into action as a billeting officer without
even waiting until he had reported his release.

Leaving Simpson with the wildly elated Lucidis, Lieutenant

Furman set off to convoy the good news to me, but the German
sentries still stood grimly at their posts in St Peter's Square, and
the gates were guarded as firmly as ever. Furman had to be content with leaving a message, and on his way home he received
another sharp reminder that the Germans were still masters of
Rome.

A German soldier prodded him with a pistol, and commanded,
"Run! Run! Early curfew to-night!" It was too much for Furman, and he kept on walking, but he realized, as he paced deliberately away from the scowling sentry, how silly it would be if,
after all that had happened, he died with a bullet in his back
for no better reason than that he insisted on moving slowly away
from a German.

Simpson remained at the Via Scialoia flat, where, ironically,
the Lucidis were also harbouring the two civilian internees who
had been released from the Regina Coeli, at Dr Cipolla's random
request, in place of Lieutenant Simpson and Captain Armstrong.
Simpson still did not know that he owed his life to Monsignor
O'Flaherty's arrangements with Piedro Koch, but if the monsignor had not been aware of Simpson's assumed name he might
not have been left behind by the Germans. In a few days we had
a tragic reminder of this.

The success of the contract between the monsignor and the
Fascist had, in fact, been considerable. Including the escapers,
nearly seventy people were left behind in the prisons, and found
their way to freedom, but as a last gesture of sadistic defiance
against the humiliating end to their long domination of the Eternal
City, the Germans took one group of prisoners from the Regina
Coeli on the road to the north.

Five miles outside Rome the following day, fourteen bullet-
riddled bodies were found. Among them was that of the officer
we had come so close to saving—Captain John Armstrong.

13

Liberation

THE sun edged over the hazy eastern hills, and the great cross of St Peter's seemed to gleam as it had never seemed to gleam before. The long night was over, yet dawn came to a strangely silent Rome on June 4, 1944.

The streets and squares were empty, and even the tireless Tiber looked still, but this was not the sullen silence of resignation to doom. It was a breathless pause, a silence of expectancy, welling up behind windows shuttered against the possibility of street fighting, behind tremulous lips that would laugh, and eyes that would weep for joy at the first sign that the dream was reality and the day of liberation had really dawned. All over Rome there were people who, like Sir D'Arcy Osborne, Mr Hugh Montgomery, Father Owen Snedden and myself, now stood waiting by high windows, having risen early, or perhaps not slept at all, in order not to miss the magical moment that marked the return of peace and dignity to Rome.

Our little group, on the topmost floor of the erstwhile hospice housing the British Legation, waited in strained silence. Our eyes were glued on the farthest corner of the wide road along which we had seen so many men and machines stream northward in the last few days. Suddenly a line of vehicles swept into view, following the same familiar course—but with such a difference: these were pursuers, not pursued. It was the veritable point of the Allied spearhead, an American tank-busting unit of about thirty vehicles, including a jeep bearing the single star of a brigadier, and I, who had never come across the American forces in battle before, thought it was quite the most beautiful sight I had ever seen.

Diplomat and butler, soldier and priest, felt a surge of common emotion: cheering, clapping, slapping each other on the back, shaking hands, laughing wildly, and all talking at once, we seemed to throw off in an instant the strain that had settled on us all. The reservation of the diplomat, the caution of the soldier, the calm of the priest, were alike swallowed up in a giddy whirlpool of delight and relief.

In a matter of minutes all Rome became flooded by a pleasant pandemonium. Into the great square of St Peter's swept tens of thousands of happy Italians, anxious, as in all moments of crisis, grave or gay, to receive the blessing of their Pope; British and American flags, home-made from rags or painted paper, fluttered out from windows everywhere; the summer morning air tingled and vibrated with an unforgettable murmur of welcome and thanksgiving. This, I thought, must be the best reward for taking arms on the side of honour and justice—to be welcomed, not as conquerors, glamorized for a moment by the tinsel and glitter of conquest, but as liberators.

Yet this was no time for philosophy. In the city local government had evaporated, and all public services were out of action. In my office the carefully-preserved organization was in danger of sliding into chaos, for past orders were easily forgotten by escapers who realized that they would soon be able to return to their own families.

Lieutenant Colin Lesslie descended from 'up the hill,' the only major billet in the city which from first to last had avoided a raid, to find out what to do with the large group of escapers under his command.

"Keep 'em there for the time being," I instructed. "But what about Anderson, the lad who had the appendix operation and a somewhat mobile convalescence? I suppose we'd better send an ambulance up to collect him."

"Not a bit of it," replied Lesslie. "Recovery complete. He's walking about with the best of them !"

Lieutenant John Furman renewed old acquaintance with Monsignor O'Flaherty's office, the entrances to the Collegio Teutonicum having been reopened at once, but found to his disgust that he was still unable to get past the Vatican Gendarmerie to the British Legation. I sent him details of a plan which we had already worked out, realizing that when liberation came the organization would need its own headquarters in the city, and he went off with authority to requisition an appropriate centre before other units snapped up all the most convenient accommodation. Furman had already earmarked the very place—a luxury flat on the ground floor of the block where the Lucidis lived. Its tenants had been a well-known Fascist family, and, as Furman expected, they promptly moved north when the Allies drew near. He

requisitioned it, moved in, and started working at once, making
his first task the obtaining of extra rations for the families who
had helped us through the dark days.

Ignoring the order to remain at their billets, escapers from all
over Rome started calling at the Vatican guardrooms for instructions, and to avoid wasting further time, I arranged with
the guards to tell all such visitors to go on living where they were
until further notice.

As soon as I could get away from the legation, I set off with
John May in his little car, which for so many months had been
confined within the walls of the Vatican, with the idea of making
a tour of as many of the billets as possible. It gave me a strange
thrill to drive in broad daylight through the gates that I had last
entered five months earlier in the garments of a monsignor, head
bowed.

Rome was hard to recognize. The tall colonnades around St
Peter's Square, which had always been a place of shadows, subterfuge and German sentries, were thronging with happily chattering Italians; the streets, empty of trams and buses, were crowded
with people, and festooned with the red, white, and blue of the
Union Jack and "Old Glory."

My aim was to go from billet to billet, instructing the escapers
to remain where they were, and pointing out that if they linked
up with any unit on their own they might delay their repatriation,
and would certainly complicate the interrogation work which
would have to be carried out. But I was able to call at relatively
few billets, because every Italian family, free for the first time in
many months from the nagging fear of torture and death, wished
only to celebrate the liberation, and my visit as commander of the
Rome Organization seemed to provide a welcome excuse for a
party with a startling rate of *vino*-consumption. Remembering
these simple, kindly folk only from the time when they had hastily
and fearfully admitted me after a secret ring at the door, I was
astonished by the warmth of their welcome, and it seemed that
every one of our 'padrones' had carefully buried at least one
bottle of good wine for just such an occasion.

Glad that John May was driving, I returned to the Vatican
to find that the genial confusion and gaiety which was transform-
ing Rome had spread like a fever into the British Legation. After
several years as a diplomatic backwater, the legation was now

the one place in Rome that was generally expected to be able to do anything for everybody, and a constant flow of visitors mingled with a flood of telephone calls, messages, and requests from the Vatican Secretariat of State.

There were visitors for me, too, including a senior British Military Intelligence officer, with whom I naturally had a good deal to discuss. Brother Robert Pace called after emerging from hiding—and then set off to visit all his old billets.

So many people were calling to see the Minister that John May found difficulty in finding room for them, and had them waiting in odd parts of the legation, including my room. I was eating an early lunch when John May ushered in a British civilian, and said by way of introduction and apology, "Mr Caccia is calling on the Minister. There's nowhere else I can ask him to wait." I greeted the visitor casually, and got on with my meal, but I might have been less off-hand if I had realized that this was the first senior representative of the Foreign Office to arrive in Rome— the man who, as Sir Harold Caccia, was later to become Britain's Ambassador to the United States.

In the mounting turmoil the Secretariat of State expected Sir D'Arcy Osborne to make his first priority the preservation of the strict neutrality of the Vatican, particularly since the Germans had taken a leaf out of the British book, closing their embassy in Rome, and moving a reduced diplomatic staff into the Vatican itself. Both British and German Ministries were now within its high walls.

Demands poured in from the Secretariat on Sir D'Arcy. The Secretariat wanted safe conduct for their supply convoys in and out of Rome, and passes for their servants, and they demanded immediate removal of the army vehicles, which had parked in St Peter's Square for the occupants to go sight-seeing—and they did not fail to remind the Minister that the Germans had never permitted such a violation of the *piazza*. Difficulties were increased by the fact that the Vatican authorities were already slightly testy with the British, because in the fighter sweeps over northern Italy, after the fall of Cassino, a few of their road convoys had been mildly shot up. These vehicles, which took supplies to monasteries or guards on leave in Switzerland, were all painted yellow and white, with the idea of giving them immunity, and Sir D'Arcy had, in fact, made strenuous efforts through the

Foreign Office to ensure their protection, but mistakes were bound to occur.

Most of the requests flooding in on Sir D'Arcy's tiny staff were reasonable enough, but his chief problem was that he had no link with the new Military Government of Rome. That was why the Minister sent for me, and asked me to act as liaison officer between the legation and the Rome Area Command. Thus I found myself appointed temporary military attaché to the Holy See.

This was agreeable, because I regained my identity, becoming at last an official resident of the legation where for so long I had been a diplomatic secret—a ghost neither seen nor acknowledged —and a new and perfectly genuine pass was issued in my name. "Mr Derry," it said in Italian, "is employed by the British Legation to the Holy See, and has liberty to pass into and out of the Vatican." So far as the Secretariat was concerned, I had moved into Rome with the skeleton military staffs, which had been waiting for weeks, ready to re-establish local government and public services as soon as the Allies marched in. These men were now engaged on the gigantic task of restoring water and electricity supplies, bringing trams and buses back into operation, setting up a food-rationing system, and substituting Allied lire (already in use throughout the southern part of Italy), for the existing monetary system.

Armed with my new Vatican papers and a letter from the British Minister, I visited the offices of the various military authorities, and obtained from them passes which enabled me to go anywhere. One problem was to establish contact between the legation and the new police authorities. Leaving my office one day to arrange this, I found myself face to face with Lieutenant-Colonel R. T. Millhouse, D.C.M., whom I had last seen in the uniform of chief constable of my home town.

"I thought you were in Newark!" I said, delighted to see him.

"I expect you did," he grinned, "but I knew damned well where you were!" Colonel Millhouse had arrived to take over as public safety officer (chief of police services), for the provinces of Lazia and Umbria, and our meeting resulted in the slashing of the red tape for the issue of passes and permits for Rome Organization helpers.

Shortly afterwards I was warned to be on call for a V.I.P. who was expected at the legation, and when I was summoned to the Minister's office I found myself face to face with the Allied Commander-in-Chief, General (later Field-Marshal Viscount) Alexander. It was a slightly embarrassing moment, because the general, rated by many as Britain's greatest soldier of the war, was neat and 'properly dressed,' by the best military standard, while I wore a tight blue suit, with a gusset let into the seat of the trousers. It was a rather bizarre ending to a bizarre command, for I had taken over while wearing a priest's soutane, and was now making my report to my Commander-in-Chief wearing clothes in which I had to sit down with caution.

Any discomfiture, however, was outweighed by pleasure at the warmth of the general's appreciation of the work of the Rome Organization, for it was clear that he had known a great deal of what had been going on behind enemy lines even before Sir D'Arcy Osborne filled in the gaps for him. The interview was significant, because it marked the end of the organization as we knew it, and the simultaneous beginning of a new organization, which was to go on for more than two years.

The general's main concern was for those who had risked their lives and suffered loss to help us. All the escapers would be transferred as soon as we could marshal them to a repatriation unit, which already existed in embryo, and would be returned to their families with a minimum of delay, but General Alexander was anxious that those who through dangerous months had made their repatriation possible should not be forgotten. He asked me to set up an *ad hoc* organization which would collect evidence, pending the establishment of a new unit, to recompense helpers—and it was a request, not an order.

"I'd like to stay, sir," I said, and I meant it. Much as the thought of home appealed to me, I could not bear the idea of walking out on all the loyal helpers who had made the organization's work possible, without first trying to do something to ensure that they were compensated. I was pretty sure that Lieutenants Simpson and Furman would be of the same mind, even though they had suffered more than I, and had even stronger cause for repatriation. I was not mistaken. They moved into the new flat at Via Scialoia, where they were joined by Captain Byrnes, with his exhumed records, and the indefatigable Greek, Theodore Meletiou, and together they started on the work straight away.

We were a unique unit (as I suppose we always had been),

answerable to none of the various authorities in Rome. General Alexander had ordered me to make my reports direct to the office of his Chief-of-Staff, General (later Field-Marshal Sir John) Harding, and results were rapid. I received an order establishing a ration strength of ten for the new unit, and giving authority for the requisitioning of property and the drawing of supplies, including the invaluable, and otherwise unobtainable, petrol and oil.

Our first task, naturally, was handing over escapers. The Allies had arrived prepared for a giant and virtually unprecedented job, and one of the first headquarters established in the city was that of the Repatriation Unit, geared ready to house, clothe, feed, interrogate, and generally administer thousands of escapers and evaders.

The unit established itself in a barracks, and took over camps as transit bases for the temporary accommodation of the ex-prisoners. By the time of the liberation, the Rome Organization had on its books the names of 3925 escapers and evaders, of whom 1695 were British, 896 South African, 429 Russian, 425 Greek, 185 American, and the rest from no fewer than twenty different countries. Fewer than 200 were billeted actually in Rome, but of the thousands in the 'country branch' most, by far, were in the rural areas immediately surrounding the city, scattered in groups varying in size from three to more than a hundred.

We handed over responsibility immediately for this underground army, but it was not quite so easy to hand over the men themselves, for after months of confinement they not unnaturally wanted a day or two to celebrate, before they reported to the formidable looking barracks. Those men who had been 'living rough' in the country were glad to move into the camps established for them, but the 'Romans' were not so keen. Most of them were living in comfortable private homes, now without fear of arrest for themselves or retribution for their hosts, and they had money of their own to spend.

This was because we had paid out, at the beginning of the month, subsistance allowances sufficient to keep them going for a fortnight—and the liberation had come a couple of days later. They very nearly had twice as much, for Lieutenant Furman wrote on May 29 :

In favour of a full month is the fact that should our condition not be changed by June 15, circulation to distribute the money may well prove more than hazardous. If our condition has changed, then we shall be somewhat out of pocket, but either the chaps themselves or their 'padrones' will benefit—a not altogether undesirable circumstance. So, on the whole, I favour a full month's payment.

This was eloquent advocacy, but I was confident of an imminent liberation, and I could not take as philanthropic a view of the distribution of the Government money as Furman, so I ordered payment for a fifteen-day period. It proved more than enough. With money in their pockets, freedom to move about as they wished, and the Italian summer sun shining on a Rome bubbling with the spirit of *festa*, our 'Romans' found it convenient to obey the last order they had received, which was to remain at their existing billets until further notice. They guessed, quite rightly, that it would take time and effort before fresh orders arrived.

Nevertheless, the Allied Repatriation Unit was so thoroughly prepared for its task that within a week all the escapers and evaders from the Rome area were transferred to Naples, whence they were, with very little delay, shipped home. In the short time that they were at the transit camps every one was interrogated by intelligence officers flown in from Bari, and extracts from their reports were sent to help the new organization in recording assistance given by Italians to the Allied cause.

The Allied Repatriation Unit subsequently functioned all over the world, dealing with many thousands of prisoners released or left behind by retreating (and later defeated) Germans and Japanese, but it was in Rome that it had its first operational experience, and I like to imagine that nowhere did it meet a stranger situation than in the Eternal City, where in one small area, nearly 4000 men had all been at large for months under the noses of the enemy.

The escaper most quickly reunited with his family was Lieutenant Paul Freyberg. General Freyberg came by car into Rome to collect his son, and a few days later Lady Freyberg opened a club in the city for New Zealand forces. In a note to me later Lieutenant Paul Freyberg wrote:

I hope you are hanging, drawing, and quartering all the various bastards who caused us annoyance, and that the old chestnut about the Mills of God will for once come true.

I was still aware that there was a war to be fought and won, but to the Romani, it was all over. To them, it was the past that mattered, and the only thing demanding urgent attention was the punishment of the collaborators and denouncers. "What are you doing about Perfetti?" I was asked two dozen times a day. Italians began to seek me out simply to tell me, repeatedly and insistently, "You must have so-and-so arrested at once."

I was pretty sure that the mills would, in due course, grind exceeding small; and, in fact, retribution was catching up with the delinquents one by one. Piedro Koch, the Fascist master-torturer, had been overtaken on his way north, and was subsequently shot. Since his wife and mother had made their own way south to Naples, Monsignor O'Flaherty was relieved of his obligation to hide them in a religious house, but they were, of course, quite safe, since the Allies did not shoot women for the offences of their husbands and sons. Pasqualino Perfetti and his old associate, Aldo Zambardi, were both arrested, and thrown into the Regina Coeli, to which their denunciations, particularly Perfetti's, had condemned so many Italians and escapers only a few weeks earlier. These two had been my first contacts on entering the town, and, personally, I owed a good deal to them, but it had not taken me long to discover that Perfetti's motive was not a desire to help the ex-prisoners so much as an affection for the money which it brought him. Zambardi's denunciations had been few compared with the bogus priest's, but, on the other hand, it could at least be said for Perfetti that he had been badly beaten up before he started his long tour, guiding the Germans to the billets, whereas Zambardi, once he had been implicated by Perfetti, told the little that he knew without further 'persuasion.' There were, as might be expected, many families in Rome whose chief ambition was to lynch Perfetti, but he was transferred to a prison in Milan, after threats by the Romans to burn the hated Regina Coeli to the ground, and that was the last I heard of him.

Dr Cipolla, the unashamed double-agent, made no attempt to get out of Rome, and was consequently arrested. I was satisfied that in all his intrigues he had never done anything to harm the organization or Allied ex-prisoners. Indeed, apart from his considerable, if self-interested, assistance at a time when a change of control in Rome was obviously near, he had helped Monsignor

O'Flaherty before my arrival, and was instrumental in obtaining the Via Chelini flat. However, the Italians had some scores to settle with him, and he came up for trial. Through Renzo Lucidi, we ensured that the brighter side of Cipolla's case was made known, and he escaped with his life, although he was sentenced to a pretty savage term of twenty-four years' imprisonment.

During the dark days of the organization it had once seemed that everybody was denouncing everybody else, and now it all happened again. Many denunciations were made in an understandable spirit of revenge, but a fair proportion of them were aimed at throwing a smoke-screen over the denouncer's own misdeeds, and I watched the tide of recrimination with mixed feelings.

The case of Cipolla was an example of the problem set by people who had, at various times served both sides, for those now denounced were rarely, like Koch, completely evil, but only characteristically human—a mixture of good and bad. Those who knew only one side of Dr Cipolla's activities, for instance, thought that he should be shot at once, but those who knew only of the other thought he should be given a medal. Aware of something of both sides, I could only ensure that those who sat in judgment were given as balanced a view as possible, and informed of any good work done for the organization. Quite often I had deliberately accepted assistance from dubious characters; more than once I had been surprised at the good results.

There was, for example, the case of Jack S. I had first heard of him around Christmas-time, while I was still moving about in Rome. Brother Robert Pace reported that this man was very anxious to help in the organization's work, and could be very useful, as he had a flat, a car, and a permit to use it. On hearing this I bristled with suspicions as sharp as the quills of an angry porcupine, for anyone who was permitted to run a car was working for the Germans or the Fascists, so I urged Brother Robert, "Don't have anything to do with this chap at all."

Soon afterwards I discovered by accident that Jack S. was, in fact, being used to bring escapers to Rome, and find billets, and when I taxed Brother Robert about this he replied somewhat sheepishly, "He is very good, and he can get around. But he would very much like to meet somebody in authority."

"No doubt," I replied, "but he isn't going to. If you must use him don't let him know anything about anybody. Let him look after the people he brings into Rome and places in billets himself, but no more."

I was still sure Jack S. was a potential danger, although I gave up hope of convincing the trusting Brother Robert. Surprisingly, however, the scheme seemed to work, and I sent money through Brother Robert, who regularly reported back on the good work that Jack S. was doing for him—never without mentioning that he was still most anxious to meet somebody in authority. I continued to ward off these requests, but they still turned up even after I had withdrawn to the British Legation.

Towards the end of February Brother Robert casually mentioned to Lieutenant Simpson that he might meet Jack S., but Simpson, cautious as ever, asked me for information first.

> I have never met this man [I replied], although he tried many times to see me. However, he has done much for our boys in the last few months. There is quite a lot of his story that does not fit in, and I know quite a lot about him that I cannot put on paper, so be careful of anything you tell him. Also, warn any of our boys who are put with him to be sure not to talk of the organization or say where any of their friends live. However, I do not wish to upset him, as he has certainly done some excellent work.

Simpson replied four days later:

> I have not met this individual yet—and am not particularly keen. "Edmund" told me yesterday that he had told his boys not to speak about the gang to J.S., but apparently some had already said so much—though nothing very important.

Shortly afterwards, through sudden pressure on billets, Simpson passed three escapers to Jack S. through "Edmund" (Father Madden) without making direct contact.

Then Jack S. was arrested, exactly as I had expected, for whenever the Germans succeeded in placing a stool-pigeon in an underground organization they usually 'arrested' him when the time came for him to present his detailed report. In that way the people on whom he had been spying might be hood-winked, and the man would be available for further service.

All the billets known to Jack S. were immediately evacuated, and a warning sent to Brother Robert, Father Madden, and all the others who had been in contact with him, to be on their guard.

Much to my surprise, as the weeks went by, not one of the billets known to Jack S. was raided, and he remained in custody instead of emerging to guide the Gestapo from place to place. I became increasingly curious, and eventually learned through the police contacts that Jack S. had been tortured and badly beaten up, but had divulged nothing about the organization. Concluding that I had misjudged my man, as I had Joe Pollak, I was delighted when, on the liberation, Jack S. was found to be among those left alive in the Regina Coeli.

A few days after the Allied occupation I was walking with a senior official of the Foreign Office in the garden of the old British Embassy, now being prepared for re-opening, when my companion produced a list of names, and handed it to me.

"These are all renegade British subjects who have, to our knowledge, worked with the enemy," he said. "We are rather anxious to get our hands on them. Know anything about any of them?"

I glanced at the piece of paper, and right at the top of the list saw the name of Jack S.

"I can put my hand on this one straight away," I said, "though I never knew he was a British subject. I thought he was Italian."

"Born in London," the Foreign Office official replied. "His father was of Italian descent, but one hundred per cent. British in outlook, and has done a lot of jolly good work. This lad didn't share his father's loyalty, but offered his services to the Italians as soon as they entered the war, collected some forged documents from the Italian Embassy before it put up the dust-sheets, and left in the last trainload of diplomats on their way back here."

"I always thought there must be somehthing odd about him," I said, "but he has done a lot of very good work for me. Why should the Foreign Office be so keen on grabbing him?"

The official looked at me coldly. "Didn't you know," he asked with incredulity, "that this man was the 'Cockney Broadcaster of Rome'?"

I was astonished. I was well aware that William Joyce, the "Lord Haw-Haw" of German propaganda broadcasts, was by no means the only British subject to have acted as a radio mouthpiece for the enemy, and I had heard of his cockney counterpart on Rome Radio, but it had never occurred to me that this man might be in my own organization.

Jack S. was, of course, arrested, because his propaganda

broadcasts, while of much less significance than those from Germany, still constituted high treason. But I could not forget that he had worked hard for British ex-prisoners over a long and dangerous period, and when at last the test had come he had shown selfless courage in refusing to denounce the British Organization, in spite of torture. I put this side of his activities before the authorities as strongly as I could, and eventually, unlike William Joyce, a Fascist with no saving graces, Jack S. did not go to the gallows. In fact, he was not even sent back to Britain to stand trial. The eminently reasonable decision made was that he should remain in internment until the Allies left Italy, and then be released, but warned that if he ever set foot on British territory anywhere in the world he would be arrested and tried for treason.

If the liberation brought some shady characters into the limelight it also allowed the secret agents with more honourable backgrounds to emerge at last from the underground. Into the light, for instance, came the picturesquely titled Liberty or Death movement of fearless Greeks, who had helped our organization from the earliest days, and whose finances, in return, had been backed by the British Government. As the Allies marched into Rome, the Liberty or Death agents had little silver badges made and displayed them proudly in their buttonholes.

Lieutenants Simpson, Furman, and myself were each presented with one of these badges, and became the first Britons in a Greek organization, most of whose members, alas, were to have angry things to say about Britain when disputes arose over Cyprus after the war. Indeed, throughout the life of the Rome Organization one of our staunchest and most gallant allies against the common enemy, was the man who became Greek Foreign Minister and one of our bitterest opponents over Cyprus—Angelo Averoff.

The friendship and, indeed, affection between us was typified by the letter which Angelo Averoff sent me with the silver badge:

> We have the honour and the pleasure to inform you that the executive committee of the organization of Liberty or Death, in full agreement with its supreme adviser, the ex-Minister for the Air Force, Mr Alexander Zannas, has elected you as an honorary member of the above, our organization. This is quite a natural thing after such a collaboration, full of friendship—that loyal friendship which characterizes the relations between our two

countries. We beg to enclose herewith the distinctive of the Liberty or Death—a distinctive which was concealed up to this day, and which we can finally bear.

For Lieutenant Furman, it was a second "distinctive," for he already had his own in the form of a little Union Jack brooch, which he had taken to wearing under his lapel during the last few weeks, and which was, in fact, in its place on both recent occasions when he was stopped and asked for his papers. This, of course, he had not mentioned to me in his reports, any more than that he had taken to carrying a tiny pistol, for he knew that my reaction would have been unequivocal. If he had been searched either brooch or pistol, and certainly the combination of the two, would have been a death warrant.

In the turmoil of the first couple of days we had so much to do that there was no time for relaxation and reunions, but there were some periods when I deliberately pushed work aside, no matter how pressing, and that was when the B.B.C. war news was due. Only a couple of days after the liberation of Rome, Father Snedden and I were having a quiet drink with John May, when we were electrified to hear the first announcement of Allied landings in Normandy, and although the brief statement gave no indication that this was the opening of the long-awaited "Second Front," the fact that it was headed "Communiqué No. 1" made it clear to any soldier that it was more than just another coast raid.

By evening it was obvious that the Allies, in full force, were fighting their way back into Northern Europe, and with the joy of the Rome liberation still warm within us, we felt that now the time had come for the party we had all been promising ourselves. With Lieutenants Furman and Simpson, Renzo and Adrienne Lucidi, the American Lieutenant Dukate, and other escapers still in Rome, plus a good number of the Italian girls who had been among our helpers, I launched the biggest party the Rome Organization ever knew. Memories flooded back as we ate and drank in the Grand Hotel, which Furman, Simpson, and I could still picture vividly under very different circumstances, crowded with German officers and leading Fascists. In the pleasant bar of the Orso our friend the barman, Felix, had proudly erected a notice informing his customers that the bar was regularly patronized by British officers during the German occupation, and to

endorse the claim the three of us signed this notice, which was a
showpiece when the bar ultimately became an officers' club.

As the British Minister's attaché, I came to the conclusion that
it was not fitting for the chief representative of H.M. Government
to remain without transport of his own. Besides, he was finding it
increasingly difficult to make all the calls demanded of him, and
after all we had authority from the highest military level to requisition enemy property.

Armed with the necessary papers, I therefore looked around
for a car for Sir D'Arcy, and it was not long before my eye fell
upon the gleaming giant left in Rome by Prince Bismarck, to
whom (though he did not know it) we were already substantially
indebted. It was a stupendous vehicle, specially built with a highly
polished aluminium Heinkel body wrapped round an enormous
Lancia engine. It had flamboyant, sweeping lines, four head-
lights at the front, and another on each side of the windscreen,
and every conceivable embellishment and extra comfort.

It was, I thought, the most beautiful motor-car I had ever seen,
so I requisitioned it on the spot, swept away in it to the Vatican,
and proudly produced it to the Minister. Like me, he needed
only a single glance at the magnificent monster to make up his
mind.

"Thank you, Major Derry," he said, with a perceptible
shudder, "but do you think you could find me something a little
less—er—spectacular?"

I was only too happy to oblige, for after a couple of miles at
the wheel of this 'Silver Bullet' I was filled with covetousness, so
I went out again, and collected a sober, stately limousine for Sir
D'Arcy—but kept the 'Silver Bullet' for myself.

I was on a journey in it one day, accompanied by a girl from
the American Embassy, when I picked up a British corporal who
had thumbed a lift. As we drove along I asked him casually
where he lived.

"Oh, you wouldn't know it, sir," he replied deprecatingly. "It's
a little place in Nottinghamshire called Newark."

"Why, that's my home too!" I exclaimed.

"And mine," said the girl, in a strong American drawl. We
looked at her blankly. "Newark, New Jersey," she added.

The car remained with me for as long as I stayed in Rome.
Prince Bismarck apparently nursed an affection for it, because

some years later he asked the British authorities if he could have it back. He was unsuccessful, I fear, for the officer in whose charge I left it had underestimated its power at a particularly sharp bend, and bent it beyond repair.

In the search for transport during the early days of the Allied occupation the officers of the Rome Organization naturally had a considerable advantage over those newly arrived in the city. Just as we knew where to find the excellent flats vacated by departed Fascists, we were able to lay our hands on enemy-owned cars, which had been stowed away in 'safe' hiding-places. Within hours of receiving permission to requisition, our organization was fully mobile, although not all the cars were gleaming giants.

Our knowledge of Rome helped us to overcome problems more difficult than the finding of cars and flats. There was the small matter of the odd 100,000 lire, borrowed in the dark days of January against a contract which I had signed, undertaking to repay in sterling within five days of the liberation. Anxious to honour this contract, I ran up against the very obstacle I had foreseen when the British military banking authority refused point-blank to release sterling under any circumstances. This problem was by no means insurmountable for an organization as skilled as ours in black-market dealing, for we knew that floating around was a good deal of English currency, which had been smuggled in or illegally cashed by Allied troops at an attractive rate of exchange. Our Italian contacts were therefore set to work in the channels they knew so well, and by the next day we had enough British notes to repay the debt in full.

Another debt, incalculable, and perhaps never quite repayable, still remained—our debt to those who risked everything to help us. The erstwhile Rome Organization was able and happy to help in this task. We were undergoing a metamorphosis, and emerged as the prototype of a new organization that was to operate all over the world as the cannon quietened and shattered cities came back to life. Sir D'Arcy Osborne and I had foreseen the need, and had discussed it frequently. We planned the broad outlines of what I had described to Lieutenant Furman as "the commission," while at the War Office, the Deputy Director of Military Intelligence, Brigadier Norman Crocket, C.B.E., D.S.O., M.C., to whom all reports of the organization's work had found their way, spent many hours working out the details, and the

Commander-in-Chief himself had given it much thought, as was evident in my interview with him.

Thus the *ad hoc* organization at the Via Scialoia flat had powerful backing, and to this was rapidly added the support of the various military organizations established in Rome. The Rome Area Command had scarcely settled in the city before it found itself deluged with appeals from Italians bearing promises of monetary payment, commendations for good service, and IOU's on odd scraps of paper signed by British servicemen. The Rome Organization had never issued chits of this sort, but many individual escapers had given them to Italians who had helped them.

It was, I think, a great advantage for the Rome Area Command to know that there was a unit to which the flood of chits could be diverted, and one that could deal with the steady stream of complaints from Italians who had been forced into hiding, and now wished to give information against collaborators. To our headquarters were diverted also the hundreds of Italians who, immediately after the liberation, began to besiege Monsignor O'Flaherty's office with appeals for some form of recognition that they had been good patriots.

The key to the truth of most of these claims still lay buried in the Vatican gardens, so, as unobtrusively as we had planted them, we unearthed the biscuit-tins containing the records of eight incredible months, and in our new task the bits and pieces of information that had been crammed into these tins proved to be buried treasure indeed.

During the months at the British Legation, just within the southern wall of the Vatican, I had often conjectured about that part of the city-state, hidden from my view by the vast basilica of St Peter's, which housed the 1000-room Papal Palace that occupies a tenth of the entire state's 110 acres. The chance to see for myself came one day when things were running smoothly, and the First Secretary, Mr Hugh Montgomery, a devout Catholic, invited me to go with him for a Papal audience.

With Mr Montgomery and Colonel Millhouse, I went through the great bronze doors at the northern end of the façade of St Peter's, up the long, wide stairs, and through a succession of chambers and galleries ornamented with the most magnificent frescoes and tapestries. It has been said that this vast palace contains more objects of intrinsic beauty than any other in the world.

In the heart of the Vatican we were ushered away from the throne-room into a small anteroom. There we waited in silence, conscious of the majesty of our surroundings, and of the fact that we were being accorded the rare privilege of a private audience.

Anxious to do the right thing, though unaware of what was expected of me, I was taken completely by surprise by the Holy Father's entrance. I had rather expected that the double doors would open grandly, picturesquely-dressed attendants would make ringing announcements, and His Holiness, surrounded by retainers, would pace in slowly and solemnly, a picture of grave pageantry. In fact, the door was almost flung open, and, as though in a bound, the late Pope Pius XII was before us, smiling, energetic, and unexpectedly human. I found myself half kneeling, not knowing what to do next, as I looked for the first time upon the scholarly, saintly features of the man who, unknowingly, had been my host for so long.

The piquancy of the situation was intensified when the Holy Father addressed a question to me directly which left me tongue-tied, but Mr Montgomery, perfect diplomat as always, cut in quickly to say, "Major Derry is doing a great deal of work as our liaison officer with the new Military Government in Rome."

His Holiness nodded approvingly, gave me a medallion commemorating the audience, and moved on to Colonel Millhouse, leaving me vastly relieved that I had not been forced to depart from the truth on such an august occasion.

For Pope Pius XII, in perfect English, had asked me, "And how long have you been in Rome?"